G. J. (George John) Whyte-Melville

Market Harborough

How Mr. Sawyer Went to the Shires

G. J. (George John) Whyte-Melville

Market Harborough
How Mr. Sawyer Went to the Shires

ISBN/EAN: 9783744752923

Printed in Europe, USA, Canada, Australia, Japan

Cover: Foto ©ninafisch / pixelio.de

More available books at **www.hansebooks.com**

MARKET HARBOROUGH;

OR,

HOW MR. SAWYER WENT TO THE SHIRES.

FOURTH EDITION.

INSIDE THE BAR;

OR,

SKETCHES AT SOAKINGTON.

BY

THE AUTHOR OF "DIGBY GRAND,"

ETC.

LONDON:
CHAPMAN AND HALL, 193, PICCADILLY.
1862.

[*The right of Translation is reserved.*]

CONTENTS.

	PAGE
CHAP. I.—ONE OF THE "OLD SORT"	1
II.—"MR. JOB SLOPER"	12
III. "YOUR HAND-WRITING, SIR"	17
IV.—MARCHING ORDERS	25
V.—"BOOTS AND SADDLES"	33
VI.—HAZY WEATHER	44
VII.—A LEICESTERSHIRE LARK	50
VIII.—A DOVE OF THE SAME	59
IX.—FOUR O'CLOCK, STABLES	66
X.—"HAIL! SMILING MORN!"	74
XI.—"A MERRY GO-ROUNDER"	83
XII.—"DEAD FOR A DUCAT"	91
XIII.—"AFTER DARK"	103
XIV.—"BEFORE THE DAWN"	114
XV.—TAKING A HINT	119
XVI.—RIDING TO SELL	125
XVII.—"TEMPTED TO BUY"	137
XVIII.—THE DOVE-COTE	146
XIX.—"THE BOOT ON THE OTHER LEG"	156

CONTENTS.

	PAGE
CHAP. XX.—DEEPER AND DEEPER	162
XXI.—THE MAGNUM BONUM	169
XXII.—A WET NIGHT	175
XXIII.—DOUGHTY DEEDS	187
XXIV.—THE BALL	192
XXV.—THE RACE	202
XXVI.—THE MATCH	209

INSIDE THE BAR.

CHAP. I.—"THE GENIUS LOCI"	217
II.—TIPS, THE HORSE-BREAKER	233
III.—MR. NAGGETT	251
IV.—TOM TURNBULL	267
V.—OLD IKE, THE EARTH-STOPPER	283
VI.—MISS MERLIN	297
VII.—MISS MERLIN	313
VIII.—YOUNG PLUMTREE	329
IX.—IN THE TRAP	345
X.—THE OLD SQUIRE	361
XI.—THE SOAKINGTON FIELD-DAY	377

MARKET HARBOROUGH;

OR,

HOW MR. SAWYER WENT TO THE SHIRES.

CHAPTER I.

ONE OF THE "OLD SORT."

MOST men have a sunny spot to which they look back in their existence, as most have an impossible future, to attain which all their energies are exerted, and their resources employed. The difference between these visionary scenes is this, that they *think* a good deal of the latter, but *talk* a good deal of the former.

With some fellows the golden age seems to have been passed at Eton, with others at the Universities. Here a quiet, mild clergyman gloats over the roystering days he spent as a Cornet in the Hussars; there an obese old gentleman prates of the fascinations of London, and his own successes as a slim young dandy about town. Everybody believes he liked that rosy past better than he did. Just as we fancy that the hounds never run nowadays as they used, when we had lungs to holloa and nerves to ride; and that even if they could go the same pace, hunters are not now to be got of the stamp of our old chestnut horse, concerning whose performances we think no shame to lie, year by year, with increasing audacity; there is nobody left to contradict us, and why should we not?

Now, Mr. Sawyer, too, will descend into the vale of years, with a landmark on which to fix his failing eyes, an era which shall serve as a date for his reminiscence, and a starting-point for his after-dinner yarns. This shall be the season when Mr. Sawyer went to the Shires. It is not yet very long ago. Perhaps it may be well to relate a few of his adventures and doings in those localities ere they lapse into the realms of fiction under the romantic colouring with which he will himself begin to paint them, when their actual freshness has worn off.

Touching Mr. Sawyer's early history, I have collected but few particulars, not enjoying the advantage of that gentleman's acquaintance till he had arrived at years of maturity. I gather, however, that he matriculated at Oxford, and was rusticated from that pleasant University for some breach of college discipline, sufficiently venial in itself, but imbued with a scarlet tinge in the eyes of the authorities. I have heard that he rode an Ayrshire bull across Peckwater in broad daylight, having previously attired himself in a red coat, with leathers, etc., complete, and clad the patient animal in a full suit of academicals. Also that he endeavoured to mollify his judges by apostrophizing the partner of his trespass, in the words Horace puts into the mouth of Europa,

"Si quis infamem mihi nunc juvencum;"

and so on to the end of the stanza. As, although Mr. Sawyer's fluency in all Saxon expletives is undeniable, I never heard him make use of any language but his own, I confess to my mind this story bears upon the face of it the stamp of improbability, and that perversion of the truth from which Oxonian annals are not entirely free.

It is a good old fashion to commence a narrative by a personal description of its hero; such as you would see in the 'Hue and Cry,' or the advertisements for that missing gentleman in the 'Times' who has never been found yet, and whose humble costume of half-boots, tweed trousers, and an olive surtout, with a bunch of keys and three-halfpence in the pockets, denotes neither affluence nor display. Upon this principle let me endeavour to bring before the mind's eye of my readers the outward semblance of my worthy friend, John Standish Sawyer, a man of mark, forsooth, in his own parish, and "justice of peace in his county, simple though he stand here."

Mr. Sawyer is a well-built, able-bodied personage, standing five feet eight in the worsted stockings he usually affects, with a frame admirably calculated to resist fatigue, to perform feats of strength rather than agility, and to put on beef: the last tendency he keeps down with constant and severe exercise, so that the twelve stone which he swings into his saddle is seldom exceeded by a pound. "As long as I ride thirteen stone," quoth Mr. Sawyer to his intimates after dinner, "no man alive can take the shine out of me, over a country. Mason! Mason's all very well for a *spurt!* but where is he at the end of two hours and forty minutes, through woodlands, in deep clay? Answer me that! and pass the bottle."

Our friend's admirers term his person square: his enemies, and he has a few, call it "clumsy:" certainly his hands and feet are large, his limbs robust, but not well-turned; and though it would make him very angry to hear me, I confess his is not my *beau idéal* of the figure for a horseman. Nevertheless, he has an honest English face, round and rosy, light-grey eyes, such as usually belong to an energetic and persevering temperament, with thin sandy hair, and a good deal of stiff red whisker.

Altogether, he looks like a man you would rather drink with than fight with, any day. Perhaps, if very fastidious, you might prefer letting him alone, to doing either. Of his costume, I shall only say that it partakes on every-day occasions of the *decidedly* sporting, with a slight tendency towards the *slang*. Its details are those of a dress in which the owner is ready to get on horseback at a moment's notice; nay, in which he is qualified, without further preparation, to ride four miles straight-on-end, over a stiff country; so enduring are its materials, and so suggestive of equestrian exercise is its general fit. Also, on Sundays, as on weekdays, in town or country, he delights in a "five to two" sort of hat, with the flat brim and backward set, which denote indisputable knowledge of horseflesh, and a sagacity that almost amounts to dishonesty.

Not that Mr. Sawyer ever bets; far from it. He elbows his way indeed into the ring, and criticizes the two-year-olds as they walk jauntily down to the starting-post, as if he speculated like the Leviathan, and owned a *string* like Sir Joseph Hawley's; but all this is simply *ex officio*. Wherever horses are concerned, Mr. Sawyer deems it incumbent on him to make a demonstration, and he goes to Tattersall's as regularly on the Sunday afternoons in the summer, as you and I do to dinner. Like the Roman Emperor, the horse is his high-priest, and the object of his idolatry.

I am afraid hunting is going downhill. I do not mean to say that there is not an ever-increasing supply of ambitious gentlemen who order coats from Poole, boots from Bartley, and horses from Mason, to display the same wherever they think they are most likely to be admired; but I think there are few specimens left of the old hunting sort, who devoted themselves exclusively to their favourite pursuit, and could not even bear to hear it mentioned with anything like levity or disrespect; men whose only claim to social distinction was that they *hunted*, who looked upon their red coat as a passport to all the society they cared to have, and who divided the whole community, in their own minds, into two classes—"men who hunt," and "men who don't."

In these days people have so many irons in the fire! Look at even the *first* flight, with a crack pack of hounds; ten to one amongst the half-a-dozen who compose it you will find a soldier, a statesman, a poet, a painter, or a Master in Chancery, whilst "maddening in the rear" through the gates come a posse of authors, actors, amateurs, artists, of every description, till you think of Juvenal's stinging lines, and his Protean Greek, who was

"Grammaticus, rhetor, geometres, pictor, aliptes,
Augur, schœnobates, medicus, magus," etc.,

and vote a fox-hunter the conglomeration of all these different accomplishments.

But Mr. Sawyer did not trouble himself much about Juvenal or his opinions. Finding his classical career a failure, and, what was more disappointing, his anticipated season with Mr. Drake cut short in consequence of his misadventure with the bull, he gave up the little reading which he had been compelled to take in hand, and confined his studies exclusively to 'Bell's Life,' 'The Field,' with its questions and answers to correspondents, suggestive alike of inventive ingenuity as of exhaustive research, and the 'Sporting Magazine.' The fact is, what with hunting three and four times a week, talking of it the remaining days, and thinking of it all the seven, with constant visits to the stable and a perpetual feud with his blacksmith, Mr. Sawyer's mind was completely filled with as much as that receptacle could be thought capable of containing.

My hero, like the champions of the Round Table, is perhaps seen to the greatest advantage on horseback. Let me introduce him to my reader, riding like a knight through the wilds of Lyonnesse, up a deep muddy lane, as he returns from hunting in the dull November twilight.

"Capital bit of stuff," says Mr. Sawyer, knocking off the ashes of his cigar with his dogskin-clad finger, and apostrophizing his "mount," a very little grey horse, with an arched neck and light mouth, and a tail set on high on his quarters. "Capital bit of stuff," he repeats, dangling his feet out of the stirrups; "as game as a pebble, and as neat as a pink." "Two hundred—two hundred and fifty! You're worth two hundred and fifty, every shilling of it" (he had bought him of a fishmonger for forty pounds and a broken-winded pony). "Worth as much as any horse *can* be to carry thirteen stone. Hang it; you'd *fetch* all the money at Tattersall's if any of *the customers* could only have seen you go to-day!"

Then Mr. Sawyer placed his feet in the stirrups, and fell to thinking of his day's sport.

They had really had a good run—a fine, wild, old-fashioned fox-hunting sort of run—from two hundred acres of woodland, down a couple of miles of bottomless ravine, and away over deep stiff ploughs and frequent straggling fences, till they reached the far-stretching Downs. Here their fox had made his point good up-wind, and the pace even of those square-headed, deep-ribbed, heavy-timbered hounds had been liberal enough to satisfy the most exacting. Mr. Sawyer remembered, with a glow of pride, how, when they descended into the low country once more, he had led the field, and jumped an awkward stile, into a lane, to the admiration of all beholders. He could *ride*, to give him his due; and, moreover, he knew what hounds were doing, and was familiar with the country. Therefore he had slipped away with them, when the pack, after three or four turns round the huge woodland, had forced their fox into the open; therefore he had kept on the down-wind side of the ravine aforesaid, and therefore he had been fortunate enough to see the fox handsomely run into, in an old double hedgerow, after an hour and forty minutes, during which he had unquestionably "gone best" from end to end. The huntsman said so—a wary ancient, who, never showing in front at any period, or running the slightest risks in the way of pace or fencing, had a huntsman's peculiar knack of turning up when he was wanted, particularly towards the finish. The doctor said so—an old rival, whose high character for riding entitled him to be generous; and the fishmonger, previous possessor of the grey, loudly affirmed, with many oaths which it is unnecessary to repeat, that "Muster Sawyer always was a hout-and-houter, and had gone audacious!" Contrary to custom, none of the rest of the field had been near enough to give an opinion, though excuses as usual were rife for non-appearance. To judge from his own account, no man ever misses a run, save by a concatenation of circumstances totally unprecedented. Besides every normal casualty, he would always seem to have been baffled throughout by an opposing fiend of remarkable perseverance and diabolical ingenuity.

As the sun went down in a deep crimson segment, like the glow of a ruby, or the danger-signal on a railway, Mr. Sawyer lit a fresh cigar, and began to ponder on the merits of his own riding and the capabilities of his stud. As the daylight waned, and the grey ash of his "choice Laranaga" (seven-and-forty shillings the pound) grew longer and longer, he began to think so much talent was quite wasted in "the provinces"—that he was capable of better things than "showing the way" to the half-dozen of red-coats and couple of farmers who constituted his usual "gallery"— that he was too good for the Old Country, as its sportsmen affectionately designate that picturesque locality in which they follow the chase—and that he was bound to do himself and the little grey horse justice by visiting the wide pastures, the prairie-like grazing-ground of the crack countries; to use his own vernacular, that he ought to "cut the whole concern for a season, and have a turn at the Shires." His cogitations took some such form as the following:—"Here am I, still on the sunny side of forty—in the prime of my life, of my pluck, of my strength, and—ahem!—of my appearance—none so dusty neither, on horseback, whatever Miss Mexico may think, with her olive skin and her stuck-up airs. After all, I don't know that I'd have had her, though she *was* a thirty-thousand pounder! I don't like 'em touched with the tar-brush. I'm all for the thorough-bred ones—women, as well as horses. Well, here I am, wasting my life in these deserted ploughs. Even if we do get a run, such as we had to-day, I have no one to talk to about it. The Grange is a crafty crib enough, and I'm as comfortable there as a bachelor need to be; but I can't go home, night after night, to bolt my dinner by myself, smoke by myself to digest it, and go to bed at ten o'clock, because I'm so bored with John Sawyer, and it's the only way to get rid of him. No, hang it! I'll emigrate; I'll go and *hibernate* in the grass. I'll make Isaac a stud-groom; I'll buy a couple more nags, the right sort too—show those dandified chaps how to *ride*, and perhaps sell the lot for a hatful of money at the end of the season, and have all my fun for nothing." Deluded man! how feasible the latter project sounds—how difficult to realize!

The idea once having taken possession of our friend's mind, soon found itself cramped for room in that somewhat circumscribed area. All dinner-time he was absent and preoccupied; even Scotch broth, a beef-steak pudding, a damson tart, and toasted cheese, did not tend to settle him. Two of the Laranagas were converted into smoke and ashes before he could come to anything like a definite conclusion. Though a temperate man habitually (for the sake of his nerves), he rang for the old brandy labelled V.O.P., and mixed himself a real stiff one, with boiling water and one lump of sugar. I have my suspicions that his final decision was partly its result. The great difficulty was where to go. A man of limited acquaintance and reserved manners has at least this advantage—that all parts of England are equally attractive as regards society. Then he had hunted too much to believe newspaper accounts of sport, so that looking up the old files of 'Bell's Life' assisted him no whit to a conclusion; also being of an inquiring turn of mind, wherever foxhunting was concerned, he had amassed such a quantity of information concerning the " flying countries," that it took him a considerable time and another glass of brandy-and-water to digest and classify his facts. Altogether it was a complicated and puzzling question. First he thought of Leamington and the Warwickshire North and South, with regular attendance on the Atherstone and one field-day per week with the Pytchley; but many considerations combined to render the Spa ineligible as his head-quarters. In the first place, the evening gaieties made his hair stand on end. Since his rejection by Miss Mexico, Sawyer was no dancing man; and indeed even in the first flush of his courtship he was seen to less advantage in a white neckcloth than a blue bird's-eye. Some men's hands and feet are not made to fit boots and gloves as constructed by our neighbour the fiery Gaul, and for such it is wise to abstain from "the mazy," and to rest their hopes of success on other and more sterling qualities than the rapid demeanour and cool assurance which triumph in a ball-room. Then, with all his fondness for the applause of his fellow-creatures, he did not quite fancy making *one* of that crowd of irregular-horse who appear on a Wednesday at Crick or Misterton, to the unspeakable dismay of the Pytchley *lady* pack, who, if there is anything *like* a scent, scour away from them as if for their very lives; and although it is doubtless a high compliment that two hundred gentlemen in scarlet should patronize the same establishment, Mr. Sawyer thought that as far as *he* was concerned, the number might as well stop at one hundred and ninety-nine.

I believe, however, that the dread of those wide and fathomless rivers which are constantly jumped, in Warwickshire, by at least *one* amphibious sportsman out of a daring field, and of which the width from bank to bank, according to the newspapers, is seldom less than seven-and-twenty or more than seven-and-thirty feet, was what principally terrified our friend. Accustomed to a leading championship at home, he shrank from such aquatic rivalry, and resolved that, with all its fascinations, Warwickshire at least should not have the benefit of his patronage.

Once, after a steaming gulp of the stimulating fluid, the idea of Melton flashed across his mind, but it was dismissed as soon as entertained. "I'm not such a fool as I look," quoth Mr. Sawyer; "and I don't mean to keep eight hunters and a couple of hacks to meet a set of fellows every day, who won't condescend to notice me unless I do as they do. Whist and dry champagne, and off to London at the first appearance of frost; ride like a butcher all day, risking twice as much neck as I do here, and then come out 'quite the lady' at dinner-time, and choke in a white tie, acting the part of a walking gentleman all the evening. No! Melton won't suit my book at any price. Besides, I'd never sell my horses there; they order their hunters down from London just as they do their 'baccy' and their breeches." So the idea of Melton was dismissed; and a vision of Oakham, or Uppingham, or even Billesdon rose in its stead. He could not quite get those tempting pastures, with their sunny slopes and flying fences, out of his head. The same objection, however, applied to the last-mentioned places that drove him from home, viz. the want of society. That deficiency seemed to threaten him wherever he set up his staff. At Wansford he would be as solitary as in the Old Country; also he would be further from High Leicestershire than he liked. The same drawback was attached to Lutterworth, and Rugby, and Northampton. It was not till the third glass that the inspiration seized him. Dashing the end of his cigar under the grate, he rose from his easy chair, stuck his hands in his pockets and his back to the waning fire, stamped thrice on the hearth-rug, like a necromancer summoning his familiar, and exclaimed aloud, "The very place! I wonder I never thought of it before. Strike me ugly, if I won't go to Market Harborough!"

Then he finished his brandy-and-water at a gulp, lit his candle, and tumbled up to bed, where he dreamed he was riding a rocking-horse over the Skeffington Lordship, with no one in the same field with him but the late Mr. William Scott, the vehemence of whose language was in exact proportion to the strength of the beverage which had constituted his own night-cap.

CHAPTER II.

"MR. JOB SLOPER."

THE ancient Persians, who seem also to have been wonderful fellows to ride, had a pleasing system of deliberation, which has somewhat fallen into disuse in our modern Parliaments. According to the old historians, it was their practice to discuss all graver matters of policy when in a state of inebriety, giving their debate the advantage of being resumed and repeated next morning; also, should they inadvertently convene a meeting when sober, to reverse the process, and ascertain whether on getting drunk over it they arrived at the same result. The system was not without its merits, no doubt, one of the most prominent of which seems to have been that it entailed a double allowance of liquor. Mr. Sawyer was sufficiently a Persian to reconsider his decision of the previous night, when he woke next morning with a trifling head-ache, and a tongue more like that of the reindeer, as preserved by Fortnum and Mason, than the organ of speech and deglutition peculiar to the human subject.

He was a hard fellow enough; but no man can smoke cigars and drink hot-stopping the last thing at night, and get up in the morning without remembering that he has done so.

A plunge into his cold bath, however, a cup of warm tea, with a rasher of bacon frizzling from the fire, and well peppered, soon restored the brightness to our friend's eye and the colour to his cheek. When he lit his cigar on his own well-cleaned door-step, and turned his face to the balmy breath of "jocund day," under a soft November sky, dappled, and mellowed, and tinged here and there with gold by the winter sun, he felt, as he expressed it, "fit as a fiddle, and hotter upon Market Harborough than ever."

He was a man of few words though, when he meant business, and only pausing for a moment at the Stable, and feeling the grey's legs, which somehow always *did* fill after a day's hunting, he took no living mortal into his confidence, not even the taciturn Isaac (of whom more hereafter); but started for a five-mile walk, to inspect the stables of a certain horse-coping worthy, with whom he had long been too well acquainted, and who generally had a good bit of stuff somewhere about the premises, provided only you could get hold of the right one.

Mr. Sawyer was not a man to order a horse out of the stable in the hunting season for any but the legitimate purpose of the chase. "Walking," he said, "kept him in wind;" and off he started down a narrow lane that in summer was thick with blackberries and blooming with dog-roses, and over a stile and across a fallow, and through a wood, at an honest five-mile-an-hour, heel-and-toe; every turn in the path reminding him, as he stepped along, of some feat of horsemanship or skilful shot, or other pleasing association connected with his country home. And this is one of the greatest advantages of hunting *from* home. After all, notwithstanding her irresistible attractions, we cannot follow Diana every day of our lives, and surely it is wiser and pleasanter to take her as we want her amongst our own woods and glades, and breezy uplands, and pleasant shady nooks, than to go all the way to Ephesus on purpose to worship with the crowd. Mixed motives, however, seem to be the springs that set in motion our human frames; and if Care sits behind the horseman on the cantle of his saddle, Ambition may also be detected clinging somewhere about his spurs.

In little more than an hour Mr. Sawyer found himself entering a dilapidated farmyard, of which three sides consisted of tumble-down sheds and out-houses; while the fourth, in somewhat better repair, denoted by its ventilating windows, latched doors, and occasional stable-buckets, that its inmates were of the equine race. Stamping up a bricked passage, on either side of which sundry plants were dying in about three inches of mould, our friend wisely entered the open door of the kitchen, preferring that easy ingress to the adjacent portal, of which a low scraper and rusty knocker seemed to point out that it was chiefly intended for visits of ceremony. Here he encountered nothing more formidable than a white cat sleeping by the fire, and a Dutch clock, with an enormous countenance, ticking drowsily in the warmest corner of the apartment.

Coughing loudly, and shuffling his feet against the sanded floor, he soon succeeded in summoning a bare-armed maid-of-all-work, with a dirty face and flaunting ribbons in her cap, who, to his inquiries whether "Mr. Sloper was at home," answered, as maids-of-all-work invariably do, that "Master had just stepped out for a minute, but left word he would be back directly: would you please to take a seat?"

This interval, our friend, who, as he often remarked, "wasn't born yesterday," determined to spend in a private visit to the stables, and left the kitchen accordingly for that purpose. It is needless to observe that he had barely coasted a third of the ocean of muck which constituted the centre of the yard, ere he encountered the proprietor himself coming leisurely to greet him, with a welcome on his ruddy face and a straw in his mouth.

Mr. Sloper was a hale hearty man of some three-score years or so, who must have been very good-looking in his prime; but whose countenance, from the combined effects of good-living and hard weather, had acquired that mottled crimson tinge which, according to Dickens, is seldom observed except in underdone boiled beef and the faces of old mail coachmen and guards. It would have puzzled a physiognomist to say whether good-humour or cunning prevailed in the twinkle of his bright little blue eye; but the way in which he wore his shaved hat and stuck his hands into the pockets of his wide-skirted grey riding-coat, would have warned any observer of human nature that he was skilled in horseflesh and versed in all the secrets that lend their interest to that fascinating animal. Somehow Honesty seems to go faster on horseback than afoot.

Not that a man of Mr. Sloper's years and weight ever got upon the backs of his purchases, save perhaps in very extreme cases, and where "the lie with circumstances" was as indispensable as "the lie direct." No, he confined himself to dealing for them over dark-coloured glasses of brandy-

and-water, puffing them unconscionably in the stable, and pretending to ignore them completely when he met his own property out-of-doors. "His eyesight," he said, "was failing him; positively he didn't know his own nags now, when he met them in his neighbour's field!"

Tradition asserted, however, that Job Sloper, when a younger man, had been one of the best and boldest riders in the Old Country. The limp which affected his walk had been earned in a rattling fall over a turnpike-gate for a wager of a new hat, and Fiction herself panted in detailing his many exploits by flood and field when he first went into the trade. These had lost nothing by time and repetition, but even now, in those exceptional cases where he condescended to get into the saddle, there was no question that the old man could put them along still; for, as lusty and heavy as he'd grown, "I'm a sad cripple now, sir," he'd say, in a mild reflective voice; "and they wants to be very quiet and gentle for me. I never had not what I call good nerve in the best of times, though I liked to see the hounds run a bit too. I was always fond of the sport, you see; and even now it does me good to watch a gent like yourself in the saddle. What I calls a *reel* 'orseman—as can give-an'-take, and bend his back like Old Sir 'Arry; him as kept our hounds for so long. If it ain't taking too great a liberty, perhaps you're related to Sir 'Arry: you puts me in mind of him so much, the way you carries your 'ands!"

The old hypocrite! Ingenuous youth was pretty sure to "stop and have a bit of lunch" after that, and after lunch was it not human nature that it should buy?

CHAPTER III.

"YOUR HAND-WRITING, SIR."

"Mornin', sir," says Mr. Sloper, scenting a customer as he accosts his guest. "Oh, it's you, is it, Mr. Sawyer? Won't ye step in and set down after your walk? Take a glass of mild ale and a crust of bread-and-cheese, or a drop of sherry or anythink?"

"No hunting to-day, Job," answers the visitor, declining the refreshment; "so I just toddled over to see how you're getting on, and have a look round the stables; no harm in looking, you know."

Mr. Sloper's face assumes an expression of profound mystery. "I'm glad you come over to-day, sir," he says, in a tone of confidential frankness, "of all days in the year. I've a 'orse here, as I should like to ast your opinion about—a gent like *you* as knows what a 'unter really is. And so you should, Mr. Sawyer, for there's no man alive takes greater liberties with 'em when they *can* go and do it. And I've got one in that box, as *I* think, just *is* more than curious."

"Would he carry *me?*" asks Mr. Sawyer, with well-affected indifference, as if he had not come over expressly to find one that would. "Not that I *want* a horse, you know; but if I saw one I liked very much, and you didn't price him too high, why I *might* be induced to buy against next season, perhaps."

Job took his hands out of his coat-pockets, and spread them abroad, as it were to dry. The action denoted extreme purity and candour.

"No; I don't think as he ought to carry *you*, sir," was the unexpected reply. "Now, I ain't a-going to tell you a lie, Mr. Sawyer. This horse didn't *ought* to be ridden, not the way *you* take and ride them, Mr. Sawyer; leastways not over such a blind heart-breaking country as this here. He's too good, he is, for that kind of work; he ought to be in Leicestershire, *he* ought; the Harborough country, that's the country for him. He's too fast for *us*, and that's the truth. Only, to be sure, we have a vast of plough hereabout, and *I* never see such a sticker through dirt. It makes no odds to him, pasture *or* plough, and the sweetest hack ever I clapped eyes on besides. However, you shall judge for yourself, Mr. Sawyer. I won't ask you to believe *me*. You've a quicker eye to a horse than I have, by a long chalk, and I'd sooner have your opinion than my own. I *would* now, and that's the truth!"

Our purchaser began to think he might possibly have hit upon *the* animal at last. Often as he had been at the game, and often as he had been disappointed, he was still sanguine enough to believe he might draw the prize-ticket in the lottery at any time. As I imagine every man who pulls on his boots to go out hunting has a sort of vague hope that to-day may be his day of triumph with the hounds, so the oldest and wariest of us cannot go into a dealer's yard without a sort of half-conscious idea that there *must* be a trump card somewhere in the pack, and it *may* be our luck to hold it as well as another's.

But Sloper, like the rest of his trade, was not going to show his game first. It seems to be a maxim with all salesmen to prove their customers with inferior articles before they come to the real thing. Mr. Sawyer had to walk through a four-stall stable, and inspect, preparatory to declining, a mealy bay cob, a lame grey, a broken-winded chestnut, and an enormous brown animal, very tall, very narrow, very ugly, with extremely upright forelegs and shoulders to match. The latter his owner affirmed to be "*an extraordinary shaped un*," as no doubt he was. A little playful *badinage* on the merits of this last enlivened the visit.

"What will you take for the brown, Sloper, if I buy him at so much the foot?" said the customer, as they emerged into the fresh air.

"Say ten pound a foot, sir!" answered Job, with the utmost gravity, "and ten over, because *he always has a foot to spare*. Come now, Mr. Sawyer, I can afford to let a good customer like you have that horse for *fefty. Fefty* guineas, or even *pounds*, sir, to *you*. I got him in a bad debt, you see, sir;—it's Bible truth I'm telling ye;—and he only stood *me* in forty-seven pounds ten, *and* a sov. I gave the man as brought him over. He's not everybody's horse, Mr. Sawyer, that isn't; but I think he'll carry *you* remarkably well."

"I don't think I'll ever give him a chance," was the rejoinder. "Come, Job, we're burning daylight; let's go and have a look at the crack."

One individual had been listening to the above conversation with thrilling interest. This was no less a personage than Barney, Mr. Sloper's head groom, general factotum, and rough-rider in ordinary—an official whose business it was to ride anything *at* anything, for anybody who asked him. He was a little old man, with one eye, a red handkerchief, and the general appearance of a post-boy on half-pay; a sober fellow, too, and as brave as King Richard; yet had he expressed himself strongly about this said brown horse, the previous evening, to the maid-of-all-work. "He's the wussest we've had yet," was his fiat. "It's nateral for

c 2

'em to fall; but when *he* falls, he's all over a chap till he's crumpled him." So his heroic heart beat more freely when they adjourned to the neighbouring box.

Mr. Sloper threw the door open with an air. It must be confessed he seldom had one that would bear, without preparation, a minute inspection from the eye of a sportsman; but he knew *this* was a sound one, and made the most of it. Clothed and hooded, littered to the hocks, and sheeted to the tail, there was yet something about his general appearance that fascinated Mr. Sawyer at once. Job saw the spell was working, and abstained from disturbing it. As far as could be seen, the animal was a long, low, wellbred-looking roan, with short flat legs, large clean hocks, and swelling muscular thighs. His supple skin threw off a bloom, as if he was in first-rate condition; and when, laying his ears back and biting the manger, he lifted a foreleg, as it were, to expostulate with his visitors, the hoof was round, open, and well-developed, as blue, and to all appearance as hard, as a flint.

"Has he *fashion* enough, think ye, sir?" asked Job, at length, breaking the silence. "Strip him, Barney," he added, taking the straw from his mouth.

The roan winced, and stamped, and whisked his tail, and set his back up during the process; but when it was concluded, Mr. Sawyer could not but confess to himself, that if he was only as good as he *looked*, he would *do*.

"Feel his legs, Mr. Sawyer!" observed the dealer, turning away to conceal the triumph that *would* ooze out. "There's some legs—there's some hocks and thighs! Talk of loins, and look where his tail's set on. Carries his *own* head, too; and *if* you could see his manners! I never saw such manners in the hunting-field. Six-year-old—not a speck or blemish; bold as a bull, and gentle as a lady; he can go as fast as you can clap your hands, and stay till the middle of the week after next—jump a town, too, and never turn his head from the place you put him at. As handy as a fiddle, as neat as a pink, and worth all the money to carry in your eye when you go out to buy hunters. But what's the use of talking about it to a judge like you? Lay your leg over him—only just lay your leg over him, Mr. Sawyer. I don't want you to buy him! but get on him and feel his action, just as a favour to *me*."

Our friend had made up his mind he would do so from the first. There was no mistaking the appearance of the animal; so good was it, that he had but two misgivings— some rank unsoundness, to account for its being there, or so high a price as to be beyond his means; for Mr. Sawyer was too fond of the sport to give a sum that he could not replace for so perishable an article as a hunter.

He was no mean equestrian, our friend, and quite at home on a strange horse. As he drew the curb-rein gently through his fingers, the roan dropped his long lean head, and champed the bit playfully, tossing a speck of froth back on his rider's boots.

"You've got a mouth, at any rate," quoth Mr. Sawyer, and trotted him gently down the hard road, the animal stepping freely and gaily under him, full of life and spirits. The customer liked his mount, and couldn't help showing it. "May I lark him?" said he, pulling up after a short canter to and fro on the turf by the wayside; during which Job Sloper had been exercising his mental arithmetic in what we may term a sum of problematical addition.

"Take him into the close, sir," was the generous reply; "put him at anything you like. If you can get him into one of these fences, I'll *give* him to you!"

So Mr. Sawyer sat down to jump a low hedge and ditch, then stood up, and caught hold of the roan's head, and sent him a cracker through the adjoining plough, and across a larger fence into a pasture, and back again over a fair flight of rails and lost his flat shooting-hat, and rucked his plaid trousers up to his knees; and Sloper marked his kindling eye and glowing cheek, and knew that he had *landed* him.

"Walk him about for ten minutes before you do him over," said that worthy to Barney, as Mr. Sawyer dismounted, and the latter brought him his hat. "And now, sir," added the hospitable dealer, "you can't go away without tasting my cheese—the same you liked last time, you know. Walk in, sir; this way, and mind the step, if *you* please." So speaking, Mr. Sloper ushered his guest into a neat little parlour with a strong odour of preserved tobacco-smoke, where a clean cloth set off a nice luncheon of bread and cheese, flanked by a foaming jug of strong ale and a decanter of oily-brown sherry.

And herein the dealer showed his knowledge of human nature, and his discrimination in the different characteristics of the species. Had his guest been some generous scion of the aristocracy, with more money than nerves, he would have *primed* him first, and put him up to ride afterwards. But he knew his man. He was well aware that Mr. Sawyer required no stimulant to make him jump, but a strong one to induce him to part with his money; so he proposed the luncheon after he was satisfied that his customer was pleased with his mount.

Neither of them touched on business during the meal, the conversation consisting chiefly of the runs that had lately taken place in the old country, with many an inferred compliment to the good riding of the possible purchaser.

Then Mr. Sawyer, produced the *Laranagas* and offered one to Job, who bit it, and wet it, and smoked it, as men do who are more used to clay pipes, and then they went back to the stable to see the roan done up.

The gallop and the ale were working in Mr. Sawyer's brain, but he didn't see his way into the roan at a hundred; so he obstinately held his tongue. The dealer was obliged to break the ice.

"I'd take it very friendly of you, sir, if you'd give me your honest opinion of that horse," said he, waving the *Laranaga* towards the animal. "I fancy he's too good for our country; and I've a brother-in-law down in Rutland as wants to have him very bad. He's just the cut, so he says, for these Melton gents; and he's a good judge, is my brother-in-law, and a pretty rider to boot. He'd give me my price, too; but then, you know, sir, askin' your pardon, it isn't always ready money between relations; and that cuts the other way again, as a man may say. What do *you* think, Mr. Sawyer?"

"I'll find out what he wants for him, at any rate," thought the customer. "What's his figure?" was the abrupt rejoinder.

Mr. Sloper hesitated. "A hundred and—" *eighty*, he was going to say; but seeing his customer's eye resting on the roan's back-ribs—a point in which the horse was somewhat deficient—he dropped at once to seventy, and regretted it the next moment when he caught the expression of the listener's face.

"It isn't *even* money," answered Mr. Sawyer, without, however, making the same sort of face he had done several times before, when he had refused to give double the sum at which he had eventually purchased. "I should say you might get a hundred and twenty for him down there, if you'd luck. But it's a great risk—a great risk—and a long distance; and perhaps have him sent back to you in the spring. If I wanted a horse, *I'd* give you a hundred for him, though he isn't exactly my sort. A hundred!—I'll tell you what, Sloper, I'll be hanged if I won't *chance* it—I'll *give* you a hundred—*guineas*—come! Money down, and no questions asked."

"I can warrant him sound," answered Mr. Sloper; "and I'd rather *you* had him than anybody. But it's childish talking of a hundred guineas and that horse on the same afternoon. However, I thank you kindly all the same, Mr. Sawyer. Barney! shut the box up. Come in, sir, and have *one* glass of sherry before you start. The evenings get chill at this time of year, and that's old sherry, and won't hurt you no more than milk. He *is* a nice horse, Mr. Sawyer, I think—a *very* nice horse, and I'm glad you're pleased with him."

So they returned into the little parlour, and stirred up the fire, and finished the bottle of old sherry: nor is it necessary to remark that, with the concluding glass of that generous fluid the roan became the property of John Standish Sawyer, under the following somewhat complicated agreement:—That he was to give an immediate cheque for a hundred and forty pounds, and ten pounds more at the end of the season; which latter donation was to be increased to twenty if he should sell him for anything over two hundred—a contingency which the dealer was pleased to observe amounted to what he called "a moral."

The new owner went to look at him once more in the stable, and thought him the nicest horse he ever saw in his life. The walk home, too, was delightful, till the sherry had evaporated, when it became rather tedious; and at dinner-time Mr. Sawyer was naturally less hungry than thirsty. All the evening, however, he congratulated himself on having done a good day's work. All night, too, he dreamed of the roan; and on waking resolved to call him "Hotspur."

When the horse came home next day, he certainly looked rather smaller than his new owner had fancied. Old Isaac too, growled out his untoward opinion that he "looked a sort as would work very *light*." But then Isaac always grumbled—it was the old groom's way of enjoying himself.

CHAPTER IV.

MARCHING ORDERS.

Isaac was a character in his way—quite an institution at The Grange, where, by dint of indomitable tenacity of opinion, and a singular talent for silence, he had contrived to extend his influence over a good many matters not in the least connected with his department. For instance, not a sheep could be killed without consulting Isaac. His word on the subject of pigs was law; and it needed but a wave of his hand to substitute for the useless, hideous, gigantic Cochin-Chinas of the poultry-yard, a certain breed of plump Dorkings, that laid diurnal eggs in their lifetime, and, after death, made almost as handsome an appearance as Norfolk turkeys on the dining-table.

Perhaps the old groom was less omnipotent in the stable than elsewhere. Mr. Sawyer, like many other proprietors of small studs, chose to have his own way with his horses, and would no more have omitted to visit them after breakfast than he would have neglected to smoke his cigar. It is only the tip-top swells, with whom our friend had not yet scraped acquaintance, who " suppose their *fellow* will have '*two or three*' at the place of meeting." But although it is doubtless a great luxury to own plenty of hunters, this very plurality often prevents a man from finding out which is his best horse. There are not a great many *good* runs over any country in one season. It is a long time before you have treated each one of your dozen to a clipper; and, till then, you only know you have a good *hunter*, but cannot tell you have got a good *horse*.

Mr. Sawyer, however, knew the merits and the failings of his own two or three nags but too well. He was pretty often on their backs, and, when off them, constantly in and out of the stable. Isaac would no more have dared to give one of them a gallop, or a dose of physic, than to have inflicted the same discipline on his master. Nevertheless he grumbled always and continuously. As I have said before, it was the one relaxation he permitted himself. Perhaps he never had a better opportunity than on the morning after the new horse came home, when Mr. Sawyer, according to custom, but with a trifle more eagerness than usual, visited his favourites in their comfortable quarters. According to custom, too, he felt their legs all round; expressed his satisfaction that the grey's had got "quite fine again," and passed over a certain thick-set underbred bay horse without a remark. Indeed, it would have been difficult to say anything complimentary of this animal; and his remaining so long in Mr. Sawyer's stable was less the consequence of his merits than that strangers seemed to have the same opinion of him as was entertained by his own master. It *is* somewhat galling, when we cannot get rid of a bad one, to reflect that it should be so difficult to find a bigger fool than ourselves. The bay, who rejoiced in the classical appellation of *Marathon*, was a slow horse, a sulky horse, and by no means a safe fencer—about as unpleasant a hunter as a man would wish to get upon, but rather a favourite with Isaac notwithstanding, as he was sound, and a voracious feeder. These three, the roan, the grey (who had no name), and the bay, with a little three-cornered jumping hack called Jack-a-Dandy, now constituted Mr. Sawyer's stud; and, as he contemplated them all hard at work with their eleven o'clock feed, he felt that spark of ambition glowing in his bosom which has lured so many great men to their destruction.

"He *looks* a clipper! don't he, Isaac?" observed the master, nodding towards the roan's long shapely quarters and square tail. "The rarest shaped one we've had in *this* stable for many a day," he added, seeing his servant's features screwed into the well-known twist that denoted disapprobation.

"Looks!" grunted Isaac, who never called his master "sir." "Looks! Ah! he'd be a nice thing enough to knock a light trap about, or do you a day now and then when the country gets dry. He'll never be fit for our ploughs—you see if he will! They'll pull him to pieces in a fortnight—you see if they won't!"

"I don't *want* him for our ploughs," answered Mr. Sawyer, waxing somewhat impatient. "I don't think I shall have another day in the old country this year. Look ye here, Isaac. I'm going to move the horses. I've three now, let alone 'Jack'" (this was an abbreviation for the hack, who seldom enjoyed his full name, being generally designated as above, or as "The Dandy")—"three right good ones. I can easily pick up another, when I'm settled. I'm going down to the grass."

"Grass!" grunted the listener. "Where be that?"

"Well, I'm going to see what sport they have in the Shires," answered his master, warming up with the subject —"going to have a look at Mr. Tailby and the Earl of Stamford and Warrington, and try if I can't make a fight good enough to see those Pytchley bitches run into their fox. I'm going to Market Harborough, Isaac. Such horses as mine are wasted in this out-of-the-way country. Why, the grey's the best I've ever had; and the roan ought to be faster than he; and even the bay would carry me better, I think, in that country than he does here."

A gleam as of pity softened old Isaac's hard blue eye, as it rested on Marathon tucking in his feed, and he pictured that devoted animal rolling and lurching, disconsolate, over the ridge-and-furrow of a fifty-acre grass-field. But he only observed sardonically,

"Markit Harboro', is it? To stand at the sign of the 'Hand-in-Pocket,' I suppose?"

"Never mind what you suppose!" answered Mr. Sawyer, now positively angry. "You do what I bid you. Move the horses down to-morrow by the rail. Take The Boy with you; and mind you keep him out of mischief. I've written to a friend of mine to engage stables. Next week we'll begin work in right earnest. Come into the house, with your book, after your dinner; and hold your tongue!"

Old Isaac knew better than to pursue the subject any further; and, truth to tell, the old fellow had a spark of his youth's adventurous spirit lingering about him still, which made him not averse to a change, although he thought the scheme wasteful, imprudent, and extravagant. He looked after his master, strolling leisurely towards the house, and observed very slowly to himself and the stable-cat:

"Market 'Arborow! Market 'Arborow! Five days a week, bullock-fences, and a wet country! Thorns, stubs, cracked heels, and hawful wear-an'-tear of horses! No—I couldn't have believed it of him!"

Eight-and-forty hours more saw old Isaac stamping drearily about on the wet pavement of that excellent sporting locality. Market Harborough, though perhaps the best head-quarters in the world for fox-hunting, can scarcely be termed a gay or very beautiful town. On a wet, drizzling afternoon in early winter, when twilight begins somewhere about 2.45, with no movable object visible save a deserted carrier's cart, and a small rain falling, which dulls the red-brick houses while it polishes the paved and slippery streets, it is, doubtless, a city suggestive of repose, not to say stagnation. Isaac's was a temperament sufficiently susceptible of all unpleasant influences; and he began to wish heartily he hadn't come. A variety of disadvantages had occurred to him since his arrival. The price of forage and stabling he considered enormous. The conveniences for hot water were not what he was accustomed to at home. Hotspur did by no means feed well in a strange box: the horse had begun to look poorer day by day since he left the dealer's. And last night The Boy, who had never been from home before, certainly smelt of gin when he came to bed.

This youth—who, if he once had a name, must have long forgotten it, since he was never called anything but "The Boy"—was a continual thorn in the head groom's side. He had originally been taken solely on Isaac's recommendation, and had caused that worthy more trouble than all the rest of the establishment put together, horses, pigs, and the Cochin-Chinas to boot. He was a light, lathy lad, with a pretty face; a good horseman, considering his strength, or rather weakness; and had a knack of keeping his hands down: but he owned the usual faults of boyhood—carelessness, forgetfulness, "*imperence*" (as Isaac called it), a great love of procrastination, and general insensibility to the beauty of truth.

"If he takes to drinking, the young warmint!" thought Isaac, "I'll larrup the skin off him!" And thus consoling himself, the old man turned his cheek once more to the chill, misty heavens, and shook his head. His horses were done up; the door locked, and the key in his pocket; The Boy also secured by the same means in the loft. Master could not arrive till eight or nine o'clock. It was the hour when, at The Grange, he was accustomed to see the pigs feed and the chickens to roost. He wished he was back in the old country: the time hung heavily on the old groom's hands.

"Nothing to do, and lots of time to do it in! that seems to be about the size of it—eh, governor?" said a voice at his elbow; and, turning round, Isaac confronted a short and dapper personage, whom, by a sort of freemasonry, he had no difficulty in recognizing as one of his own profession.

At any other time he would have treated this worthy's advances to acquaintance with sovereign contempt; but his spirits were depressed and his heart solitary, so he vented a grunt of acquiescence, which, for him, was wonderfully polite.

"I think I see you arrive yesterday, with two or three

nags," continued this affable functionary, "when I was out a hairin' some o' mine; and you're puttin' up close by my place. Come in, governor, and take something hot, to keep the cold off till we becomes better acquainted."

With this hospitable offer, Isaac found himself following his new friend into a cosy little tap-room, with red curtains and a sanded floor, which apartment they had all to themselves; and whilst "something hot"—a delicious compound of yolk of egg, brown sugar, warm beer, and cordial gin—was being got ready, he had time to study the exterior of his new acquaintance.

Probably the utmost ingenuity of the tailor's art must have been exhausted in constructing trousers so tight as the pair which clung to that person's legs. Not a crease had they, nor a fold anywhere; and, unless the man slept in them, it was difficult to conceive how they could conveniently be used as articles of daily apparel. The person's boots, too, were neat, round-toed Wellingtons; his waistcoat descended far below his hips; and the waist-buttons of his grey-mixture coat were unusually low and wide apart. A cream-coloured silk neck-cloth, secured by a horse-shoe pin, set off a pale, sharp-looking countenance, speaking of hot stables and dissipation, while the closest possible crop of hair and whiskers did justice to a shaved hat with an exceedingly flat brim. A few splashes of mud on the boots and trousers showed he had been lately on horseback; and he held up one of his thin little legs as he took his seat, and contemplated the stains with a grin of morbid satisfaction.

"Blessed if ever I see this country so deep!" he remarked, after a pull at the flip. "How *my* horses will stand it, I know no more than the dead, the way the governor rides.

We're *only* nine this year; and he's an awful hard man upon a horse."

" Nine!" exclaimed old Isaac, smacking his lips after the draught, which warmed the very cockles of his heart; and, being a man of few words, only added, "Well, now, to *be* sure!"

"He *is* awful hard upon 'em—that's the truth," continued the narrator. " It was only last week he says to me, 'Tiptop,' says he—*my* name's Tiptop—'what made Boadicea' (that's our bay mare by Bellerophon out of Blue Light) —'what made Boadicea stop with me under Carlton Clump to-day? Either she wasn't fit,' says he, 'or she isn't worth five shillings.' 'Well, sir,' says I, 'the mare's a gross feeder,' says I, 'and you ride with *rayther* a slack rein.' 'Slack rein be hanged!' says he. 'If ever such a thing happens again, you'll get the sack,' says he. So I up and told him I was ready to go whenever he could replace me; and the upshot of it was as he apologized quite like a gentleman; for, indeed, he wouldn't know whatever to do without me. He's a good man—my governor—enough; but he's hasty—very hasty. Why, to see him coming over a gate into the turnpike-road, as I did t'other day, on Catamount—that's our chestnut, as ran fourth for the Liverpool—you'd say he'd no discretion whatever; but they've all got their faults—all on 'em. What's yours? Can he ride?"

Discreet Isaac answered with a counter-question. "What's your governor's name?" said he, peeping once more into the waning pewter measure.

" The Honourable Crasher," replied Mr. Tiptop, not without an air of exultation. " A brother he is to the Hearl of Heligoland. Now I've told *you* all about it, old bloke. There —you ease your mind in return, and give us *your* name."

"I'll let you know when I've seen the register," answered Isaac. "But it's a long way to the parish as owes me a settlement; and I'm afraid you'll have to wait, Mr. Tiptop, till I can communicate with you by post." Saying which Isaac finished the flip at a gulp, and walked off to seven-o'clock stables without uttering another word.

CHAPTER V.

"BOOTS AND SADDLES."

LONDON is in the way to everywhere. I have an old friend, —an honest Lincolnshire squire,—who, paying his sister a visit in Norfolk, always goes and returns by London. I do not think it is necessary to traverse Oxford Street in order to proceed from the Old Country to Market Harborough; and yet on the day that witnessed his faithful groom's introduction to Mr. Tiptop, John Standish Sawyer might have been, and indeed *was*, seen crossing that crowded thoroughfare, with hasty steps and an air of considerable preoccupation.

The fact is, Mr. Sawyer was full of business. In the first place, it is needless to observe, he had been to have his hair cut—a rite seldom neglected by the true Englishman when entering upon a new phase in his career. Also he had to purchase many articles of wearing apparel, such as are only to be procured in the Metropolis. Since his rejection by Miss Mexico (for previous to that casualty he had been rather a gaudy dresser than otherwise), our friend, although preserving an equestrian exterior, had suffered his wardrobe to run considerably to seed. In truth, there was little temptation to extravagance on that score at The Grange. But now that he was about to take his place, as he observed, amongst the sporting aristocracy of Great Britain, it would be necessary to call in the aid of such artists as consider themselves the especial providers of boots, breeches, etc., for the first flight.

When I met him he was hurrying towards the well-known emporium of Messrs. Putty & Co., now universally acknowleged to be the only firm in London at which a truly workmanlike top-boot—combining, as their advertisement expresses it, " comfort to the wearer, with satisfaction to the looker-on"—is to be obtained. I could not resist my friend's imploring request to accompany him into the shop, and favour him with my experience on a subject which cannot be mastered without considerable observation and reflection.

Like most people from the country, Mr. Sawyer feels somewhat shy in the presence of a fashionable London tradesman. When he entered the warehouse, a languid gentleman, with one shoeless foot placed on a square of brown paper, was drawling out his directions to Messrs. Putty's foreman, an exceedingly smart and voluble disciple of St. Crispin.

" Not too thick," said the languid man, in a tone of utter physical exhaustion. " Man can't ride nicely, if he don't feel his stirrup through his boot;" and Sawyer nudged my elbow with a delighted wink, that seemed to say—" This swell, too, is a votary of Diana!"

The languid man's silk-stockinged foot having been reshod, he rose with great difficulty, and moved feebly in the direction of his brougham, from the window of which he adjured the shopman, in a faint voice, to forward "the tops when finished to my address at Market Harborough," and sank back amongst the cushions, completely overcome.

The talismanic syllables raised the curiosity of my friend. "Who is it?" he whispered eagerly to the returning shopman; and that worthy, placing a chair and a fresh square of brown paper for his new customer, replied somewhat condescendingly—"*That*, sir? That's the Honourable Crasher, sir; hunting gentleman, and *very* particular about his tops. What can I do for *you*, sir?"

I had now an opportunity of observing the great warmth and thickness of the worsted stockings in which my friend kept his legs encased; also the stout proportions of those useful limbs, more adapted perhaps for the Highland kilt, than any other costume. Mr. Putty's foreman saw at a glance the difficulties he would have to contend with, and prepared to subdue them.

"Very muscular gentleman!" said he; passing his tape round my friend's calf. "Great pedestrian powers, I should say. Inconvenient in the saddle; but will endeavour to rectify that. Excuse me, sir: take the liberty of asking whereabouts you generally hunt."

"Hunt?" repeated the customer. "Oh! Leicestershire —Northamptonshire—all about there—in the neighbourhood of Market Harborough." Mr. Sawyer spoke in a vague general sort of way, as if he was in the habit of pervading the whole of the grazing districts.

A cloud gathered on the foreman's brow.

"The Shires!" he rejoined, with a perplexed air; "that increases our difficulties very much indeed. I could have made you, now, a particular neat *provincial* boot; but with this pattern it's exceedingly difficult to attain the correct appearance for the flying countries. I'll show you a pair here, sir, that the Honourable Crasher sent back this very morning, because they fell away the eighth-of-an-inch at the setting-on of the leg, and the Honourable's girth is at least two-and-a-half less than yours. You wouldn't like a pair of Napoleons, I presume. Very fashionable just now, sir. All the gentlemen wear them in the Vale of Aylesbury."

I confess I rather expected an outburst at this suggestion: my friend sharing with me a strong prejudice against what have been termed " Butcher-boots ;" but

"Prolonged endurance tames the bold,"

and Sawyer submitted with considerable patience to the foreman's promise, that they would do all in their power to make him two pair of top-boots, only inferior to those of the Honourable Crasher, and send them down to him in a little over a fortnight; or, "*not* to disappoint him, say *punctually* that day three weeks."

A thorough revisal of gloves, neckcloths, etc., is soon made; and after a hearty luncheon at the railway station, I put my friend into a first-class carriage attached to the fast train, and wished him "Good sport," and "Good-bye," with a feeling somewhat akin to envy, as I remained in smoky London, and he was whirled away into the soft fragrant country saturated with rain, and smiling itself to sleep in the calm grey light of a mild winter's afternoon. He had but one fellow-passenger, of whom more anon.

I wonder whether the reflections of other men in a railway-carriage, bowling through the midland counties at the rate of forty miles an hour, on such a day as I have described, are like my own. I honestly confess that a very few ideas, if they are favourite ones, are sufficient to fill my brain. As I speed along the level embankments, which give one such a commanding view of the surrounding country, I cannot help imagining myself on the back of a good horse, sailing away from field to field after a pack of hounds. How well I can see my way!—how easy the fences look!—how readily I distinguish the place I should make him take off at, and the exact spot on which he would land, choosing unhesitatingly the soundest ridge, on which I should increase my pace so confidently down to that glassy brook, that looks as if you could hop over it from here, but which memory tells me is at least fifteen feet of water! How easy to get a start from that spinny, shaped liked a cocked-hat, of which the three corners have puzzled me so often, never hitting the one the hounds came out at, though I have tried them all in turn! How contemptible the size of this woodland, in which I have yet known a fox hang for hours together! What a run I have in imagination! and how well I see it! Alas! like everything else coloured through that deceitful medium, how different from the "cold reality"!

Nevertheless, much as I sympathize in his bride's consternation, I cannot deny a fellow-feeling with that bridegroom of whom it is related that, on a wedding-trip of many hours by the side of his late-won treasure, during which he ceased not to scan the adjacent fences with a practical eye, he uttered never a word during the entire journey, save this one remarkable sentence, "There's my place! Where would *you* have it?"

Some such ruminations as the above probably engrossed the whole of my friend's intellects, till the courteous offer of 'Punch'—containing, as usual, one of Leech's inimitable hunting sketches—drew his attention to his fellow-traveller, under whose multiplicity of wrappers he had no difficulty in recognizing the placid features of the gentleman he had that morning noticed in the boot-shop. It was, indeed, none other than the Honourable Crasher; by this time completely worn out, and who, to do him justice, was a gentlemanlike, well-featured fellow enough, if he had not always looked so dreadfully tired.

The reply to such a courtesy, where there were no ladies in the carriage, could only be, " Have you any objection to smoking?" And as nobody ever *does* object nowadays to that soothing practice, and the "forty-shilling penalty" is, I trust, simply a dead-letter and a fallacy, the *Laranagas* were produced, and a couple of them soon got very freely under way.

No introduction from a mutual friend is equal to that of a cigar. Any two votaries of the "pleasant vice," at least during the time they are engaged in its practice, are sure to fraternize, and in five minutes Mr. Sawyer and the Honourable Crasher were hard at it, I need scarcely observe, on the subject of fox-hunting; the former resolving, as far as possible, to pick the brains of his new acquaintance (if he could find them) on that exhaustless topic; the latter positively warming into a languid enthusiasm on the only subject to which he could direct his whole attention for ten consecutive minutes.

Racing men are bad enough. Politicians are sufficiently long-winded. A couple of agriculturists will keep the ball rolling pretty perseveringly on the congenial themes of "cake," mangold wurzel, short-horns, reaping-machines, and guano; but I have heard ladies, who are perhaps the best judges of volubility, affirm that, for energy, duration, and the faculty of saying the same thing over and over again, a dialogue between a couple of fox-hunters beats every other kind of discussion completely out of the field.

Mr. Sawyer took the initiative by pointing to the fox's tusk which fastened the string in his new friend's hat.

"Done anything this last week?" said he, with that mysterious air specially affected by all individuals who are connected, however remotely, with horseflesh, and which, I believe, has much to answer for, in the impression of consummate roguery which it conveys to the uninitiated. "It's been good scenting weather in my part of the world. Hounds must have run hard on the grass."

The Honourable Crasher emitted a large volume of smoke, ere he roused himself for the effort, and replied: "Good thing, last Friday, with the Pytchley, from Fox Hall. Do you know that country?" he added, thinking, if his listener did *not*, he might save himself the trouble of detailing it.

"I am on my way down to hunt there now," rejoined our friend, "so I take an interest, naturally, in your sport. Last Friday, you say? Ah! that was the day we had such a fine run over *our* country. Two hours and forty-seven minutes, and killed our fox—*and killed our fox*," he repeated, as if such a climax was sufficiently rare to merit more than common attention.

Nothing but the spirit of emulation between different packs could have embarked the Honourable Crasher on a long story; but he woke up from his lethargy at this juncture, and observed,

"Two hours and forty-seven minutes? Indeed! It must have been a fine run; but slow, I conclude—slow. I never care much for anything over an hour. It's labour and sorrow, *walking* after hounds, to *my* mind."

"Slow!" retorted Mr. Sawyer indignantly. "Not at all; I was riding the best horse in my stable, and he had to do all he knew to live with them. Fine country, too—wild fox-hunting country—not a soul in the fields; very deep, and a good deal of fencing. I don't know that I was ever better carried," he added meditatively, hoping to bring the conversation round to the merits of the grey.

But the Honourable Crasher had his story to tell too, and broke in with unusual vehemence:

"*Ours* was about the quickest thing I ever rode to. Found in Faxton Corner; fox never hung a second, and the hounds ran him over those large grass fields as if they were tied to him, all down by— Dear me, I forget the names of the places, and I never *can* describe a run; but if you don't know the country, it don't signify. In short, they ran him all about, you know, over a capital line, and turned him up in the open, at the end of seven-and-twenty minutes, without a check, and very straight, you know, and all that; satisfactory to everybody, and not at all bad fun, and so on." The Honourable C. was rapidly collapsing, running down like the last notes of a musical box. Ere he arrived at this very explicit conclusion, he had become perfectly torpid again.

Finding his neighbour would not listen to *his* story, Mr. Sawyer thought he might as well get what he could in the way of information, and began accordingly to propound a series of questions, only interrupted by the occasional apparition, at the window, of a broad chest and ruddy bearded face belonging to the guard, who, seeing the gentlemen still smoking, vanished again incontinently. The examination proceeded much as follows, the catechumen, though waking up at intervals, becoming more and more comatose.

Mr. Sawyer: "It is very stiff, isn't it, that Pytchley country? Large fences that won't bear liberties being taken with them?"

The Honourable Crasher: "Yeas, I should say, it wanted a hunter to get over it."

Mr. S.: "Do you consider it as difficult to cross as the Quorn?"

The Hon. C.: "Yeas—no—that's to say, I ride the same horses in both; I don't know that there's much difference."

"Whom do you consider your best men now, in your field?"

"Oh! there are lots of fellows who can ride, *if they get a start*. It's impossible to say; there's a good deal in luck, and a good deal in horses." [N.B. This is hardly a sincere speech of the Hon. C.'s. He does *not* think either luck or horseflesh constitutes a *customer*, and has not the slightest doubt in his own mind as to whom he considers about the best performer in that or any other country; only modesty forbids him to name the individual.]

Mr. S., a little dissatisfied: "I suppose the Leicestershire men are spendidly mounted?"

Hon. C.: "No; I should say not. I never remember seeing so few good horses. I shouldn't know where to get a hunter if I wanted one!"

Mr. Sawyer thought of the roan, and ran his eye over his friend's slim figure and horsemanlike shape. "He'd carry him like a bird," thought the owner, "and I shouldn't mind letting him have him for two hundred, or say, if I dropped into a good thing with him, two hundred and *fifty;*" but he only observed, "I suppose you are *very* well mounted yourself?"

"So-so," was the reply. "I'm rather short just now; only ten. Good useful brutes some of them; but I shouldn't say *my* lot was quite first-class, by any means!"

Again Mr. Sawyer found subject for rumination. Ten!

Only ten! and not first-class ones neither, though it was probable that a man who had ten hunters in his stable would not find it worth while to keep a bad one; and then he thought of his own three, and the severe infliction it would be to have to ride Marathon over the fences, which, as he looked from the window, loomed larger and larger in the twilight, as they approached the grazing districts. No secret, it has been said, is so close as that between a horse and his rider; and Mr. Sawyer hardly liked to confess, even to himself, the very inferior brute he had got in the bay. Somehow all the difficulties into which he had put him seemed to rise in his mind's eye, like an accumulation of photographs, as he sat back amongst the cushions, and, withdrawing his gaze from the outward world, fixed it on the lately-lit lamp above his head.

He remembered, not without a shudder, what a cropper the brute gave him at that stile in the potato-garden, which at least he might have scrambled over, if he had only risen six inches. He recalled the famous run he lost from the Forty-acres, because no persuasion would induce Marathon to face the bullfinch enclosing that meritorious fox-covert, and which a donkey could get through, if he would only look at it. He reflected how the animal perversely

"Struck all his timber, fathomed all his ditches;"

how he had never cleared a brook with him, or gone a run to his master's satisfaction; and how even old Isaac allowed his favourite "wur a better nag in the stable nor he wur in the field;" and so musing, he shuddered to think of their joint endeavours to get out of a fifty-acre pasture, with an ox-fence all round it, and the gate locked!

To avoid such horrible visions, he would have plunged

once more into conversation, but looking at his neighbour, observed he was now deep in "The Idylls of the King,"— an epic which served at least to keep the Honourable Crasher awake, thereby substantiating a theory I have heard broached by certain philosophers, and which I am not entirely prepared to dispute, viz. that there is something of poetry in every man who rides hard across a country.

Certainly not a Knight of the Table Round could have been more daring in the saddle than the Honourable Crasher, for all his dissipated looks and languid manners; nor could he have been so engrossed in the fate of "The Lily Maid of Astolat," nor so lost in the description of the black barge floating dreamily down with its snowy burden (perhaps the most beautiful piece of word-painting in the language), had he not acknowledged in some corner of his much-neglected intellect that *divinæ particula auræ*, which may often be found, like a sweet wayside flower, blooming in the most unexpected and uncultivated localities.

Though Mr. Sawyer was himself innocent of all such weaknesses, he had the grace not to interrupt his fellow-traveller, and consequently not a word more was spoken till they exchanged a courteous "Good-evening," as they glided into the Market-Harborough station, and the new arrival wondered in his own mind how it was possible for any one man to require such a quantity of clothing as must be contained in the numerous portmanteaus which the guard's van produced, and which were claimed by the Honourable Crasher as his own.

"He can't have been a week in town," thought our honest friend, "for he was hunting here only last Friday, and he's taken more clothes with him than I've got for my whole kit in the world!"

He had, however, his own affairs to attend to—himself and his modest luggage to stow away in a damp fly, with a broken-winded horse; his dinner to order at the principal hotel, where he meant to reside—at least, till he found out if he liked his quarters. For so old a traveller, he committed in this matter a somewhat unaccountable mistake. Dazzled by the magnificence of his manners, and the sumptuous verbal bill of fare which the waiter stated to be available, he left the details of his meal to that functionary—an oversight which produced a somewhat untoward result, inasmuch as that, after a visit to his stables, a minute inspection of his horses, and a long consultation with Isaac, concerning which of them he should ride on the morrow, interspersed with many complaints and prognostications of evil from the latter, when he returned to his apartment very hungry and in want of comfort, he found the following banquet prepared for his delectation: A slice of soft cod, one raw mutton-chop relieved by an under-done ditto, two sorts of pickles, and some exceedingly strong cheese.

CHAPTER VI.

HAZY WEATHER.

When Mr. Sawyer awoke in the morning, his first impression was, that he had never left The Grange, but that the pattern of his bedroom paper was strangely altered, and the situation of his couch had been mysteriously changed in the night.

It was not till he had turned over, and yawned twice or thrice, that he comprehended the actual position in which he was placed. Then, for the first time, the magnitude of the undertaking on which he had embarked presented itself to his mind; and then did he realize the deficiencies of his stud, the difficulties he was about to encounter, the rashness and perplexity of the whole proceeding. A feeling of loneliness stole over him; and he even experienced a want of confidence in himself. For an instant, he almost wished he was back at home, and the dastardly possibility of returning there flashed across his mind. All these unworthy thoughts, however, were dissipated by the entrance of Isaac, with a pair of boots in one hand, and a glimmering bedroom candle in the other, as the mists of morning are dispelled by the rising sun; and, even as the shrinking combatant gathers confidence from the flash of his drawn sword, so, at the first glimpse of those long-rowelled spurs of which Marathon knew too well the persuasive powers, John Standish Sawyer was himself again.

"Half after eight, sir," said Isaac, setting down the candle, and proceeding to pour cold water into the tub—a process that by no means tempted his master to rise on the instant. "Half after eight, sir; and the grey's got a bit of a cough. It's that strange stable as done it. And you was to let me know in the morning which of them I was to take on."

"What sort of a day is it?" asked our friend, in a sleepy voice, turning, like Dr. Watts's sluggard, into a more comfortable position. At that moment, it would not have broken his heart to be told that it was too hard to hunt.

"Can't see your hand," was the encouraging reply: "it's one of these regular Leicester-sheer fogs, as the grooms tells me, as is wery prevalent hereabouts. The lamps is lit now in the streets; but it'll be wusser up on the high ground. They'll hunt, though, just the same, says they. Weather never stops them here, unless it be the severest of frost and snow, as I understand. Shall I open the shutters, sir?"

Isaac threw them back as he spoke, and drew up the blind, disclosing to Mr. Sawyer's view about eighteen feet of tiles, a weathercock pointing east-south-east, and a chimney adorned with what is called an "old woman"—an ingenious contrivance to prevent it from smoking, but in this instance, to judge by the smell of soot which pervaded the apartment, by no means a successful piece of mechanism—the whole wrapped in a mantle of the densest and *wettest* fog he ever remembered to have seen.

"Sure to be late such a morning as this," thought Mr. Sawyer, preparing for another comfortable half-hour in bed; but then he reflected that he must send Isaac forward with a horse, also that he should have to find his own way to Tilton Wood, on his hack—a sufficiently intricate proceeding as studied overnight by the map, but which might become excessively puzzling when reduced to practice, through large pastures and unknown bridle-gates, on such a morning as the present.

"Take on the grey!" said he, peremptorily, ignoring the cough; "and order breakfast for me in three-quarters of an hour."

The fact is, Mr. Sawyer had but the grey to ride. He did not quite fancy giving the roan his earliest trial in what he understood to be a hilly country; and as for making his first appearance in High Leicestershire on Marathon—really, though both were pretty strong, neither his nerves nor his self-conceit would have stood such a test.

Somehow, everything went wrong, as is apt to be the case

in a strange place, and when we are particularly anxious for the reverse. He cut himself shaving. His leathers were damp, and badly cleaned; looser, too, at the knees, and tighter in the thighs, than he liked. Also, he couldn't find his button-hook; and any one who has put on boots and breeches without the aid of that implement, will sympathize with his distress. Isaac knew where it was, doubtless; but, ere his master arrived at the stage of toilet at which it was required, Isaac and the grey had made their *first* wrong turn in the fog, about a mile from the town, on their way to Tilton Wood.

Altogether, by the time The Boy, with rather heavy eyes and an unwashed face, had brought round Jack-a-Dandy, our friend was in that mood which is best described as having "got out of bed with the wrong foot foremost."

Once in the saddle, however, things mended rapidly. No *horseman* could get upon Jack-a-Dandy without feeling what a good little animal it was; and, indeed, Jack's career had been a somewhat adventurous one. Thorough-bred, but too small to be put in training, he had fallen into the hands of a steeple-chasing horse-dealer, who sank his pedigree, and put him in one or two good handicaps as "his daughter's pony." Master Jack could jump like a deer, and, with nine stone seven on his back, was quite able to make hunters of considerable pretensions look extremely foolish. This could not go on for ever, and the dealer broke, after which, Jack carried the drunken whip of a pack of Irish foxhounds for two seasons, and, when that establishment "busted up," found his way once more into his native country, as leader in a young gentleman's tandem, who tried to graduate at Oxford. Pending the failure of that acolyte, he had a good deal of fun at Bullingdon, winning cleverly whenever he had a chance, and only left the University because his master did, who took him to London, and, despite certain eccentricities, rode him in the Park. When that youth was compelled to obtain his passports for the Continent, Jack, in company with several other valuables, was seized by the creditors; and I fancy he had a very bad time of it for two or three years, till he turned up at Smithfield, nothing but skin, bone, and blemishes, with a pair of raw shoulders that would have made you sick. Here Mr. Sawyer, struck with his "make-and-shape," bought him, after a good deal of haggling, for thirteen pounds ten shillings, throwing in half-a-crown for luck, and standing two pots of beer and a glass of brandy-and-water, besides the man's expenses who brought him to the West-end. Altogether, he cost him less than fourteen sovereigns; and he justly considered him very cheap at the money. Though his knees were broke, and he was fired all round, he never stumbled or was lame; and if you didn't mind a succession of kicks for the first half-mile, and a mouth which bad usage had rendered perfectly callous, he was as pleasant a hack as you could wish to get upon. Jack never wanted to pull, if the rein was laid on his neck; but the moment it was caught hold of, his old associations took it as a signal to *go*, and go he *would*, accordingly. With regard to his appellation—the last among many *aliases*— when his master called him "Jack," old Isaac called him "The Dandy," and *vice versâ*.

There are a good many ways from Market Harborough to Tilton Wood. Of course, the morning being very thick, and Mr. Sawyer a perfect stranger to the country, he chose the most intricate, hoping to pass between the Langtons— of which, for the more complete bewilderment of strangers, there are five or six—and so to reach Stanton Wyville, whence he meant boldly to leave the lanes, and strike out into a line of bridle-gates, by the corner of Stanton Wood, which might or might not eventually land him somewhere about Skeffington.

Deluded man! Ere he reached the grass-track he meant to follow, the fog was denser than ever. He managed to get through one bridle-gate, after catching his horse's rein on the post—an insult which The Dandy resented by putting his head down, and racing wilfully and aimlessly into the surrounding obscurity—and then found himself riding round and round the same field, with extraordinary perseverance, and not the remotest chance of escape.

He would have liked, now, to get back again into the lanes; but he could not even hit the gate at which he entered, and had embarked upon the tedious process of coasting the field methodically, for that purpose, and giving up all idea of hunting for the day, when, much to his relief, he spied a gigantic object looming through the fog, which, on a nearer approach, proved to be nothing larger than a horseman, cantering confidently towards him.

On inspection, this timely arrival turned out to be the Honourable Crasher, with an enormous cigar in his mouth, looking more tired than ever, and, apparently, quite unconscious of the fog and everything else. With an effort, however, he recognized his fellow-traveller of the day before, and courteously offered to guide him—a proposal which the latter accepted with great readiness.

"I had *almost* lost myself," said he, "what with this thick fog, and not knowing the country."

To which the Honourable Crasher replied, "Y-e-e-es—it makes one cough, but it's all plain sailing now," and broke into a gallop.

E

Poor Mr. Sawyer! If he had only known it! His guide was one of the many gentlemen who could hunt twenty years from the same place, and never know their shortest way from one point to another.

CHAPTER VII.

A LEICESTERSHIRE LARK.

By good luck our pair of lost sheep soon hit the bridle-gate Mr. Sawyer had been seeking in vain.

"I suppose it's all right," said the Honourable Crasher, putting his horse into a canter, with the loose rein and easy off-hand seat peculiar to a gentleman riding to covert.

Mr. Sawyer, following close in his wake, devoutly hoped it was so; but had little leisure for considering the subject, inasmuch as his energies were completely engrossed by the delicate task of gammoning The Dandy that he didn't want to pull at him. He knew too well, by the way his little horse's ears were laid back, that he was fully prepared, and only sought an excuse, to come with a rush at the shortest possible notice.

They went on pleasantly enough for a mile or so, the Honourable leading, and commencing a variety of courteous remarks to his follower, which invariably broke off in the middle. At last, the former pulled up with an air of uncertainty.

"Very odd," he said; "often as I've come this way before, I never remember the gate locked." He had put his whip confidently under the latch, and his horse's chest against the top, without the slightest effect. "'Pon my soul, it seems rather absurd, but I do believe *we've* lost our way."

"*We*," thought Mr. Sawyer; "and this fiend in top-boots laughs as if it were a joke!" but he only said aloud, "I shall get down and take it off its hinges."

The Honourable's reply was simple and conclusive. He pointed to the upper hinge, craftily turned downward, so as effectually to prevent all tampering with it, and observed in a tone of melancholy apology, "The fence seems *rather* a bad one" (it was an "oxer," about seven feet high, and impervious to a bird!). "Do you think your horse could get over the gate after mine? This is only a five-year-old, and very likely to break it," he added, with the manner of a nurse tempting a child to take its dose.

I have said Mr. Sawyer was a brave man, and so he was; but I am bound to confess the proposition startled him not a little. Put yourself in his place, courteous reader, and say whether a foggy morning, an uninhabited country, and the necessity of riding a horse barely fourteen-two over a gate more than four feet high, after a languid desperado in pursuit of an uncertainty, was not a somewhat alarming contingency. Nevertheless, there was nothing else for it. The Honourable turned his horse round, took him in a grasp of iron, and put him rather slowly at the gate, which the animal, a well-bred, raking-looking chestnut, with a long bang-tail, got over exceedingly badly, striking the top bar with fore and hind legs; but neither disturbing the Honourable Crasher's seat nor the imperturbability of his demeanour in the slightest degree. He looked back, however, to see his companion come, and even condescended to express a feeble approval of his performance, without removing the cigar from his mouth.

It is but justice to The Dandy to observe, that he no sooner obtained "the office" from his rider, and saw what was expected of him, than he cocked his ears, took the bit in his teeth, and bounded over the gate like a buck, indemnifying himself for the effort, by breaking clean away with his rider as soon as he landed, and going by the Honourable Crasher and his chestnut like a flash of lightning.

I have often observed that the blood of a languid person, if once he or she gets it "up," boils more fervidly than that of less peaceful temperaments; perhaps it is altogether a thicker fluid, and consequently more retentive of caloric. Be this as it may, no sooner did the Honourable Crasher behold Mr. Sawyer speeding by him like an express train, than, roused by the example, and further stimulated by the insubordination of the chestnut, he sat well down in the saddle; and, taking his horse by the head, soon caught up and passed the astonished Sawyer, merely remarking, "We've got a *little* out of the line; you seem to be riding a good fencer, and had better follow me!" and then proceeded to lead his victim perfectly *straight* across country, in the direction of Tilton Wood; the fog, too, was by this time clearing off considerably, or it might be they had emerged from the region of its influence, and the stranger had not even the advantage of its friendly veil to hide from him the dangers by which he was encompassed.

To this day Mr. Sawyer has not left off talking about this his first ride over High Leicestershire. After a bottle of port, he even becomes heterodox for so good a sportsman, and vows he would rather gallop to covert over those grass-fields, than see a run in any other country in the world. I have my doubts, however, whether he enjoyed it so very much at the time. Jack put him down twice; first at an ox-fence, of which the rail was from him, and which, although his leader hit it very hard, deluded the unsuspecting Dandy; and secondly, by landing on a covered drain, which gave way with him, and superinduced one of those falls that are generally designated "collar-boners." On this occasion the Honourable Crasher brought him back his horse, with quite a radiant expression of countenance.

"What a good little animal it is!" said he, throwing the reins back over its neck. "I'm trying to 'crop' this beggar of mine, and I very soon *should*, if I had to follow *you*."

In effect, the chestnut's head and bridle-band were plastered over with mud, although his rider's coat was as yet unstained.

At Skeffington, they relapsed into a quiet trot, and rode on together, feeling as if they could hardly realize the fact, that twenty-four hours ago they were utter strangers to each other.

It is odd how people cast up at a meet of fox-hounds, from all sorts of different directions, even on the most unpromising mornings. Though the fog was as thick as ever at the top of the hill, and Tilton Wood, at no time the best of places to "get away from," was perfectly invisible at two hundred yards' distance, there was already a good sprinkling of sportsmen assembled at the fixture. Two or three "swells" from Melton, very much the pattern of the Honourable Crasher, had arrived on their smoking hacks, and were greeted by him with considerable cordiality. Truth to tell, the Honourable dearly loved what he called "a customer," meaning simply an individual who was fool enough to rate his neck at the value he did his own; and, indeed, he never would have taken so affably to Mr. Sawyer, on such short notice, had the latter not been fortunate enough to possess an excellent hack hunter in Jack-a-Dandy, and bold enough to make very free use of that jumping little animal; the hounds, too, had already arrived, and in the glimpse which Mr. Sawyer caught of them as he rode up, he was sportsman enough to remark that they looked speedy, stout, level, and uncommonly fit to go. Such a pack, he thought, would not even have disgraced the Old Country! the huntsman also seemed to afford the happy combination of a *riding* as well as a hunting one; and the other servants were remarkably well mounted, and looked like business. Mr. Sawyer began to feel quite keen, and to look about for Isaac and the grey, who had not made their appearance; the other Harborough hunters, however, had not yet come up; their grooms had, probably, taken the chance of a late meet to refresh in a body somewhere on the road; there was nothing for it but to light a cigar, and wait patiently for more daylight.

Two or three clever-looking horses with side-saddles, denoted that if the weather had been more propitious, the same number of fair equestrians would have graced the field. Mr. Sawyer particularly remarked a very neat chestnut, apparently, like the groom who led it, exceedingly loath to be ordered home. A peremptory gentleman, in particularly good boots and breeches, with a clerical white neckcloth, and black coat, who had just arrived on wheels, seemed to be the proprietor of this shapely animal. Mr. Sawyer caught himself vaguely wondering whether it belonged to his wife or daughter, and laughed at his own preoccupation as he thought, "What *could* it signify to him?"

It is very tiresome work, that waiting for a fog to clear off before hounds are put into covert. In all other anti-hunting weather, you know, to a certain extent, what you are about; the frost, that sent you to look at the thermometer last night before you went to bed, is either all gone by twelve o'clock, or the matter is set at rest the other way, and you make up your mind not to hunt again till the moon changes. It is the same thing with snow; and, moreover, if you *can* hunt on the surface of mother earth when wrapped in her spotless shroud, she rewards you by carrying a capital scent. But in a fog everything is uncertain and obscure; it may clear off in ten minutes, or it may not be so dense elsewhere. It seems a pity to go home, when the very signal for a return may herald a change of weather; and yet it is a melancholy amusement to walk hounds and horses round a wet field till far on in the afternoon. Everybody is of a different opinion too, usually regulated by personal convenience; those who live a long way off are all for having a try, whilst the man who has ridden his hunter a mile or two to the place of meeting, and can keep him fresh for next day, opines that " It is madness—folly—you'll disturb your country—you'll lose your hounds—you might as well go out hunting in the middle of the night," etc.

On the present occasion it was obvious that the day was getting worse. Sheets of mist came driving up the valleys, and wreathing round the crests of the wooded hills; the slight breeze seemed but to bring up fresh relays of vapour, and every visible object, trees, hedges, gates—nay, the very ears of the horses, and whiskers of their riders, were dripping and saturated with moisture. The Master of the Hounds, a thorough sportsman, never to be beat by a difficulty, announced his intention of waiting whilst any one else remained; but it soon appeared that ere long he would have the field to himself. The Melton gentlemen lost no time in galloping home on their hacks, to while away the hours till dinner-time with a "smoking rubber." Half-a-dozen yeomen adjourned to a neighbouring farm-house to have what they called "a snack" and drink a goodly allowance of port and sherry in the middle of the day. Even the clerical gentleman, owner of the chestnut ladies'-horse, thought it wouldn't do; and just as Isaac on the grey turned up at the head of a strong detachment from Harborough, with whom he had fortunately fallen in, after losing his way twice, it was finally decided that the hounds should go home, and the day's hunting be given up.

Warmed by his ride to covert, and hopeless of finding his way back, except in the same company, Mr. Sawyer lost no time in exchanging The Dandy for the grey. "If we are to lark home," he thought, "I may as well ride a nag I can trust; but if ever I pin my faith upon one of these thin-booted gentlemen to show me the way again, why, I shall deserve the worst that can happen to me—that's all!"

Now, although the appearance of a stranger does not create such a sensation in Leicestershire as in more remote countries, yet the Honourable Crasher was so well known, that it was natural some inquiries should be made as to his companion; for the Honourable C., who was thoroughly good-natured, had no sooner fraternized with our friend than he began to consider him in some sort, and in his own off-hand way, as under his especial charge. Mr. Sawyer's exterior, too, although not extraordinarily prepossessing, was undoubtedly workmanlike. As he settled himself in the grey's saddle, and altered the stirrups which Isaac could never be persuaded to pull to the same length, the clerical gentleman ranging alongside of the Honourable whispered to the latter:

"Who's that fellow? Is he staying with you at Harborough?"

The Honourable laughed feebly.

"Don't know him from Adam," he replied, as if there could be any connection between the two. "He don't seem half a bad fellow, though," he added, "and I shouldn't wonder if he could ride."

Now, the clerical gentleman, who was, indeed, no other than the well-known Parson Dove, had struck up a firm alliance with the Honourable Crasher, cemented on both sides by a keen love for fox-hunting, or perhaps I should rather say, for galloping and jumping over a country—the Parson, be it observed, being the best *sportsman* of the two. On an occasion like the present, he hoped to secure his friend's company at luncheon, by which stroke of policy he should please Mrs. Dove, who was not unprepared, and also show him a certain four-year-old, by which the Reverend set great store. Nay, it was by no means impossible that the Honourable, who never missed a chance of placing his neck in jeopardy, or the stranger who looked *hard*, might be induced to buy the animal for purposes of tuition. So he ignored all about Adam, and simply said, "It's not a quarter-of-a-mile out of your way to stop at the Rectory; indeed, you go by my stableyard. Won't you and your friend come in and have a glass of sherry and a biscuit?"

Mr. Sawyer was a man who had no objection to a glass of sherry and a biscuit at any time, let alone such a cheerless day as this. The hospitable offer, too, was made in so loud a voice that he could not but accept it as addressed to himself; so he drew his horse back to the speaker, and thanked him for the offer, which he expressed his willingness to accept. The Honourable Crasher perceiving that he had been led into the virtual introduction of a man whose name he didn't know, put a bold face on the matter, devoutly hoping the patronymic might never be asked, and the three turned in at a hand-gate, and jogged on amicably through the fog, in the direction of the Rectory.

As Mr. Sawyer ran his eye over the person and appointments of his future host, he could not but acknowledge to himself that never, no, *never* in his life had he seen such a thoroughly *workmanlike* exterior: from the clean-shaved ruddy face, with its bright-blue eye and close-cropped grey hair, down to the long heavy hunting-spurs, the man was faultless all over. Nobody's leathers were so well made, so well cleaned, so well put on as Parson Dove's; and, though he affected brown tops, it is well known that they were such unequalled specimens as to have caused one of his intimate friends who particularly piqued himself on "boots," to give up all hope, even of imitation, and relapse into "Napoleons" in disgust. Why, the very way he folded his neckcloth was suggestive of Newmarket, and no scarlet coat that was ever turned out by Poole looked so like hunting as that well-cut unassuming black. His open-flapped saddle, his shining stirrup-irons, his heavy double-bridle, were all in keeping with the man himself, and it is needless to state that he was riding a thorough-bred bay, with a pair of fired forelegs, and about the best shoulders you ever saw on a hunter.

All this Mr. Sawyer had time to observe ere they rode into a neatly-bricked stableyard, where they gave their horses to a couple of smart grooms, and followed the owner through the back door, past the cleanest of kitchens and tidiest of sculleries, into the more aristocratic part of the mansion.

CHAPTER VIII.

A DOVE OF THE SAME.

I THINK it is the observant author of 'Soapy Sponge,' who makes that sporting tourist declare that "women never look so well as when you come home from hunting." Certainly the contrast between a cold cheerless day out-of-doors and the luxurious atmosphere of a well-warmed, well-ventilated house, inclines a man to view everything through a complimentary medium, even without taking into consideration the delightful exchange of a hard slippery saddle for the cushions of a comfortable arm-chair, or the warmth of a blazing fire. The inside of the Rectory was as pretty and as snug as it was possible for any house to be. Parson Dove was one of those men in whom the bump of *comfort* is strongly developed, and whether he bought a warming-pan or a wine-cooler, he was sure to get the best, and the best-looking, article that was to be had for money.

As the three sportsmen clanked along the carpeted passage to the drawing-room, they heard the notes of a pianoforte sounding from that apartment, and Mr. Sawyer had barely time to summon all his fortitude, for the subversion of his constitutional shyness, ere he found himself ushered into that sanctuary, in the wake of the Honourable Crasher, whom, truth to tell, just at that moment, he felt he would have followed with less apprehension over another locked gate, or treacherous "oxer." It was not so formidable an undertaking, after all. There were but two ladies, and both seemed delighted at the acquisition of visitors on so dull a morning. The introductions were got over, none the worse that nobody knew the stranger's name; and both Mrs. Dove, an ample lady, with the remains of considerable beauty, and "My daughter Cecilia," of whom more anon, seemed resolved to make themselves agreeable to their guests—Mamma rather inclining to the Honourable Crasher, who was an old friend, and had often dropped in to luncheon before; whilst the siren Cecilia, fresh from the execution of that "sweet thing" they had heard on the pianoforte, seemed willing to devote herself to the amusement and possible subjugation of the stranger.

There are some men on whom young ladies feel instinctively they are but wasting their time, and it is curious how seldom their perceptions deceive them on this point. Of such was the Honourable C. Good-looking, amiable, to all appearance well-off, and not over-burdened with brains, he possessed all the attributes of an "eligible *parti*," and yet somehow the most match-making of mothers, and the most enterprising of daughters, always gave him up as a bad job, after the first ten minutes. There was something about him that betrayed to female shrewdness he was not "a marrying man," and as they judiciously abstain from playing a game in which the loss is not exclusively on the side of the adversary, they let him alone accordingly.

Now, it was otherwise with Mr. Sawyer. Although you and I would have voted him a confirmed bachelor, might even have judged him uncharitably as somewhat rough and unpolished and unrefined, might have scouted the idea of his being in any respect "a ladies' man," and laughed outright at his competing with such a double-distilled dandy as the Honourable C., we should thus have only exposed our ignorance of the secret springs and impulses that move that mysterious piece of mechanism—the female mind. Miss Dove, in the absence of any other and nobler game, had not the slightest objection to exercise the different weapons in her armoury on her Mamma's friend's friend.

These were of a sufficiently deadly character. Miss Cecilia—or "Cissy," as they called her at home—without being strictly pretty, was a very attractive young lady. She had a pair of wicked black eyes, with rather thick eyebrows; a high colour; white teeth, which she did not scruple to display on all available occasions; and a laugh so clear and ringing and inspiriting, that it put a man in good humour in spite of himself. Even in the bitterest of frosts, Papa could not be cross for five minutes together, when "Cissy" set to work to tease him into affability. Also, Miss Dove's figure was exceedingly round and symmetrical; not an angle nor a corner in those graceful, flowing lines. Her foot and ankle were undeniable, and her hands white and well-shaped. Altogether, she would have passed muster as good-looking in London: it is needless, therefore, to say that she ought to have been placarded "dangerous" in Leicestershire. Nor had this young woman neglected such opportunities of improving her natural advantages as had come in her way. She could play and sing with much taste and tolerable skill; she could waltz down a strong man in pretty good training, without drawing her breath quicker for the exertion; she could ride with a degree of nerve and judgment seldom enjoyed by the softer sex; and, finally, she had a way of looking down, to show her long eyelashes, which in many instances had been productive of much loss and confusion to the adversary.

It was, you see, scarcely a fair match to pit all these qualities against honest John Standish Sawyer, with his coarse hands and feet, his short, square-tailed coat, ill-made boots and breeches, red whiskers, and general diffidence.

As he sat before her, with his cap between his feet (I need hardly observe that, like the other ornaments of the Old Country, he wore a velvet hunting-cap), and the horn handle of his whip in his mouth, she took the lead in the conversation; indeed, I am prepared to lay my reader considerable odds, that, whenever he meets a lady and gentleman together, the former is talking, and the latter listening.

Miss Dove began at him without delay:

"You've only just arrived, I hear; and, indeed, what unpromising weather you find us with! I told Papa, this morning, I was sure we shouldn't be able to hunt; and I went and took my habit off directly after breakfast. If there's one thing I abominate more than another, it's a fog; and at Tilton Wood, too, of all places in the world! I've no idea of leaving a good fire, to go and sit there with the others, like a lot of crows in a mist; and this weather always lasts three days; and to-morrow they meet at the best place they have; and I hope you like our country?"

Mr. Sawyer could not conscientiously affirm that he had yet *seen* it; so he mumbled out an unintelligible answer, and the young lady went off again at score:

"Harborough's getting quite a gay place, I declare. So many gentlemen come there now, to hunt; and it's so convenient for the railroad; and I dare say you know Mr. Savage, and Captain Struggles, and Major Brush; and are you going to give us a Harborough ball?"

Mr. Sawyer was sufficiently experienced to take heart of grace at this juncture, and reply, "Oh, certainly—certainly! I'm sure it will be a capital ball. May we hope, Miss Dove, that you will come to it?"

The eyelashes went down immediately; and Miss D. was, no doubt, on the eve of making an appropriate reply, when the announcement of luncheon, and the simultaneous return of *Paterfamilias*, broke up the pair of *tête-à-têtes*, and the party adjourned to the dining-room, all, apparently, on pretty good terms with themselves—Mr. Sawyer inwardly proud of having got so well out of the ball difficulty; "Cissy" a little elevated with the conviction that she had made a fresh conquest (not that it was any novelty, but the feeling is always more or less agreeable); Papa ready for luncheon, and sanguine about the four-year-old; Mamma enchanted to have caught a good listener; and the Honourable Crasher in his usual state of easy and affable *nonchalance*.

It is only right to observe that the Rev. had exchanged his hunting costume for a suit of more clerical attire, yet, somehow, had failed to put off with his leathers an atom of his equestrian air. Even in the fullest canonicals, you never could have taken Mr. Dove for anything but a sportsman.

Why are people always so much pleasanter at luncheon than at dinner? Notwithstanding John Bull's predilection for the latter meal, as a mode of testifying his regard, his civility, and his own respectability, I cannot help thinking that foreigners are right to ignore that heavy system of dinner-giving which we islanders regard as the very framework of our social system. There is always more or less of pomposity, and consequent restraint, attendant upon a regular set dinner in the country. A few thorough people of the world, "worldly," know how to ask exactly the right three couple or so, and put them down to a hot dinner at a round table, such as is the very acme of all festive boards; but this is a rare quality in host and hostess. Usually, you are placed next to a guest you don't know, and opposite to one you don't like. Your soup is cold, your venison underdone; and the eyes of three or four servants intently watching every mouthful you swallow is destruction to a delicate appetite. In some old-fashioned houses, you may even recognize the burly coachman assisting his fellow-domestics to wait upon the company; and although, for my own part, I confess to a liking for "the smell of the stables," I cannot but admit that the flavour is somewhat spoilt by being mixed with that of a "*salmi de gibier*," or a sweetbread plastered round with spinach.

But luncheon, on the contrary, is a light, exhilarating, free-and-easy meal. Even Mr. Sawyer, as he finished his leg of pheasant and glass of brown sherry, felt wonderfully restored by his repast. "Cissy" was a good "doer" (ladies generally are, about two o'clock), and, till she had disposed of her meal, gave her neighbour a little breathing-time, and leisure to look about him.

I have often thought, although I am by no means the first person who has made the observation, both in and out of print, how true it is that it may be a huge disadvantage to a girl to be seen in company with her mother. It is sometimes discouraging enough to reflect that the coveted treasure must eventually expand into a facsimile of the dragon on guard. Fancy, if the fruit in the Gardens of the Hesperides had been eggs instead of apples, each golden shell enclosing the germ of just such a monster as was grinning at the gate! To be sure, the resemblance may cut the other way as well. I *have* seen mammas whom the fairest of Eve's daughters might be proud to resemble; but it is sometimes hard upon the young Phœbe to have perpetually at her side the shapeless Mother Bunch, into the facsimile

of which she must eventually grow. Mr. Sawyer, gazing
intently on his hostess discussing her cutlet and glass of
port-wine with considerable relish, *acknowledged*, though he
he would not *accept*, the warning.

Miss Dove took after Mamma rather than Papa. The
matron's red face was a brilliant colour in the girl; and the
exuberant proportions of the one, suggestive of good-humour,
good-living, and motherly content, were but the full, flowing outlines of perfect symmetry in the other.

However, they all got on remarkably well. Even the
Honourable Crasher made a feeble joke, of which the point
somehow escaped his listeners—without, however, destroy-
ing his own enjoyment in its delivery. By the time Papa
proposed an adjournment to the stables, to inspect the four-
year-old—"Cissy" pleading for two minutes' law, to put
her hat on—they were all in high good-humour. If "one
spur in the head" be "worth two in the heel," I think it is
equally true that a slight stimulant about 1.30 is twice as
effectual as a feast at 7.45.

The four-year-old was a fine, lengthy, *lashing*-looking
young horse, to use a graphic expression, more akin to the
kennel than the stable. He had all that thickness of outline and *coarseness* of particular points which sportsmen so
like to see, when pedigrees are unimpeachable, and which
are sure to grow out into eventual strength and symmetry.
Mr. Sawyer would perhaps have admired him more, had his
attention not been distracted by the apparition in the young
one's box of the following choice assortment: viz. one pair
of Balmoral-boots (arched instep and pointed heels, after
Leech); one scarlet *jupe*, short and full; one morning-
gown, very rich and voluminous, tucked and girt up all
about ditto; one pair of neat little gloved hands, with tight-

F

fitting bust and arms to match; and one rosy, smiling, happy face; the whole crowned by *such* a hat and feather as said "*Suivez moi!*" far more peremptorily than ever did Henri Quatre's great white *panache*. After that, he looked very little at the four-year-old.

Poor Mr. Sawyer! When his horse was led out, to take him back to Harborough, she patted its grey nose, and called it "*a darling*." "A darling!" and the ungrateful brute snorted all over her pretty face and hands! Well, he patted its neck himself, as he rode out of the yard.

The day seemed to have improved somehow, though the fog was equally dense, and twilight—or rather no-light—had set in. That cigar, too, which the Honourable gave him just under Langton, he thought, was the best he had ever smoked in his life.

CHAPTER IX.

FOUR O'CLOCK, STABLES.

I SHOULD be sorry for my reader to suppose that John Standish Sawyer was what is termed "a susceptible man." On the contrary, since his well-remembered rejection by Miss Mexico, an event of which it is unnecessary to specify the date, he had steeled himself resolutely against the fair, and devoted his energies, if possible, more exclusively than ever to the worship of Diana. Cold as she is at times, and rigorous as are her icy frowns, corrugating that beaming face into unpropitious wrinkles, at least she is a mistress who never deceives. The thermometer at your dressing-room window tells you exactly the humour in which you will find her, and we do not hear the old, whose season of enjoyment has passed away, regretting the hours and days they have spent in her service. "If I had my time to come over again," I heard a hale octogenarian declare not long ago, "I should make *one* alteration. I should flirt a little *less* and hunt a great deal *more.*" He had been a four-days-a-week man all his life, and in his youth a fierce admirer of the ladies. The foregoing, nevertheless, was the result of his experience.

Mr. Sawyer, like any other male biped, was not above being flattered and pleased by the notice of such a girl as Miss Dove. It smoothed his feathers, so to speak, and encouraged him to think better of himself. The Honourable Crasher, too, who had quite taken a fancy to his new friend, asked him to a *tête-à-tête* dinner at his lodgings on the night after the Tilton Wood meet; and as the wine was remarkably good, and the host, in his sleepy, quiet way, rather pleasant company, he spent an agreeable evening enough.

For the next two or three days there was a catching kind of frost, of the most provoking description, just hard enough to stop hunting, yet with a deceitful appearance of "going" which prevented sportsmen from leaving their quarters for London. During this interregnum Mr. Sawyer had leisure to unpack his things, arrange his books—consisting of 'Colonel White's Observations on Fox-hunting,' 'Ask Mamma' (illustrated with coloured prints), and a few back numbers of the 'Sporting Magazine,'—inspect his stables, watch the roan putting on flesh, and the departure of the grey's cough, besides making acquaintance with the persons and studs of Mr. Savage, Captain Struggles, and Major Brush—gentlemen possessing, one and all, an inexhaustible fund of spirits, an untiring delight in horseflesh, numerous suits of wearing apparel, such as nearly approached the character of fancy dresses, and, to all appearance, a lack of nothing in the world except ready money. They fraternized willingly enough with our friend, smoked cigars with him at his hotel in the morning, took him over their stables at dusk, did *not* try to sell him any of their horses, which would indeed have been a hopeless enterprise, and generally made the world as pleasant for him as was in their power. Mr. Sawyer began to think he had landed in Utopia at last—that he had reached the Happy Land, where, metaphorically speaking, it was to be "beer and skittles" all day long. The only drawback to his felicity was the sustained discontent of old Isaac, and an increasing tendency to inebriety on the part of The Boy.

Perhaps my reader will best understand his situation from a description of a visit paid, according to custom, by the whole gang to the stables of the Honourable Crasher. Time 4.30, on a dark afternoon, with every appearance of a thaw.

Boadicea, by Bellerophon out of Blue Light, is being stripped for Mr. Sawyer's inspection. As a compliment to the stranger, he is further invited to "walk up to the mare, and feel how fit she is!" at the risk of having his brains dashed out; Boadicea, by Bellerophon out of Blue Light, resenting such liberties with the ferocity of her British namesake, and kicking with considerable energy when her ribs are tickled. Mr. Tiptop, by far too great a man to touch a rug or hood, gives his directions from the offing, with his hat very much over his eyes, removing it only when addressed by his master, his legs very wide apart, and his hands thrust deep into the pockets of his tight trousers.

Captain Struggles, a heavy gentleman, who rides light-weight horses, and wears a shooting suit of the broadest cheek fabricated, takes a straw out of his mouth, and observes, " That's about the sort, I think, when you want to do the trick over *this* country. Ain't it, Tiptop?"

Mr. Tiptop is always mysterious and oracular concerning the Honourable's stud. Somebody, he thinks, ought to preserve the secrets of the stable, and Crasher himself is the most indiscreet of mortals on such subjects. So the groom raises his hat with both hands, puts it on again, and replies, " We like to get all of *ours* as nearly as possible about that mould. There's a young horse as is quite one of *your* sort, Captain, in the next box." Whereupon Mr. Sawyer, who has no patience with Tiptop, winks at Major Brush, and the latter bursts out laughing.

The conversation now becomes general, and not altogether devoid of personality.

" *Your sort* are rather of the weedy order, Struggles," observes the Major. " Too light for *this* country, as you'll find out before you're many days older, now that we've got the ground to ride as it should do, up to our girths. Besides, those thorough-bred rips never have courage to face large fences. Don't you agree with me, Mr. Sawyer?"

The Major has not yet forgiven Struggles for stopping him on the last day they were out, at the only practicable place in a bullfinch, on which the heavy weight and a very little chestnut stallion were see-sawing backwards and forwards, like some exquisitely-balanced piece of machinery. Mr. Sawyer, thus appealed to, gives his opinion, thinking of the roan the while: " They *must* have power, I fancy, for these flying countries, but they must have blood *too*. I should like to show you a horse I've just bought, that I mean to hunt to-morrow if the frost goes. My stables are 'close at hand.'"

It is resolved that Mr. Sawyer's shall be the next stud inspected; but such an unheard-of breach of etiquette as leaving their present haunt until every individual horse has been stripped, cannot be entertained for a moment; so Mr. Savage, in his turn, enlivens the process by attacking poor Struggles: "You never got to the end that Keythorpe day, after all," says he. "What's the use of these long pedigrees of yours, if they can't stay? I have always understood their only merit as hunters is, that you can't *tire* the thoro'-bred ones. But confess now, Struggles, you stopped before the hounds ran through the Coplow!"

"No distance at all!" chimes in Brush.

"And the ground must have been quite light before the rain," adds Mr. Sawyer, who thinks he *must* say something, and who has not been permitted to remain in ignorance of this Keythorpe day, now more than a fortnight old.

Struggles turned from one to the other of his tormentors, with a grin on his jolly face. "Little Benjamin couldn't have been so beat, when I caught your horse for you," said he to Brush; "or when I went by *you*, Savage, in the lane, and that was after five-and-twenty minutes, with fifteen stone on his back, amongst those hills. No, no, my boys! Fair play's a jewel, and neither of you were there to see whether I'd had my gruel or not. *Stop* indeed! I'd lay odds none of old Catamaran's stock would cut up soft, if you rode them till the day after to-morrow. Stop! I'll be hanged if I didn't *trot* when I got on the high-road coming home."

"Never mind! we know," interposed Mr. Savage—a tall pale man, with a hawk's eye that nothing escaped. "Why, you were *seen*, my good fellow!—*seen* with your own back against your horse's, shoving him through a fence. They said if you hadn't been the heaviest of the two, you'd have been there now."

Like almost all stout men, Struggles was the essence of good-humour. He burst into a hearty laugh, but persevered in his denial. "*Who* saw me?" said he; "who saw me? He must have been in a right good place, though I say it."

"Parson Dove saw you," rejoined his accuser. Whereat Mr. Sawyer felt his heart give a thump. "Parson Dove made a capital story about it. He said he never saw a horse so *badly in* with so heavy a backer. I shouldn't wonder if he put it in his sermon on Sunday. However, he'll be out to-morrow—he and Miss Cissy, and the lot of 'em. I'll appeal to him if what I say isn't true."

Mr. Sawyer listened attentively. Then he should see Miss Dove again on the following day, and in the enjoyment of what she had confided to him was a favourite pastime. Involuntarily he found himself thinking of the black eyes, with their long eyelashes, and wondering whether she would look well in a riding-habit.

Meantime the Honourable Crasher, in the last stage of exhaustion, was endeavouring to discover which of his horses Tiptop would let him ride on the morrow. The fixture was at a capital place, with the Pytchley, and promised a large field. Notwithstanding his *insouciance*, the Honourable C. could not but feel that he should like something both safe and fast, if, as was more than possible, he would have to ride for his life during the first ten minutes.

"Tiptop," said his master, raising himself from his seat on the corn-bin, and taking the cigar from his lips, "Tiptop, as they're all pretty fit, you may send on Catamount and Confidence to-morrow."

"Catamount's hardly got over his physic yet, and I'm keeping Confidence for you on Thursday," replied the master of the horse.

"Well, then, the mare and old Plantagenet?" urged the Honourable. "I can ride Plantagenet first, and send him home by two o'clock."

"The mare's had a gallop this morning, and we wants Plantagenet second 'oss for Friday," objected Mr. Tiptop.

"Well, then, Life Boat," pleaded the proprietor. "I haven't had a ride on Life Boat this season. And, let me see, the Banker would do very well for second."

"I thought of Topsy-Turvy and Chance," enunciated Mr. Tiptop, somewhat imperiously; and the Honourable's face lengthened considerably at the announcement. To do him justice, he was one of those sportsmen so well described in the old Cheshire hunting-song—

> "To whom nought comes amiss—
> One horse or another, that country or this;
> Who through falls and bad starts undauntedly still
> Ride up to the motto—*Be with them I will!*"

But Bellerophon himself was mortal, and Topsy-Turvy was a *very* awkward mare to ride in a crowd. With great pace and jumping powers she had all the irritability of her high-born race, and more than all the jealousy of her sex. Horses in her rear annoyed her—alongside, or in front, they drove her mad: so she was never thoroughly comfortable, unless sailing away by herself with the hounds—a place, it is only fair to add, that she was quite capable of keeping. Chance, by Gamester out of Happy-go-lucky, was no safer a mount. Just out of training, she went nevertheless at her fences with considerable audacity; but was prone to over-jump herself when she didn't run through them. As Struggles observed of her, "It was a safe bet to lay five to two on the Caster."

However, the Honourable never dreamed for an instant of disputing Mr. Tiptop's *fiat;* so he consoled himself by thinking what a start he *would* get! and how he hoped the hounds would keep out of his way. By the time Topsy-Turvy's clothes had been replaced, and a handsome pony examined and approved of, the party, much to old Isaac's disgust, adjourned to Mr. Sawyer's stables, where they were good enough to express their approval of the roan and his companions in that conventional tone which is so much less flattering than one of sincere abuse. These gentlemen hardly knew Mr. Sawyer well enough yet to give their honest opinion; and perhaps it was fortunate for the sake of Isaac's peace of mind that they did not.

"*Useful* horses, Sawyer!" observed Mr. Savage, considerately sparing the groom the labour of stripping them.

"*Useful* horses," repeated Captain Struggles and Major Brush in a breath; the latter adding, "and seem pretty fit to go." While the Honourable Crasher, who had not ventured further than the door, remarked that he "thought Jack-a-Dandy the best shaped one of the lot;" but conceded, in a faint whisper, that the rest of them looked "very like hunters: remarkably *useful* horses indeed!"

Our friend was not deficient in penetration, and by no means a person to have been nearly a week in The Shires without finding out what this epithet means. "When a man tells me he has got a *useful* horse," Mr. Sawyer was once heard to observe, "I interpret it that he is the owner of a *useless brute*, which he wishes to sell *me!*" And Mr. Sawyer was not deceived by the politeness of his companions. He held his tongue, however; but more than once he caught himself brooding over the offensive adjective during the evening.

"If the roan is only half as good as I take him to be, and I can but get a start to-morrow," thought our friend, "I'll show them what my *useful* horse can do! Miss Dove will be out, too, and that cursed fellow of Putty's hasn't sent down my new boots! Never mind—I've got the right spurs at any rate, and it won't be my fault to-morrow if I don't 'go for the gloves,' as we used to say in the Old Country."

He dined at home, and reduced the allowance of sherry considerably; also consumed but one of the Laranagas before going to roost at the sober hour of 10.30. Mr. Sawyer seldom took his nervous system into consideration; but on this occasion, with all his self-confidence (and he had as much as his neighbours), he was indeed resolved not to throw a chance away.

CHAPTER X.

"HAIL! SMILING MORN!"

When we read in 'Bell's Life,' the 'Morning Post,' or the Northampton paper, that the Pytchley hounds will meet on Wednesday at Crick, we confess to the same sensation which the old coachman is said to experience at the crack of the whip. We call up a picture tinged with the colours of a memory that Time has no power to fade. It seems again to be a soft-eyed morning in the mild winter or the early spring, and the sky is dappled with serene and motionless clouds; whilst here below, a faint breeze from the south whispers of promised fragrance, only biding its time to exude from Earth's teeming bosom —she sleeps, the mighty mother; but even in repose she is clad in majestic beauty, and instinct with vitality and hope. On such a morning the blood dances through their veins, and her children would fain leap and shout aloud for joy. What freshness in the smell of the saturated pastures! What beauty in the softened tints and shadows of the landscape—leafless though it be! How those bare hedges seem ready to burst forth in the bloom of spring, and the distant woods on the horizon melt into the sky as softly as in the hot haze of a July noon. The *thud* of our horses' hoofs strikes pleasantly on the ear, as we canter over the undulating pastures, swinging back the hand-gates with a dexterity only to be acquired by constant practice, and on which we plume ourselves not a little. He is the sweetest hack in England, and shakes his head and rolls his shoulders gaily, as we restrain the canter from becoming a gallop. Were he *not* the *sweetest*, etc., he would begin to plunge from sheer exuberance of spirits; we could almost find it in our heart to indulge him. The scared sheep scour off for a few paces, shaking their woolly coats, and then turn round to gaze at us as we fleet from field to field. A couple of magpies, after a succession of jerks and bows, while they make up their minds, dive rapidly away over the hedge to our *right;* a direction (for we confess the superstition) ominous of sport. A scarlet coat glances along the lane in front; and, as this is our last bit of grass, and moreover the furrows lie the right way, we catch hold of *the sweetest's* head, and treat ourselves to a gallop. Soon we emerge on the high-road, and relapse into a ten-mile-an-hour trot; the *sweetest,* who thinks nothing of twelve, going well on his haunches, and quite within himself. All the best fellows in England seem to have congregated in this highway. Some in dog-carts, some in phaetons, half-a-dozen on a four-horse drag, and others on horseback, like ourselves. With the latter we speedily join company. Yesterday's gallop—the Ministerial Crisis—the Rifle Volunteers—all the topics that interest us for the time, are touched on, and we learn the latest news of each. By a quarter before eleven we have had pleasure enough for the whole twenty-four hours, and yet our day is only just beginning. Now the plot thickens rapidly. Grooms with led horses are overtaken by their masters, and we recognize many a well-known flyer and honest servant's face.

"How fresh the old horse looks, John : none the worse for the Lilbourne day, when he carried your master so well!"

"Never was better, sir," answers gratified John, with a touch of his hat; partly out of compliment to ourselves, partly out of respect for the good horse. Now we observe a scarlet group collected in a knot, where the hounds meet in the centre of the village, and the church clock points to five minutes before eleven, as we bid the cheery huntsman "Good-morning," and exchange our hack for our hunter.

Mr. Sawyer probably felt very much the sort of sensations I have endeavoured to describe, as he dashed along on the free-going Dandy, in company with some of his new companions. If so, he kept them to himself. Our friend was a man of few words at the best of times; and when, as in the present instance, "big with high resolve," taciturnity personified. Also, notwithstanding the want of the new boots, he had "got himself up" to-day with peculiar care. The result, I am bound to admit, was not entirely satisfactory;

and, when that is the case, a man's loquacity is apt to decrease in proportion. However, the roan, or "Hotspur," as we must now call him, made a pretty good figure, as far as appearance went, even amongst a bevy of celebrated hunters, and his master felt a considerable accession of confidence when he found himself fairly mounted and ready for the fray. Miss Dove, too, had arrived in company with her papa. There was no doubt about it: she *did* look remarkably well in her riding-habit.

Mr. Sawyer, a little nervous and rather ashamed of it, doffed the velvet hunting-cap, and rode up to accost her. I need scarcely observe that the young lady's greeting was of the coldest and most reserved. The last time she had been all smiles and sunshine: so, on the principle of rotation, today must be one of frigidity and decorum. It's a way they have, you see; and one that seldom fails to put the inexperienced to utter confusion. A man cannot be said to know what the ague really is till he has suffered from the fits—both hot and cold. Take warning, John Standish Sawyer! you who have once before burnt your fingers, and had cause to dread the fire. Miss Mexico, with her quadroon stain and her thirty thousand pounds, was a queerish one to manage; but she was a fool to Miss Dove.

"Confound the girl! what does she mean by it?" said the humiliated swain to himself, as the hounds moved off towards the gorse. He felt a little disgusted, and *not* a little irritated: just in the humour that makes a man ready for a bit of excitement rather keener than ordinary. He thought he had never felt *so like riding* in his life before! With the natural instinct of one who knew himself capable of going in the first flight, the observant Sawyer proceeded to scan narrowly such of the surrounding sportsmen as looked to him like "meaning mischief." Out of a hundred riders it was not so difficult as might be supposed to pick a proportion of flyers, and the proportion, as my hunting readers will not dispute, was little over ten per cent. Shall I name them? Shall I add ninety enterprising and energetic gentlemen to the list of my mortal enemies? Heaven forbid that I should do anything so invidious and ill-advised! Mr. Sawyer did not know them, and why should I? Each of the hundred, doubtless, believed himself one of the chosen ten. I fancy that every man who goes out hunting thinks he only wants an opportunity to show his back to the rest of the field. I fancy that when the opportunity *does* come, he lets it slip in hopes of a better, and that no one attributes to want of nerve, horsemanship, or common sense, that failure, on which it would be no bad investment to offer each equestrian nine to one! Well, everybody has an equal chance on a fine scenting day, when the fox has slipped quietly away, by good fortune only seen by a countryman, with a quinsy, who couldn't halloo to save his life. When the two or three couple of leading hounds have flashed a hundred yards or so over his line, thus enabling the body of the pack to join them, and stoop all together to the scent, when after a cheery twang, the huntsman returns his horn to its case, and the master, relieved, for an instant, from the weight of care, which none but an M. F. H. knows, takes his place alongside of his favourities, and observes mentally, though he wouldn't say it aloud for a thousand, "Now, my fine fellows, ride on their backs if you *can!*" In short, at that delicious moment when the wise bethink them of a fox's point, and a convenient lane, and the enthusiasts glance exultingly at each other, and say, "All right, old fellow! I *think* we're landed!" then hath each a fair

field and no favour; and if a man's hardihood, or his vanity,
or his ambition, prompt him to assume a place in the front
rank, he has nothing to do but go and try.

As Mr. Sawyer rode down to the Gorse, he was pleased
to feel Hotspur step so lightly and vigorously under him.
The horse shook his bit, and cocked his ears, and reached at
his bridle to get near the hounds. He *felt* like a good one,
and we all know what confidence that sensation imparts to
the rider. Mr. Sawyer forgot all about Miss Dove, and
the unprovoked manner in which she had snubbed him. It
was cheerful to hear one or two complimentary remarks
exchanged between the passing sportsmen.

"That's a clever horse," said a tall heavy man, himself
admirably mounted, indicating the roan with a nod, and addressing a supercilious-looking person in a black coat, whose
attention was much taken up with the appearance of his
own legs and feet, which he was looking at alternately *en
profile.*

"Rather," answered the supercilious person, glancing up
for an instant from his occupation—"Who's the man?
Never saw such a man; never saw such boots; never saw
a fellow so badly got up altogether."

At this juncture the Honourable Crasher, cantering by
on Topsy-Turvy, accosted our friend with good-humoured
familiarity, and the supercilious man, changing his mind all
in a moment, about Mr. Sawyer and his boots, resolved to
take the first opportunity of making the stranger's acquaintance. In effect he followed the last comer to prosecute
this intention. The Honourable C. disappearing through
a bullfinch, on Topsy-Turvy, whom he thus hoped to put
in good humour, was ere this in a field alongside of the
hounds, which he was likely to have all to himself.

Soon a hand-gate stems the increasing cavalcade, and the stoppage becoming more obstinate, owing to Mr. Sawyer's abortive attempts to open the same, a good deal of conversation, rhetorical rather than complimentary, is the result.

"Put your whip *under* the latch," says one.

"Got the wrong hand to it," sneers another.

"What a tarnation muff!" vociferates a third.

"Ware heels!" exclaims a fourth, as a wicked little bay mare, in the thick of them, lets out with unerring precision; and one man says, "What a shame it is to bring such a devil as that into a crowd!" and another opines that "The kick will be out of her before two o'clock!" and the owner, profuse in apologies, is only thinking of slipping through the gate, and going on to get a start.

Meanwhile Hotspur makes himself profoundly ridiculous, pushing the gate when the latch is down, and wincing from it when he ought to shove; also finding himself totally unassisted by the crook of his master's whip, which keeps slipping on the wet green wood, waxes irritable, rears up, and threatens to vary the entertainment, by performing a somersault into the next field.

"Let me do it for you, sir," says a good-natured young farmer; and Mr. Sawyer wisely abandons his office of door-keeper, and after about forty people have hustled by him, manages at last to edge his way through.

By this time the hounds have been put into the gorse. Nineteen couple are they of *ladies*, with the cleanest of heads and necks, straight and fair on their legs and feet as so many ballet-dancers, and owning that keen wistful look, which is so peculiar to the countenance of the fox-hound. They dash into the covert as if sure of finding, and Parson Dove, standing erect in his stirrups, watches them with a glow of pleasure lighting up his clean-shaved face. "There's a fox, Charles, I'll lay a bishopric!" says he, and a whimper from Truelove confirms the parson's opinion on the spot.

"Not a doubt on it! sir, not a doubt on it! one if not a brace!" replies that functionary, with immense rapidity. He loses very little time indeed, at his phrases, or his fences, or anything else. In another moment he is up to his girths in the gorse, cheering on the beauties, who are working up the scent with a vast deal of musical energy. The master casts an uneasy glance at the crowd; countless anxieties and apprehensions cross his mind. One way the fox will be headed, another the hounds will be cut off, a third leads up to the village, and we all know how fatal are houses and pigsties at the commencement of a run. But the fourth side is clear; happily the hounds are even now bustling eagerly towards it.

Diverse occupations engross the attention of the field; few of them seem to be much taken up with the business in hand. Here a gentleman is giving a farmer's horse a gallop, preparatory, as it would appear, to a purchase. There another is detailing the last news from Warwickshire, to an applauding audience. Struggles, on his feet, is adjusting a snaffle-bridle more comfortably on the head of a game little thorough-bred. Savage is discussing the merits of a new novel with a literary friend. Major Brush is taking up a link in Miss Dove's curb-chain; that damsel, very killing indeed, in a little hat and feathers, is surrounded by admirers, and yet, *lassata, nondum satiata*, is inwardly regretting that she had snubbed poor Mr. Sawyer so gratuitously at the meet. You see, however low one may rate the value of his vassalage, still a victim always counts *for one;* and it is a pity needlessly to throw away the veriest weed that helps

G

to make up one's chaplet. Truth to tell, Mr. Sawyer was not thinking about her. He had crept on, as he thought, unobserved, to a place from which he could command the proceedings, and try to get a good start. Nevertheless, a watchful eye was on his movements. The master was even then deliberating whether he should holloa to him to "Come back, sir," and was hoping in his own mind, "that chap in a cap wouldn't go on, and head the fox!"

The Honourable Crasher and Topsy-Turvy had already fallen out, as to a cigar, which the former wanted to light. No! the mare would *not* stand still, and an impatient jerk at the curb-rein had not tended to adjust this difference. So she was backing and sidling and shaking her head, and making herself intensely disagreeable, whilst the Honourable, who soon recovered his equanimity, scanned a certain stile just in front of her with a critical eye, and employed himself by vaguely calculating how many yards before she came to it she was likely, in her present humour, to "take off;" also whereabouts he should land if they *did* make a mess of it, and whether *more* than two or three fellows would be on his back at once.

He has by no means solved the problem, when a violent rush is made towards the lane. Somebody has seen somebody else gallop, who has seen a sheep-dog run; this is a sufficient reason for some eighty or ninety horsemen to charge furiously in the same direction; their leaders finding no hounds, then pull up, and the crowd proceed leisurely back again. But this false alarm has been in favour of the fox, who perceiving a clear space before him, and having obtained, by a dexterous turn round the covert, a little law of his pursuers, takes advantage of the lull, to slip away unobserved by any one but the first whip, and that official is far too discreet to make a noise. He telegraphs mutely to the huntsman, who has *the ladies* out of covert, and dashing to the front, with three blasts of his horn. Ere the Honourable Crasher has had time to indulge Topsy-Turvy with a fling at the stile, which she jumps as if there was a ten-foot drain on each side, the pack are settled to the scent, and racing away a clear field ahead of every one but the huntsman and whip. The Honourable Crasher, however, is coming up hand-over-hand, Topsy-Turvy laying herself out in rattling form. The master, with a backward glance at the crowd, is alongside of him, and Mr. Sawyer, sailing over the first fence, in such good company, with a tight hold of his horse's head, and an undeniable start, thinks he is "really in for it at last!"

CHAPTER XI.

"A MERRY GO-ROUNDER."

A MILE-AND-A-HALF of grass, some six or eight fences, and the sustained brilliancy of the pace, have had their usual effect on the moving panorama. A turn in his favour, of which his old experience has prompted him to take every advantage, enables Mr. Sawyer to pull Hotspur back to a trot, and look about him. He is in a capital place, and has every reason to believe the new horse is "a flyer." Hitherto, he has only asked him to gallop, best pace, over sound turf, and take a succession of fair hunting fences in his stride. Hotspur seems to know his business thoroughly, and though a little eager, he allows his rider to draw him together for his leaps, and the way in which he cocks his ears when within distance denotes a hunter. Mr. Sawyer is full of confidence. He has been riding fence for fence with the Honourable Crasher, whose pale face wears a smile of quiet satisfaction. The latter has indulged Topsy-Turvy with two awkward bits of timber, and an unnecessary gate; the mare is consequently tolerably amiable, and, though she throws her head wildly about if any other horse comes near her, may be considered in an unusually composed frame of mind. The huntsman has been riding close to his hounds, in that state of eager anxiety which the philosopher would hardly consider enjoyment, and yet which is nevertheless not without its charms : all his feelings are reflected, in a modified form, in the breast of the master. The latter, riding his own line, as near the pack as his conscience will permit him, is divided between intense enjoyment of the gallop and a host of vague apprehensions lest anything should turn up to mar the continuance of the run. He has already imbibed a qualified aversion for Mr. Sawyer, whom the instinct peculiar to his office prompts him to suspect as "a likely fellow to press them at a check;" while he knows his friend Crasher so well, as to feel there is but one chance with that mild enthusiast, viz. that Topsy-Turvy should come to a difficulty before the hounds do. Besides these four, Captain Struggles and Major Brush are very handy, whilst Mr. Savage heads another detachment in the next field, of which Miss Dove, riding with considerable grace, is at once the ornament and the admiration. Her father has lost his place from a fall, but is coming up with steady skill and energy, going as straight as if he were close to the hounds, and ready to take every advantage. At the first turn in his favour he will be with them as if nothing had happened. In addition to these, many score of sportsmen are scattered over the neighbouring district, and a serried mass of scarlet, which may be termed not inaptly, "the heavy brigade," is moving in close column down a distant lane.

All this our friend observes at a glance, but his attention is soon arrested by the business in his front.

The hounds, having over-run the scent a trifle, swing to the line again with dashing confidence, and take it up once more with an energy that seems but increased by their momentary hesitation.

They might have been covered by a sheet hitherto: now they lengthen out into a string, and the leaders scour along, with their noses in the air and their sterns lowered. Every yard increases their distance from the pursuing horsemen.

They are pointing to a dead flat surface of old yellow grass, with patches of rushes and ant-hills interspersed. There would appear to be a mile or more of plain without a fence; but Mr. Sawyer spies a tell-tale willow here and there, and he wishes in his heart that he was quite sure Hotspur could jump water!

Presently the hounds disappear, and emerge again, throwing their tongues as they take to running, and looking darker and less distinct than before.

"Is there a ford, Charles?" halloos Major Brush, who has shaken to the front, and would fain continue there without a wetting.

"Never a one for miles," answers Charles with inconceivable rapidity, catching his horse by the head, and performing a running accompaniment with his spurs.

In a few seconds, he is over with a considerable effort, a certain scramble and flourish when they land, showing there are very few inches to spare.

The ill-fated Major has no idea of refusing. His horse, however, thinks differently; so they compromise the matter by sliding in together, and climbing out separately, draggled, disgusted, and bemired.

"There is no mistake about it," thinks Mr. Sawyer; "I must jump or else go home!" He may take a liberty, he hopes, with a friend; so he puts the roan's head close behind the Honourable Crasher, and devoutly trusting that gentleman will get over, drives Hotspur resolutely at the brook.

Topsy-Turvy, wild with excitement, throws her head in the air, and takes off a stride too soon. Consequently she drops her hind-legs, and rolls into the opposite field. The roan, who jumps as far as ever he can, lands on Crasher's reins, of which the latter never lets go, and drives them into the turf.

"Line, sir! line!" expostulates the Honourable, not knowing who it is. "Oh! it's you, is it?" he adds, picking himself up, and re-mounting. "All right! Go along, old fellow! The hounds are running like smoke!"

Mr. Sawyer apologizes freely as they gallop on. In his heart he thinks Crasher the best fellow he ever met, and contrasts his behaviour with that of Sir Samuel Stuffy in the Old Country, on whom he once played the same trick, and whose language in return was more Pagan than Parliamentary.

The master and Struggles get over also, the latter not without a scramble. Those who are not in the first flight wisely diverge towards a bridge. For five minutes and more there are but half-a-dozen men with the hounds. These run harder than ever for another mile, then throw their heads up, and come to an untoward check.

"What a pity!" exclaims Mr. Sawyer. Not that he thinks so exactly, for Hotspur wants a puff of wind sadly.

"Turned by them sheep!" says Charles, and casts his hounds rapidly forward and down wind. No; he has not been turned by the sheep: he has been coursed by a dog. Charles wishes every dog in the country was with Cerberus, except the nineteen couple now at fault.

"Pliant has it," observes the master, as Pliant, feathering down the side of a hedge, makes sure she is right, and then flings a note or two off her silvery tongue, to apprise her gossips of the fact. They corroborate her forthwith, and the chorus of female voices could scarce be outdone at a christening. Nevertheless, they are brought to hunting now, and must feel for it every yard they go.

But this interval has allowed some twenty equestrians, amongst whom a graceful form in a habit is not the least conspicuous, to form the chase once more. Great is the talking and self-gratulations. Watches are even pulled out, and perspiring arrivals announce the result of their observations, each man timing the burst to the moment at which he himself came up.

"How well your horse carried you!" said a soft voice at Mr. Sawyer's elbow; "didn't he, Papa?" added the siren, appealing to the Reverend Dove, who was eagerly watching the hounds. "We all agreed that the velvet cap had the best of it."

She wanted to make amends to him for her rudeness in the morning, and this was the opportunity to choose. The hardest male heart is sufficiently malleable under the combined influence of heat, haste, and excitement, though how this girl should have made the discovery it is beyond my ingenuity to guess. How do they discover a thousand things, of which we believe them to be ignorant?

Mr. Sawyer smiled his gratitude, as he opened a gate

for the lady, and very nearly let it swing back against her knees. He had not acquired sufficient practice yet at his gates, that's the truth; and perhaps there were other portals wherein his inexperience had better have forbidden him to venture. Miss Dove was fast luring him into a country which, to use a hunting metaphor, was very cramped and blind, full of "doubles," "squire-traps," and other pit-falls for the unwary.

Hounds are apt to be a little unsettled after so rapid a burst as I have attempted to describe, and it takes a few fields of persevering attention to steady them again. After this, however, I think we may have remarked they make but few mistakes, and a fox well rattled, up to the first check, huntsmen tell us, is as good as half killed.

The description of a run is tedious to all but the narrator. What good wine a man should give his guests, who indulges in minute details of every event that happened!—how they entered this spinny, and skirted that wood, and crossed the common, and finally killed or lost, or ran to ground, or otherwise put an end to the proceedings of which the reality is so engrossing and the account so tedious. I have seen young men, longing to join the ladies, or pining for their cigars, forced to sit smothering their yawns as they pretended to take an interest in the hounds and the huntsman, and the country, and their host's own doings, and that eternal black mare. I can stand it well enough myself, with a fair allowance of '41 or '44, by abstracting my attention completely from the narrative, and wandering in the realms of fancy, cheered by the blushing fluid. But every one may not enjoy this faculty, and you cannot, in common decency, go fast asleep in your Amphitryon's face. Again, I say, nothing but good wine will wash the infliction down.

Let him, then, whose port is new, or whose claret unsound, beware how he thus trespasses on the forbearance of his guests.

Of course they killed their fox. After the first check they gradually took to hunting, and so to running once more, Mr. Sawyer distinguishing himself by describing a very perfect semicircle with Hotspur, over some rails near Stanford Hall. The roan was tired, and his rider ambitious, so a downfall was the inevitable result. Nevertheless, he fell honourably enough, and hoped no one but himself knew how completely the accident was occasioned by utter exhaustion on the part of his steed.

There is no secret so close as that between a horse and his rider. Up to the first check, Hotspur had realized his owner's fondest anticipations. "He's fit for a king!" ejaculated the delighted Sawyer, when they flew so gallantly over the brook. Even after the hounds had run steadily on for the best part of an hour, the animal's character had only sunk to "not thoroughly fit to go;" but when they arrived at the Hemplow Hills, and the pack, still holding a fair hunting pace, breasted that choking ascent, he could not disguise from himself that the roan was about "told out." They are indeed no joke, those well-known Hemplow Hills, when they present themselves to astonished steeds and ardent riders after fifty minutes over the strongest part of Northamptonshire. A sufficiently picturesque object to the admirer of nature, they prove an unwelcome obstacle to the follower of the chase, and it was no disgrace to poor Hotspur that, although he struggled gamely to the top, he was reduced to a very feeble and abortive attempt at a trot when he reached the flat ground on the summit. Ere long this degenerated to a walk; and I leave it to my reader, if a sportsman, to imagine with what feelings of relief Mr. Sawyer observed the now distant pack turning short back. The fox was evidently hard pressed, and dodging for his life.

The Rev. Dove, with an exceedingly red face, a broken stirrup-leather, and a dirty coat, viewed him crawling slowly down the side of a hedgerow. In an instant his hat was in the air, and Charles, surrounded by his hounds, was galloping to the point indicated. Two sharp turns with the fox in sight—a great enthusiasm and hurry amongst those sportsmen who were fortunate enough to be present, and who *rode*, one and all, considerably faster than their horses could go—a confused mass of hounds rolling over each other in the corner of a field—Charles off his horse, and amongst them, with a loud "Who-whoop"—and the run is concluded, to the satisfaction of all lookers-on, and the irremediable disgust of the many equestrians who started "burning with high hope," and are now struggling and stopping over the adjoining parish, in different stages of exhaustion. The Honourable Crasher congratulates Mr. Sawyer on his success; also takes this opportunity of introducing his friend to the M. F. H. A few courteous sentences are interchanged; Messrs. Savage, Struggles, and Brush propose a return to Harborough; cigars are offered and lit; everybody seems pleased and excited. John Standish Sawyer has attained the object for which he left home—he has seen a good run, made a number of pleasant acquaintances, launched once more into that gay world, which he now thinks he abandoned too soon. He *ought* to be delighted with his success; but, alas for human triumphs!

"Ay! even in the fount of joy,
Some bitter drops the draught alloy;"

and our friend, with many feigned excuses, and a dejected expression of countenance, lingers behind his companions, and plods his way homewards alone.

CHAPTER XII.

"DEAD FOR A DUCAT."

It is needless for me to observe that Mr. Sawyer was one of those individuals who are described in common parlance as not having been "born yesterday." He had lived long enough in this superficial world of ours to recognize the prudence of "keeping his own counsel," just as he kept the key of his own cellar at The Grange; and he would no more have thought of entrusting his dearest friend with the one than the other.

Accordingly, when he felt certain ominous thumps against the calves of his legs, which denoted that "Hotspur was suffering from palpitation of the heart," he resolved to conceal if possible from every eye that untoward failing of so good an animal. And, with considerable judgment, he waited till his friends were out of sight ere he dismounted, and led his jaded steed into a barn, which he espied at hand, there to recover himself a little under shelter, and then, if possible, to make his way home in the dark, and trust to chance for some excuse to account for his delay, when he met them again at the dinner-table.

Perhaps the reason is, that in these fast times condition is so much better understood—for we cannot admit the uncomplimentary excuse that hounds do not run now as formerly—why horses *stop* so much less often in the hunting-field than they did in the palmy days of Musters and Assheton Smith, and "the d—d Quornites," who were always either "showing" or "being shown the *trick*" some fifty years ago. *Then* a hunter's reputation was as fragile as a sultana's, and was guarded as jealously. Not only must he be "*sans peur*," but also "*sans reproche.*" And the efforts of these lords to preserve the character of their treasures were as ingenious as they were ludicrous. One facetious nobleman actually got a tired favourite home next day right through the streets of Melton, disguised as the middle horse of a cart-team; nor did all the lynx-eyes, ready to watch for the "casualties" consequent on a clipper, discover the identity of one of the best nags in Leicestershire, under the weather-beaten winkers and shabby harness of a four-horse waggon. Mr. Sawyer trusted to the cloud of night for the same immunity.

He had just stabled his steed in the warmest corner of the shed, and, having taken off his own coat to fling over the animal's heaving quarters, was beginning to speculate on the probable rheumatism that would succeed this imprudence, when, to his astonishment and disgust, the door was darkened by another figure, and his solitude disturbed by the entrance of a man and horse, in all probability seeking the same shelter for the same cause.

The new-comer was a remarkably good-looking person, extremely well got-up, particularly as regarded his nether extremities, and our friend at once recognized him as having been very forward with the hounds at different stages of the run. His horse, a well-bred bay, was "done to a turn." When Sawyer looked at its drooping head and heaving flanks, it seemed to put him quite in conceit with the roan. For a moment neither spoke a word—then the absurdity of the situation seemed to strike them simultaneously, and they both burst out laughing.

"What? They've cooked *your* goose as well as mine!" said the stranger, in off-hand tones, producing at the same time a silver cigar-case, on which our friend could not help fancying he descried a coronet, and proceeding to light a most tempting-looking weed.

"A very likely day to do it, too," he added, glancing, as Sawyer thought, somewhat contemptuously at himself and steed. "The pace for the first twenty minutes was *alarming*, and the country awfully deep. I should say you'll hardly get that horse home to-night."

The suggestion was neither flattering nor consolatory. Mr. Sawyer felt half inclined to be offended; but he thought of the silver cigar-case, and swallowed the retort uncourteous that rose to his lips. He was a true Briton, and not above a weakness for the peerage. "This good-looking man," he argued, "notwithstanding his black coat, must be a Viscount at least!"

"I'm going as far as Market Harborough," he observed meekly. "It cannot be more than seven or eight miles. I shall hope to accomplish that."

"Lucky for *you!*" replied the other. "I want to get to Melton, if I can. I've a hack here at Welford, if this beggar can take me there. He's short of work, poor devil! and could hardly wag coming up the hill. I should say *your* horse would die."

This was an unpleasant and rather startling way of putting the matter. Mr. Sawyer had not indeed considered it from that point of view. Though a man of energy, he felt somewhat helpless; as who would not in a similar position? Eight miles from home, in a strange country, encumbered with a dying horse!

"What had I better do?" inquired he, rather plaintively, of the unknown.

Nobleman though he were, the latter seemed to be an energetic personage enough, and pretty familiar with the usages of the stable. Between them they made poor Hotspur as comfortable as circumstances would admit, the unknown conversing with great condescension and volubility the whole time.

"What you want for this country," said he, rubbing away the while at Hotspur's ears and forehead, "is a strong stud. If you've sport hereabouts, it pulls the horses so to pieces. Now this is a nice little well-bred horse enough, but he hasn't *size*, you see, and scope; there's nothing of him; consequently, when you drop into a run, he goes as long as he *can*, and it's all U P! *Mine*, now, would have gone on for ever, if he'd had *condition;* but I only bought him ten days ago, and he's never had a gallop. Nothing like *good* ones—*big* ones—and plenty of 'em! Look at him now; he's getting better every moment."

Without subscribing entirely to this statement, Mr. Sawyer humbly asked his new friend if he himself was very strong in horses?

"Not *very*," was the reply. "I've got eleven, however, at my place, which I shall be very happy to show you whenever you like to come over. Every one of them up to more than your weight," he added, casting his eye over Mr. Sawyer's much-bemired figure. "I shall be happy to give you a mount on any one of them you fancy; and you will know them better than I can tell you."

Our friend was penetrated with gratitude. Visions stole over him of an eligible acquaintance, that would soon ripen into friendship, with this most affable of peers; of a charming country-house, agreeable women, billiards, music, dry champagne, and flirtation—himself an honoured guest; of an introduction, perhaps, through his noble ally, into the best London society and everything that he had always thought most desirable, but hitherto considered beyond his reach. "Doubtless," reasoned Mr. Sawyer, "he has remarked *my riding*, and taken a fancy to me. On further observation, he finds my manners are those of a perfect gentleman; and he is determined we shall become friends. How lucky Hotspur was so beat that I came in here!"

Accordingly, he thanked his new acquaintance with considerable *empressement*, and assured him that "he should take the first opportunity of taxing his hospitality."

The unknown looked a little astonished. "Well," he replied, "if you don't mind roughing it a bit, I dare say I can find room for you, even in *my* little crib; but you can see the horses out hunting, and ride them too, just the same."

"How considerate these noblemen are!" thought Mr. Sawyer, "and how playful! I dare say his 'little crib,' as he calls it, is three times the size of The Grange. But he insists on mounting me, all the same." So he thanked him once more, and proposed that, as it was dark, and the horses were somewhat recovered, they should endeavour to make their way home.

"When will you come?" asked the unknown, as they emerged into the open air—both horses coughing, one lame before, and the other all round. "I've a bay that would carry you admirably, and a brown, and indeed, a chestnut that you would like. I'd take five hundred for the three; and they're so perfect, a child might ride them."

"What a cordial, good fellow!" thought Mr. Sawyer again. "He wishes me to enjoy my visit, and ride his horses with thorough confidence; so he tells me of their great value and perfect tuition. I have indeed 'lit upon my legs,' as the saying is." "Thank you," he replied aloud. " My time is my own ; and I will pay you a visit whenever it is perfectly convenient to you to receive me. My name is Sawyer; and I am staying at Harborough. Perhaps you will kindly write and let me know."

"Very well, sir," answered the other, muttering something about "business," but touching his hat, as Mr. Sawyer thought, with all the politeness of the old school, as their ways diverged; and he jogged off to get his hack, leaving our friend to plod on afoot by the exhausted Hotspur, in the darkening twilight, cheered but by one solitary star, which threatened to be soon eclipsed by the clouds that were rising fast in the sighing night-wind.

It was no such enviable position, after all. Seven miles at least had Mr. Sawyer to go; and he must walk, or ride at a foot's pace, every yard of the way. The sky was ominous of rain ; the Laranagas were all smoked out ; and poor Hotspur was unquestionably "done to a turn."

These are the moments which the most thoughtless of men cannot but devote to reflection. There is nothing like *pace* to drive away unpleasant considerations; but when two miles an hour is the best rate we can command, black Care is pretty sure to abandon his seat on the cantle of the saddle, and, springing nimbly to the front, grins at us in the face. I remember well how a fast-going youth—a friend of my boyhood, now, alas! gone to Jericho *viâ* Short-street, and with whom I have spent many a pleasant hour that might have been better employed—used to read with great energy whilst he was *dressing*. It was the only time, he said, that his conscience could get the better of him, and during which he had leisure to think of his sins and his debts. He smothered the accusing voice and its painful accessories by a course of severe study, and so got the anodyne and the information at once.

Mr. Sawyer's reflections were cheering enough till he began to get tired. He liked the idea of visiting the hospitable nobleman with whom he had lately parted, and pictured to himself the very pleasant visit he hoped to pay him, and the accession of importance with which such an acquaintance would doubtless invest him amongst his Harborough friends. He only wished he had inquired his name; but then, he was evidently a personage whom everybody knew, and it was better not to betray his ignorance. Also, when the written invitation arrived—as unquestionably it would—with its armorial bearings, and signature in full, he would know all about it. Before he had tramped through the mud for a mile, he began to think he had rather "got into a good thing."

Ere long, it began to rain—first of all, an ominous drizzle, that seemed like continuing; then a decided pour, such as runs into the nape of a man's neck and the tops of his boots, and wets him through in about a quarter of an hour. It was not much fun, churning the fluid in his soles; so he climbed stiffly into the saddle, and was disagreeably aware that Hotspur, besides being thoroughly tired, was also undoubtedly *lame*.

By degrees, his spirits fell considerably. He began to think of the Honourable Crasher, with his off-hand manner and his nine hunters. He remembered a certain fable of the earthenware vessel that sailed down-stream amongst the iron pots. How was he to hold his own in the fast-going set which he had entered? He had better, perhaps, have

H

contented himself with the Old Country, and stayed quietly at home. The comforts of The Grange presented themselves in painful contrast to the muddy road along which he was plodding—even to the smoky bedroom and dingy parlour which would receive him at Harborough. Though the rain had moderated, he jogged along the dark highway, now squelching into puddles at the side, now cursing the stones lately laid down in the middle—in either case, to the equal discomfiture of poor Hotspur—and felt himself more unhappy and out of humour every yard he went.

Presently, the horse quickened his pace of his own accord; and the sound of hoofs behind him produced its usual inspiriting effect on the rider.

"Company, at all events," observed Mr. Sawyer, aloud. "Hold up, you brute!" he added, as Hotspur made an egregious "bite," that nearly landed him on his nose.

Ere long, the new arrivals ranged alongside of him. They were a lady and gentleman, on exceedingly tired horses. What a piece of luck! They were no other than the Reverend and Miss Dove!

"She knew me at once, though it's so dark," thought our friend, with considerable gratification, as the damsel, adapting her own pace to that of the jaded Hotspur without difficulty, accosted him by name.

"How lucky, too!" said she, in her joyous tones. "We shall keep each other company all the way to Harborough. Papa and I were just saying how lonely the road was, after dark; and our poor horses are so tired, they can hardly walk"

"Lucky indeed, for *me*," replied Mr. Sawyer, gallantly, adding with considerable *empressement*—for it was dark enough to give a shy man confidence—"Do you know, I was just thinking of you?"

The Reverend had dropped behind to light a cigar. Miss Dove seemed to have no objection to receive this statement; of the truth of which I have myself, however, strong doubts. She edged her horse a little nearer her companion, and answered laughingly,

"Indeed! A penny for your thoughts, then. I should like to know what you *could* have been thinking about *me* in the dark, after a day's hunting."

"I was thinking how well you rode," answered Mr. Sawyer, who, not much versed in the ways of womankind, saw he might have said something more flattering, but, like a frightened bather, put one foot in, and then withdrew it. It was not *his line*, you see, as he said himself; and consequently he felt a little awkward at first with the ladies.

The latter, however, are in all cases strenuous advocates for the "sliding scale" rather than the "fixed duty." I think I have observed that they are usually as ready to bring a shy man "on" as they are to keep a forward one back. There is a certain temperature at which they consider you malleable; so they heat you up, or cool you down to it, with no small chemical skill. Sometimes, but rarely, they burn their own fingers in the process.

"I was wondering how *you* would get home," said the young lady very innocently after a pause. "Your poor horse looked so very tired; but, then, he carried you famously. Papa and I knew you by your cap—didn't we, Papa?"

Papa, who had now come up, corroborated his daughter; but the Reverend was somewhat abstracted and unobservant. He was not quite satisfied with the way his horse had carried him. He doubted whether the animal had pace. He doubted whether he had blood. He doubted whether he had courage. In truth, he was thinking just then whether he hadn't better sell him to Mr. Sawyer.

That worthy was recovering his lost ground, by expressing many tender hopes that Miss Dove was not very tired. " She had had such a long day; and it was so wet for a lady to be out; and how would she ever get home all that way into Leicestershire ?"

" Oh, we have a carriage at Harborough," answered the fair object of all these anxieties; " and I don't mind being late half so much as Papa does. I do so like being out at night. Do you know, though I am so fond of riding, I am rather *romantic*, Mr. Sawyer ?"

" Oh, indeed! Yes, of course," rejoined our friend, seeing another opening, but not getting at it quite so readily as if it had been in a bullfinch. " It's very pleasant sometimes, particularly in the summer; and horses always go best at night. But, there's no moon now," he added, looking wistfully first at the heavens, and then, as far as the darkness would permit, in his companion's face.

" I'm certain you're a great quiz," answered Miss Dove to this harmless observation. " I told Mamma I was quite afraid of you, the day you came to luncheon at the Rectory. I dare say you think us all wild savages here, compared with what people are in your own country. By the bye, your country place is somewhere near London, I think you said ?"

Mr. Sawyer did not remember saying anything of the kind, but he looked insinuating, which he need not have done, as it was so dark, and replied,

" Forty minutes by rail. I can run up, and do my shopping, and back again, between luncheon and dinner. I'm only half a mile from a station."

Then he had a country place. So far, so good. In discussing him with Mamma, the latter had inclined to think *not*, but Miss Dove held strongly to her own opinion. She knew the country gentleman's cut, she said; and in this instance she was right.

"Do you farm much?" was her next inquiry, putting the unconscious Sawyer through his facings, as only a woman can.

"Not much," replied our friend. "I let most of my land; but I keep enough in my own hands to supply the house. One must have a few cows, you know, for milk and fresh butter."

It was evidently all right. A man who had land to let and land to keep, and a place of his own, was clearly none of your penniless interlopers such as visit the grass at intervals, like the locust, and eat it bare, and fly off and are seen no more. Here was a bee worth catching; with a hive, and honey, and flowers of its own—a good, honest humble-bee, with plenty of buzz, and no sting.

By this time the lights of Harborough were twinkling in the distance, and the Rev. Dove, whose horse had coughed more than once, thought it advisable to trot forward and get the carriage ready; whilst his daughter and Mr. Sawyer came on at a foot's pace, the latter gallantly affirming that he would take the greatest possible care of his charge, and wishing, as soon as they were alone, either that somebody else would overtake them, and so break the *tête-à-tête*, or else that he could find something to say, else she must think him so confoundedly stupid. It was agreeable too, when he got a little more used to it. The girl talked on in her gentle, pleasant voice, of the hounds, and the people, and the country. Her tones had caught the languor of slight fatigue, and were very soft and silvery to the ear. More than once he wished it was not too dark to see the long eyelashes resting on her cheek, those silky excrescences having made no slight impression on Mr. Sawyer. He felt quite sorry when the turnpike denoted their approach to the confines of the town at which their ride must cease. He could not conceive now how he could have been so out of spirits not an hour ago.

"When shall I see you again?" he ventured to ask as their horses' hoofs clattered on the stony pavement, and he saw the lamps of the Reverend's carriage glowing like the eyes of some monster ready to carry off his Andromeda. As he spoke he even ventured to place his hand on her horse's neck; and this was a great stretch of gallantry for Mr. Sawyer.

"Oh, you'll be at the ball," answered Miss Dove, without withdrawing her steed from the range of her companion's caresses. "You'll be at the ball, of course, even if we don't meet out hunting before that."

"Ball!" repeated our friend in amazement. "What ball do you mean?"

"Why, the Harborough Ball," answered the young lady. "Everybody will be there; Captain Struggles, Major Brush —even Mr. Crasher, though he won't do much in the way of dancing. Why, it is held at your hotel. The music will keep you awake all night, so you may as well go."

"I will, if you'll dance with me," rejoined Mr. Sawyer, with the air of a man who is "in for a penny, in for a pound."

And he felt queerer than he had ever done about Miss Mexico when she murmured a gentle affirmative. Nay, when he had put her carefully into papa's carriage, and tucked her up as assiduously as if she was going to the North Pole, he actually whispered, "You won't forget your promise?" while he shook hands, and wished her "Goodbye." Nor did the scarce perceptible pressure with which that promise was ratified tend to restore our friend's equanimity in the least.

He was not a ball-going man: far from it. Also, I question whether it is not a breach of privilege that your rest at an hotel should be broken for a whole night by the thumping of feet, the squeaking of fiddles, the Scotch Quadrilles, and the monotonous 'Tempête;' whilst your dinner and general comfort for two days previous to, and two days after the solemnity, is reduced to positive misery. Nevertheless, Mr. Sawyer caught himself repeating more than once during the evening—which, by the way, he spent in an atmosphere of smoke, with Struggles, Brush, Savage, and the Honourable Crasher—"Ball! ball!—was ever anything so lucky? Go!—of course I'll go! In fact, I promised: and perhaps she'll dance with me *twice!*"

CHAPTER XIII.

"AFTER DARK."

I NEVER can understand upon what principle the rate of a groom's wages is always inversely proportioned to the work he performs. For instance, Major Brush's excellent domestic —a bât-man, of lengthy proportions and military exterior— brushed his master's clothes, prepared his master's breakfast, took the first horse to covert, and rode the second on occasion, cleaning either or both, if necessary, when they came in, upon a stipend which would barely have kept Mr. Tiptop in Cavendish and blacking.

The latter worthy, with a whole troop of helpers under his command, never seemed to have a moment to spare for anything but the routine duties of his station. As for riding a second horse, or remaining out on a wet day, beyond his accustomed dinner-hour, his master would as soon have thought of bidding him dig potatoes! No: if Mr. Tiptop went out hunting at all, it was generally on a *third* horse in excellent condition, that wanted a couple of hours' preparation for the day after to-morrow, when the rider, in a long-backed coat, a shaved hat, and the best boots and breeches the art of man can compass, might be seen at intervals, during a run with the first fox, now opening a hand-gate, now creeping cautiously through a gap, and anon cantering, with a Newmarket seat, and his hands down, up some grassy slope, in front of soldiers, statesmen, hereditary legislators, and justices of the peace, as if not only the field, but the county, was his own.

Old Isaac, on the contrary, though subject to occasional "rustiness," and imbued with a strong aversion to what he called being "put upon," was ready and willing to turn his hand to anything, if he thought such versatility would *really* conduce to Mr. Sawyer's advantage. With the assistance of The Boy—who, indeed, since his arrival at Harborough, had been constantly inebriated—the old man looked after the three hunters, the hack, and his master, with considerable satisfaction. He had even spare time on his hands, now that he was removed from the responsibility of the pigs, the poultry, and the potatoes at The Grange.

It was in one of these moments of leisure that the bold idea of getting the better of Mr. Tiptop entered the old groom's mind. I need not, therefore, specify that, under his calm demeanour, Isaac concealed a disposition of considerable enterprise and audacity.

Now the manner in which he proposed to take advantage of the acquaintance he had lately struck up with Mr. Tiptop was as follows:—By dint of his own sagacity and diplomatic reticence, he resolved that he would prevail on that gentleman to persuade his master that the redoubtable bay horse Marathon should be transferred to his own stables; and, to explain Isaac's anxiety for this consummation, I must be permitted to describe the appearance and general capabilities of that peculiar animal.

Marathon, then, was a long bay horse, about fifteen-two, with short legs, a round barrel, well ribbed up, and an enormous swish-tail, of which he made considerable use. He was one of those doubtfully-shaped animals which are condemned alike by the eye of the totally inexperienced and the consummate judges of horseflesh, but which are much coveted by that large class of purchasers with whom " a little knowledge is a dangerous thing."

And here I must remark how correct is usually our first impression of a horse; and how seldom ladies—who judge of these, as of all other articles, at a glance—are mistaken in their opinion of the noble animal, if indeed they condescend to turn their attention to his " make and shape."

The worst point about Marathon was his head, which was coarse, and denoted a sulky temper; but he carried a beautiful coat; could stride away for a mile or so, on light ground, with his hind legs under him, in the form of a racehorse; and in short was never so graphically described as by Mr. Job Sloper, when he sold him for sixty guineas and a set of phaeton harness to his present owner: " If that there horse aint worth five hundred, why, he aint worth fifteen sovereigns—that's all."

And Mr. Sawyer has since confessed to himself, on more than one occasion, that Job Sloper was right.

Mr. Tiptop liked Isaac, because he thought him an original; and the swell groom, who was as epicurean in his tastes as if he had been a Peer, took the pleasure of his friend's society over a can of egg-flip and a pipe of Cavendish daily, after evening stables; during which convivialities, the hard-headedness peculiar to the aborigines of the Old Country was of infinite service to the latter, who wormed out all the secrets of the Honourable Crasher's stable, without betraying his own.

"And there *is* some talk of a steeple-chase amongst these nobs, is there?" said Isaac, ordering at the same time a third can of "the flip," and knocking the ashes from his pipe with an exceedingly horny finger.

"*Talk* of it! indeed there is," answered Mr. Tiptop, whose face was beginning to redden with his potations. "And a precious exhibition it will be, too. Ride! There isn't one of 'em as don't believe he's down to every move in the game; and I'd take that boy of yours—though he *is* but a boy, and not the best of hands, neither—and teach him to outride every man of 'em in a fortnight! Such a mess as they made of it last year! Blessed if I wasn't quite ashamed of the Honourable, to see him rollin' about in a striped jacket, like a zebra in convulsions! What's the use getting a horse fit, when the *man's* blown in three fields? But I don't mind telling *you*, now," added he, confidentially, and fixing his eyes on the tallow candle that stood between them—"I don't mind telling *you*; for there's money to be made of it. He'll win it this year, if he'll only sit *still!*"

"Win it, will he?" rejoined Isaac. "Well, I shouldn't wonder, so as he comes in first. But it takes a smartish nag, Mr. Tiptop, to win a steeple-chase. Have you *tried* yours to beat everything in the town?"

"Well, I think I've the length of most on 'em," answered Mr. Tiptop, smiling at the candle with a most reflective expression of countenance. "You've got a bay as might run up, if he was lucky. Why don't you make *your* master put him in?"

"He's as deep as a well, is *my* master," answered old Isaac. "Nobody never knows what *he's* up to. Bless you! I can't help thinking as he must have bought the bay a-purpose for this here race: but *I* don't know, no more than the dead; and I dursn't ask him, neither."

Mr. Tiptop reflected profoundly for several minutes, during which period Isaac's countenance would have been a study for an artist who wished to represent a face totally devoid of thought. Then he asked—

"Have *you* ever tried the bay?"

"*Never*," answered the senior, who piqued himself on his veracity. "Master brought him back from Stockbridge, last spring, pretty nigh done; and when I asked him what he'd been up to, he bid me mind my own business. The poor critter! he'd had a benefit, *sure-lie!*"

This was undoubtedly true, Marathon having turned restive at a cross-road on the occasion in question, and, after a quarter of an hour's fight, given in, completely exhausted.

"If he can beat our mare a mile, at even weights, he'll win it, as safe as safe!" observed Mr. Tiptop, now speaking very thick, and with a good deal of gravity.

"I dursn't give him *a mile*," answered Isaac, with an

emphasis on the substantive which argued that he was open to persuasion for a shorter distance.

Mr. Tiptop regarded him attentively for several seconds, during which time he thought him first a flat, then the sharpest customer he had ever come across, and lastly an ignorant yokel and greenhorn once more.

"If *you'll* chance it," said he, "I'll chance *our* mare. We might try them early to-morrow morning."

Old Isaac pretended not to understand. Mr. Tiptop, with many flourishes, rose to explain.

"You go to exercise," said he, "a little before it's light, in the big close just outside the town. Put a fourteen-pound saddle on your nag; and don't say nothing to nobody. I'll be there in good time, just to give our mare a turn up the close. Nobody needn't be a ha'porth the wiser. Once we know the rights of it exactly, we can do what we like. You're game to the back-bone, old cock, *I* know! *You* won't split!"

"But master's going to hunt the bay horse to-morrow," interposed Isaac, preserving his appearance of puzzled integrity with admirable composure.

"Never mind," answered Mr. Tiptop: "you come all the same." And, leering grimly at the tallow candle, Mr. Tiptop made his exit, and betook himself heavily to bed.

In the meantime, the hunting gentlemen, at their hotel, had been talking over the probabilities of getting up a steeple-chase, and the chances of the different horses and riders, whose merits they discussed with considerable freedom, and no small amount of that playful *badinage* which moderns term "chaff."

Struggles, who rode over sixteen stone, was repeatedly entreated to enter, and cordially assured that he would carry all the money of the party; but Struggles, besides his enormous weight, was too good a sportsman to take pleasure in such a mongrel affair as a horse-race across a country.

"I'd sooner go to a badger-bait," said he, "or a cock-fight. I'd sooner hunt a cat in a kitchen, or a rat in a sewer. It's neither one thing nor the other; and I'll have nothing to do with it!" an announcement which was received with derisive cheers by his companions, amongst which Struggles calmly lit a fresh cigar, and filled his tumbler once more with brandy-and-soda.

The Committee, as they called themselves, had met, according to custom, for their nightly *weed*. They were indulging freely in the use of narcotics and stimulants, to the detriment of their digestions, and the destruction of their nerves. They lived by rule, these choice spirits, and restricting themselves, as they believed, with considerable self-denial, to about a bottle and a half of wine apiece at dinner, considered that such abstinence entitled them to smoke any quantity of cigars, and drink any amount of pale brandy, choice Hollands, and such alcoholic fluids diluted with soda-water, out of glasses the size of stable-buckets.

Men who spend their evenings after this fashion, are apt to be surprised that they cannot cross a country with the coolness and judgment of their earlier years. They wonder why they are beat by Farmer Styles, who rides a raw four-year-old, but who gets up with the sun, and has his beer with his dinner at one o'clock. They envy my Lord's iron nerves and fresh-coloured face, notwithstanding his grizzled hair, and do not consider that the peer has gone to bed with a clear head and a good conscience every night for the last forty years. Some days they get their courage up, and go as well as ever; but these inspiriting occasions become fewer and fewer, and at last they either give up their favourite amusement altogether, or, worse still, spend a large proportion of their time and income in a pursuit from which they have long ceased to derive either pleasure or profit.

The Honourable Crasher, though he smoked a great deal, had neither spirits nor inclination to drink much; consequently, notwithstanding his languor and apparent debility, he had preserved the integrity of his nervous system. Mr. Sawyer too, with a vigorous constitution, unimpaired by previous excesses, was not materially affected by these orgies, although his mouth was very dry in the mornings. All the rest, for the first ten minutes, rode more or less in a funk.

Nevertheless, volumes of smoke curled around the Committee, and the thirst for brandy-and-soda seemed unquenched, unquenchable.

They had discussed the usual topics which enliven the dullness of a bachelor party. They had gone through the different subjects which arise in inevitable rotation. From the merits of horses and the shortcomings of riders, they had proceeded to the fascinations of the other sex, and from that again had, of course, returned to the inexhaustible theme, the merits of horses, once more.

Major Brush, slightly excited, was the first to cross-question Mr. Sawyer about his stud. Hitherto they had treated our friend with the deference due to a stranger; but he was now to be considered one of themselves, and bantered or otherwise accordingly.

"You never ride that bay horse of yours, Sawyer," said the Major, in an off-hand, free-and-easy sort of way. "I like him in the stable, better than anything you've got."

"Good horse," replied Mr. Sawyer laconically. "Goes as fast as you can clap your hands."

Now considerable anxiety had already been excited amongst the grooms of Harborough concerning the powers of the said bay horse. Old Isaac, by an affectation of extreme secrecy, had led one and all to believe there was what they termed "something up" about Marathon; and it was but that morning the Major's faithful bât-man had thought it right to give his master a hint that "Muster Sawyer had one as they were keepin' *dark*," so that the subject created immediate interest amongst the party. Mr. Savage put down the evening paper, behind which he had been observing his friends, with a certain satirical amusement; Struggles paused in the act of raising his tumbler to his lips; and even the Honourable Crasher roused himself sufficiently to turn in his rocking-chair, and gaze with an expression of sleepy curiosity at the owner of the mysterious bay horse. Major Brush pursued his inquiries:

"Have you ever hunted him?" said he, "or do you keep him to look at?"

Dark and grim on Mr. Sawyer's mind rose many a vision of disappointment and discomfiture, and sporting casualties, such as come under the generic term "grief," originating in Marathon's incapacity; but he only replied,

"I've too few to keep any for show. I leave that to you swells with your large studs. All mine are forced to come out in their turn."

The careful ambiguity of our friend's answer put the whole company on the *qui vive*. There was evidently something about this nag that was to be *kept dark*. Even Struggles, the simplest and frankest of men, began to think Mr. Sawyer was what he called "a deep 'un." The astute Savage now stepped in for cross-examination.

"Shall you enter one for our steeple-chase, Sawyer?"

said he, with an off-hand air. "Anything that can *really* gallop would be sure to win; and as it is to be entirely amongst ourselves, and we shall all ride, it will be rather good fun."

"When is it?" asked Mr. Sawyer, with admirable simplicity, as if this very steeple-chase, and a certain ball which he had made up his mind to attend, were not the two topics by which he had of late been chiefly engrossed.

Everybody now spoke at once. "Time not fixed," said one. "Directly the weights are out," said another. "Whenever we can find a handicapper to give *universal* satisfaction," sneered a third; whilst the Honourable Crasher, turning once more in the rocking-chair, and losing a slipper in the effort, quietly remarked, he "would take ten to one even then that he named the winner."

"Take him, Sawyer!" exclaimed Major Brush. "Take him at once! and enter the bay horse. Owners to ride, of course. He's got nothing but Chance, now that Catamount's lame," added the gallant officer, in a stage whisper, and with a degree of friendly *empressement* born of rosy wine.

The Honourable smiled feebly, but vouchsafed no reply. It was indeed too true, and as he had rather set his heart on winning this steeple-chase, the truth was unacceptable, as usual. Mr. Sawyer seemed to ponder deeply on what he had heard.

"I should lose so much hunting," said he, after a pause, during which he had smoked with considerable perseverance and an aspect of profound reflection. "Why, a horse would not have the ghost of a chance, would he, unless he was put in training?"

Doctors differ upon most subjects. "No training like

regular hunting," said Struggles, who meant to have nothing to do with it. "Take him out often, and send him home early," advised Major Brush, who was generally of opinion that nothing more would be done after 1 P.M. "The halfbred ones seldom stand regular preparation," opined Mr. Savage, "I should keep him here under my own eye;" while the Honourable Crasher murmured something about "Newmarket being the only place to get a donkey fit."

Mr. Sawyer turned from one to the other, as if weighing carefully what each had said; then he flung his cigar-end into the grate, finished his liquor at a gulp, and observing, "Well, I must think about it; in the meantime I'm going to hunt him to-morrow," wished his friends "Good-night," and departed for what he was pleased to term his "downy."

As Struggles and Brush, who occupied adjoining bedrooms, shouldered each other up the narrow passage that led to their apartments, the former declared with a stupendous yawn, "He didn't quite know what to make of their new friend, but fancied, whether the bay was a *dark* one or not, his owner was well able to take care of himself." To which the Major, whose eyes seemed much dazzled by the candle in his hand, of which he was spilling the wax with considerable liberality over the passage-carpet, replied, "We shall find out all about him to-morrow, old boy, if we keep our eyes open—that's all: if we only keep our eyes open!" And for the better furtherance of this wideawake scheme, the Major, whose eyes were already nearly closed, proceeded to turn in, after an attempt to undress, in which he only partially succeeded.

Mr. Sawyer, winding up his watch and depositing it carefully on his toilet-table, observed a face of considerable wisdom in his looking-glass, as he reflected on the interest

I

which seemed to have been created about Marathon. He balanced the pros and cons: he enumerated, not without disgust, the numerous failings of the horse; then he shook his head twice or thrice, gravely, as was his habit, when, to use his own expression, "he thought he saw his way."

CHAPTER XIV.

"BEFORE THE DAWN."

An unshaved face, blotched and parti-coloured from waning inebriety, up-turned and open-mouthed in all the imbecility of profound sleep; a recumbent form snoring loudly under a patchwork quilt, and supported by a rickety bedstead, on an uncarpeted floor, in a room with a sloping roof, of which the only furniture seemed to be a box, originally intended for horse-clothing; a five-pound saddle, a pair of spurs, and a black bottle containing a tallow candle that had guttered itself out some two hours previously—all this does not sound like a cheerful and inspiriting scene about five o'clock on a winter's morning. Nevertheless, such did not fail to call a grim smile into Isaac's harsh countenance, as he contemplated it, on this, his first visit to Mr. Tiptop's apartment. Isaac had been revolving the swell stud-groom's proposal of the evening before, and had come to a decision in his own mind ere he went to sleep, the result of which was his matutinal appearance in the chamber I have endeavoured to describe. He was not a man to waste much time in the contemplation even of a more agreeable sight than that which now met his eyes. He shook Mr. Tiptop roughly by the shoulder till that worthy sat up in bed, and blinked at his visitor's candle with a ludicrous expression of astonishment and dismay.

"What's up?" he exclaimed at last, as he began to be sensible of the old man's identity. "Blessed if I didn't think the stables was a-fire, and all our horses grilling, till I see it was you. Will you take any refreshment?" added Mr. Tiptop jocosely, pointing to an earthenware ewer containing cold water—and not much of that; "or is there anything I can do for you besides telling you what o'clock it is?" he added, yawning, and betraying strong symptoms of a desire to go to sleep again.

Old Isaac laid his finger to his nose.

"Get up," said he in a cautious whisper. "It *is* just to know *what's o'clock* as I've come here. You lay your hand on a fourteen-pound saddle, and there need be no mistake about the weights. My nag's ready, and turned round. You go and get yourn. There's a bit o' moon left: not quite burned down yet. We can get it over and done with, and the horses back in the stable afore the others is up."

Mr. Tiptop was a man of considerable energy when anything like a robbery was on the cards: he was, however, hardly prepared for such a display of alacrity on the part of his companion. He put one skinny leg out of bed, and then paused, staring vaguely at his visitor.

"Come, look alive!" said old Isaac, fishing a pair of breeches from the floor; "there ain't a minute to lose. Where's the key o' *your* stable?"

The weaker nature obeyed instinctively: Tiptop put on his breeches, and produced the key.

"Not a word to living mortal!" urged the old man impressively. "It's as much as my place is worth. I've left The Boy safe locked up. You go and get *your* horse, and meet me in the close. There's just light enough to gallop 'em. Look alive, man! Whatever should I do if master was to get wind of this here?"

Isaac seemed unusually perturbed as he preceded Mr. Tiptop down the creaking stairs, and wended his way to his own stable, leaving the latter—still rather confused—to saddle and bring out the redoubtable Chance.

The Honourable Crasher's groom felt for the first time in his life somewhat puzzled, and taken aback. He had not calculated on such promptitude and decision from a "yokel." Also, his intellects had hardly recovered the potency of the flip, a beverage of which it requires several hours' sleep to obviate the effects. Altogether he was sensible of less than his usual self-confidence. In his hurry, too, and by the imperfect light of a stable-lantern, he put the wrong saddle on Chance, who, by the way, was not a very pleasant animal to caparison, save by her own accustomed attendant—a greyhaired, withered old helper, then probably dreaming of the better days most of these ancient stablemen have seen. The snaffle, too, that he wanted was not in its accustomed place. Altogether, it took him some considerable time before he could lead the horse out into the wan light of a morning moon. This interval, however, had enabled him to recover the good opinion he generally entertained of Mr. Tiptop. As he got upon Chance's back, and felt the animal step lightly and jauntily under him, the conviction came strong upon his mind that in some way or other he was sure to get the better of the yokel.

As the conscience-stricken Marmion riding his red-roan by night into the enchanted ground was aware of a phantom cavalier looming dimly in the distance in guise of his deadliest enemy, so Mr. Tiptop, opening the gate of the close which he had appointed for a trysting-place, distinguished the outline of the man and horse with whom he was about to try the speed of his thorough-bred. As he neared his antagonist, he observed that the animal he bestrode was sheeted and hooded, and otherwise so swaddled up in clothing, that there was nothing visible of it, save its legs; and in the uncertain twilight the general effect of the pair much resembled that of those hobby-horses which so delighted our ancestors in their Christmas revels.

"Look alive!" exclaimed Mr. Tiptop, somewhat angrily, as a black cloud swept across the moon, and a raw morning breeze dashed a score of sharp rain-drops into his feverish face. "It will be light in half an hour, though it's as dark as pitch now. Ain't you going to strip him?"

"Strip him!" repeated Isaac, keeping off at a respectful distance the while. "Not I; he always runs kindest in his clothes. Don't ye come anigh!" he added, as Mr. Tiptop ranged alongside. "He's werry handy with his heels when he's at exercise. Are you ready?"

Now the close, as such open spaces are termed only in the midland counties, was a field of sound old grass, comprising little less than a hundred acres, and was much affected as an exercising ground by the grooms of such sportsmen as had chosen Market Harborough for their head-quarters. This was sufficiently attested by the trodden state of its hedges, betraying the hoof-marks of many a good nag, whose speed had been tried here far oftener than was dreamt of by his master. Do you think we know the merits of our steeds one-half as well as do their own immediate attendants? Why are the hacks always in such good condition, and constantly falling lame so unaccountably? Is it that on their homeward way they are matched continually against each other, and against Father Time, whereby many pots of beer and goes of brandy are lost and won on the result? To a man who *really* cares for his horses, a groom he can depend upon is worth his weight in gold.

Both Isaac and Mr. Tiptop knew perfectly well that a straight run-in, the long way of the furrows, up to a certain white gate which they would pass on their right hand, was as near half a mile as possible. The latter, keeping out of reach of his opponent's heels, proposed a longer distance; but Isaac, declaring it was simply a question of speed, as they both knew their horses' performances in the hunting-field, overruled his friend on this point.

"When you're ready," said the old sinner, who could hardly see his listener in the increasing darkness, "we'll start, and run it from end to end. Mind, Mr. Tiptop, I trust to your h'onour!"

"In course!" replied Mr. Tiptop, who was considering whether he could make a better thing of it by acting, as he himself would have said, entirely on "the square," or otherwise.

Accordingly they took up their positions some ten yards apart, but strictly on the same level, and went off with a rush, amicably and honourably, when they were both ready.

It would be doing injustice to Mr. Tiptop to say that, when he really chose, he was not a consummate horseman, either across a country or over the flat. On the present occasion he was resolved to do all he knew, and he sat down upon Chance, and got at her in the most masterly manner. The mare, however, like many that have been in training, was a lurching, shifty goer, taking several strides before she got fairly into her speed. Mr. Tiptop, notwithstanding his proficiency, saw the dark figure of his opponent a dozen lengths ahead of him, and could not overhaul him, do what he would. His finish, no doubt, was inimitable, but it failed to land him first past the goal. Old Isaac, there was no disputing it, won cleverly by a couple of lengths.

Mr. Tiptop couldn't make it out. "They've got a flyer," said he to himself; "and they *know it!*"

He would fain have talked it over with Isaac then and there; but the veteran, simply remarking that "he was quite satisfied, and it would be daylight in ten minutes," passed through the white gate already mentioned, and trotted back to the town at a pace which Mr. Tiptop's regard for Chance's legs forbade him to imitate.

Both horses were safe home in their stables before the helpers were up.

CHAPTER XV.

TAKING A HINT.

No man alive subscribed more heartily than did the Honourable Crasher to Mr. Sheridan's aphorism, that "If the early bird catches the worm, what a fool must the worm be to get up earlier than the bird!" It was always a matter of great difficulty to get the Honourable out of bed, and not to be managed without considerable diplomacy. The stud-groom and valet laid their heads together for this purpose with laudable ingenuity, the former entertaining a professional regard for the hack's legs, the latter being much averse to the idea of a hurried toilet. He liked to turn the Honourable out as a gentleman should be dressed, resplendent in scarlet, and with faultless boots and breeches. In his own opinion, proper justice could not be done to the garments he had prepared, under an hour and a quarter; and when the place of meeting was a dozen miles off, and the church clock chiming half past nine found his master still in bed, the valet might be seen pervading the passages with tears in his eyes. The *ruse* he found most efficacious was to tap at the door soon after eight, and say it was near ten. The Honourable's watch was pretty sure to have been left downstairs, or, if in his bedroom, to have stopped, unwound; and often as the trick had succeeded, Crasher never seemed yet to have found it out. Even if he rose in time, however, he was a sad dawdle. There were letters to be read, and sometimes answered. He would breakfast in a gorgeous dressing-gown, and smoke a cigar over a French novel afterwards, never dreaming of getting into his hunting things till he ought to have been more than halfway to covert. Sometimes, and this was the sorest grievance of all, he would take a fancy not to hunt, and then changing his mind at the last moment, order round one of the unfortunate hacks, and go off like a flash of lightning.

On the morning to which I have already alluded, Mr. Tiptop, cleaned, breakfasted, and considerably freshened up, having completely recovered the effects of his early gallop, seen everything set straight about the stable, and dispatched two of his master's horses to Shearsby Inn, was vainly waiting for an audience at the Honourable's bedroom door about ten A.M.

The valet, a staid elderly man, who, as Mr. Tiptop would have said, made a point of "standing in" with all the upper servants, treated the stud-groom with considerable deference. They had exhausted their usual topic of the weather, the probability of sport, and their master's propensities for repose, and were now beguiling the time, by listening at his chamber door alternately, till the welcome sound of much splashing and hard breathing announced that the Honourable had tumbled out of bed into his tub.

After awhile the valet gave a low tap at the door, accompanied by a cough.

"Who's there?" said the inmate of the chamber, sedulously drying his elegant proportions before an enormous fire.

"Beg your pardon, sir," answered the well-drilled servant. "Mr. Tiptop, sir, wishes to speak to you, sir."

"Tell him to go to the devil," rejoined the Honourable, struggling leisurely into a clean shirt.

There was no occasion for the polite valet to repeat this message, inasmuch as Mr. Tiptop was there to hear it for himself. The servants looked at each other, and laughed in their sleeve.

Presently, the valet, who knew to a second how long each stage of the toilet ought to last, knocked again.

"What is it?" murmured the Honourable very indistinctly, for the sufficient reason that he was sedulously brushing his teeth.

"Mr. Tiptop, sir, wishes to know if he can see you before you go down to breakfast."

The stud-groom was well aware that no confidential communication could take place during that meal, disturbed as it usually was by the arrival of other late starters, dropping in, to hurry their friend.

"Come in," gurgled the Honourable: and his stud-groom made his appearance, smoothing his shiny head as all grooms do.

"What's the matter, Tiptop?" inquired his master, poising the tooth-brush between finger and thumb. "Are all the horses lame?"

"No so bad as that, sir," answered Tiptop, respectfully, revolving in his mind how he should begin what he had to say. For all his languor, there was something about Crasher that made people very loath to take a liberty. "I only wanted to tell you, sir, of a horse I've seen as you ought to buy. I thought I'd make bold to tell you before any of the other gentlemen got word of him. He's a flyer, sir—that's what he is!"

Now, in all matters relating to the stable, Mr. Tiptop ruled paramount, the Honourable's system being to make his groom look out for horses, and if he liked their appearance himself, to buy them at once. With regard to riding, I have already said, he could make them all go, if they had any pretensions to hunters about them.

"Whose is he?" was the next question asked; for the Honourable was now finishing his toilet in such a hurry as would have made you suppose he never was late in his life.

"Mr. Sawyer's, sir," answered Tiptop. "It's the bay. He'll be on him to-day at Barkby Holt."

"Very well," answered the Honourable, buttoning on a watch-chain, with half-a-dozen lockets attached, as he emerged from his room. "Tell Smiles to get breakfast *directly*, and send the hack round in ten minutes!"

Mr. Tiptop looked after him admiringly, as he clanked downstairs. "He means *business* this morning," thought the groom, "and I'll lay a new hat he buys the bay horse!"

Now if Mr. Tiptop had felt he had the best of the morning trial, it had been his intention to pull his horse back, and gammon his friend Isaac that he was beat, with the laudable determination to get the better of that worthy, as well as of the general public, by making good use of his knowledge previous to the race. When, however, he found that her antagonist had the heels of Chance, whom he had already tried with the other grooms to be quite the best in the town, he altered his tactics altogether. Obviously they ought to have both the flyers in the same stable; and it would be wiser to stand in with Isaac, and make the old groom a sharer in the profits, as he was already in the information which their early rising had enabled them to obtain. Mr. Tiptop forgot that it is as dark before dawn as it is after nightfall. He might, perhaps, have been further enlightened, had he, instead of waiting at his master's door till the Honourable's teeth had been polished to the required degree of whiteness, been able to assist at an interview which took place at the same hour between Isaac and his master, in a room where the latter had just finished breakfast.

The old groom made no apology for entering; as was his custom, he plunged at once *in medias res*.

"I've sent *two* out for you to-day," said he, marching up to Mr. Sawyer's chair, and confronting him with a grin, such as might be cut out of mahogany.

"And left *one* in the stable! you old idiot!" exclaimed the indignant Mr. Sawyer. "What the deuce have you done that for?"

"You'll want a second horse to-day," answered the groom. "You'll have a bid for Marathon before you've been on him half an hour. Leastways, if you've the discretion not to go a-showing of him up."

"What do you mean?" asked Mr. Sawyer, with a dawning of intelligence overspreading his countenance, for he knew his servant's diplomatic talents of old.

"Only that they're all of 'em wanting a nag to win this here donkey-race, as I call it; for none but a donkey would be concerned in such a tomfoolery; and Mr. Crasher, he's satisfied by this time that Marathon's the one as just *can*. You sit still upon him to-day, and keep jogging of him about, to *qualify* like, till the hounds find, and then open your mouth, and take what they offer you."

Mr. Sawyer had implicit confidence in his old servant; still he could not help wishing to be further enlightened.

"You must have told some precious yarns," said he, "to make people believe Marathon could *run up* with a man in mud-boots!"

"I never said a word!" answered Isaac; "people may believe their own eyes. Mr. Tiptop and I, we tried 'un this very morning again Chance; and though she's the best in the town, we beat her by more than a length."

"Marathon beat that mare!" exclaimed Mr. Sawyer, now completely taken aback. "What *do* you mean?"

Old Isaac's features were distorted once more into the mahogany grin.

"Well, if Marathon didn't, Jack did," said he quietly. "You couldn't tell one from the other in their clothing when it's dark, and the Dandy would win the Derby if it wasn't over half a mile."

It was too true: though the smart little nag never could stay a mile at a racing pace in his best days, he was as quick on his legs as a rabbit, and nothing could touch him, for five furlongs. Swaddled up in his clothes under the dubious twilight of a winter's morning, Mr. Tiptop never suspected him, and went home with the conviction that Marathon, and none other, was the horse that had beaten his favourite.

Mr. Sawyer laughed to himself as he rode Jack very gingerly on to Barkby.

CHAPTER XVI.

RIDING TO SELL.

IF Mr. Sawyer had kept a hunting journal (which he didn't) he would have noted down the meet at Barkby, as one of those gorgeous spectacles, which make an ineffaceable impression on the eye of the unpractised beholder. There appeared to be more hounds, more horses, more servants, more carriages, and altogether a larger staff and retinue attached to the establishment, than he had ever hitherto seen paraded for the purpose of killing a fox. Nevertheless, with all this show, there was no mistake about the workmanlike tendency of the turn-out. If the pack was numerous, it was also exceedingly level and in faultless condition; the huntsman and whips looked as if they must have been born and bred for the especial offices they respectively filled, and the second-horse men, notwithstanding their numbers, appeared to be all cut from the same pattern. As for the hunters, Mr. Sawyer would have wished no better luck than to ride the worst of them at a hundred and fifty guineas. One magnificent bay with a side-saddle, destined, no doubt, to carry a beautiful and precious burden, quite put him out of conceit with Hotspur and the grey. As for Marathon! why he would never have got on him, in such company, had not the pleasing reflection crossed his mind, that perhaps to-day he should get rid of the brute altogether.

He had ridden The Dandy very leisurely to covert, in consideration of the animal's services before dawn, and had sent on the grey with an occasional helper from the inn, under the superintendence of The Boy, who was perched on Marathon; old Isaac, who wanted to buy some hay cheap, having given himself leave of absence for the day. The helper, with many injunctions to go steadily, was entrusted with the homeward-bound hack; and The Boy shifted to the second horse, whilst Mr. Sawyer himself bestrode the redoubtable bay. All these arrangements, with the accompanying pulling up of curb-chains and letting down of stirrup-leathers, took some little time. Before our friend was fairly mounted and under way, the hounds had gone on to draw, and he found himself nearly the last of the lengthening cavalcade. Under existing circumstances, this was no great disadvantage, and the quieter he kept the bay, he thought, the better was his chance of selling him; yet he could not help wishing old Isaac had left the whole business alone. He might then have been forward with the hounds, looking out for a start on whichever horse he liked best, uninfluenced—as a man always should be, really to enjoy fox-hunting—by the sordid considerations of £. s. d.

Marathon was very fresh, and set his back up, squeaking in a most undignified manner, and swishing his heavy tail till it reached his rider's hat.

A horse galloping up from behind set him plunging with a violence that was scarcely pleasant, even to so practised a rider as our friend. He returned the greeting of the new comer—no less a personage than the Honourable Crasher, late as usual, and cantering to the front on Boadicea by Bellerophon out of Blue Light—with the preoccupied air of a man who expects every moment to be on his back.

The Honourable, slightly amused, pulled up alongside. "Halloa, Sawyer," said he, "you'll be hard to beat to-day: the steeple-chaser seems uncommon full of running."

"It's only his play," answered Mr. Sawyer, modestly; indulging Marathon, who was preparing for another kick, with a vicious jerk of the curb. "I can't get my old groom to give him work enough, and he's sent me a second horse out to-day!"

This was meant to imply that the kicker was too valuable an animal for a mere hunter, and the Honourable interpreted it accordingly. As he rode alongside, he scanned the bay's points with the critical eye of a purchaser. A horse never looks so well as when he is trotting beside you on a strip of grass, excited by the presence of hounds. If backed by a good horseman, the veriest brute, under these circumstances, makes the most of his own appearance. Marathon going within himself, playing lightly with his bit, and bringing his hind legs under his girths at every step, was a very different horse from the same Marathon extended and labouring, in a sticky ploughed field. I have already said he possessed many qualities sufficiently taking to the eye. As the Honourable examined him from his muzzle to his hocks, he could not but acknowledge that the horse looked uncommonly like a galloper. "If he can only jump," thought Crasher, "and get pretty quick over his fences, he ought to be a *rattler*. I suppose I shall have to buy him."

Meantime Mr. Sawyer, who, as he remarked of himself, "was not such a fool as he looked," but on the contrary resembled those "still waters" which the German proverb says "run so deep," conversed affably with his friend on a number of topics totally unconnected with horseflesh or the pleasures of the hunting-field. For once in his life, he did not want to get a start, that's the truth; and as his companion was one of those indolent, easy-going people whose fancy can be led astray without difficulty in any given direction, they were soon deep in a variety of subjects, originating no doubt with Mr. Sawyer, but to which, I am bound to say, he had never devoted much of his time or attention. They touched upon the last misadventure brought under the notice of Sir Cresswell Cresswell—discussed the agricultural prospects of the season, and on this theme it would be difficult to say which was most incapable of giving an opinion—argued on the importance of a movement for taking the duty off cigars, and lastly got involved in the interminable question of what use the Volunteers would be, in the event of an invasion, and whether or not they would be killed to a man, when their conversation was cut short by an obvious bustle and confusion about a mile ahead of them, denoting that a fox had not only been found, but gone away.

"Done to a turn!" exclaimed the Honourable, interrupting his own explanation of how he should handle skirmishers if he was a general officer, which, by the way, it was fortunate for the skirmishers he was *not.* "What a bore! We shan't catch them in a week!" he added, turning Boadicea's head at the fence, and starting her at score through a deep ploughed field. In a few strides he had forgotten skirmishers, and Marathon, and Mr. Sawyer, and everything in the world except that he had lost his start.

The latter, watching the line "fine by degrees and beautifully less" on the horizon, rather congratulated himself, that his chance was completely out, and that there was now no temptation for him either to exert his own energies, or draw upon the failing powers of Marathon in the pursuit of that which he felt could scarcely be called *pleasure*. He jogged along the lane accordingly, contented enough, thinking what fun he would have on the grey, in the afternoon, with a second fox!

But a few of us can have hunted much without remarking a peculiarity connected with the chase, that occasions constant irritation and annoyance to its votaries. Have you never observed, that if you lose your chance of getting away with hounds, whether from procrastination, inattention, or the laudable objection entertained by a rational man to ride at a large fence, do what you will, you only succeed in increasing the distance between yourself and the object you wish to reach? In vain you "nick," and "skirt," and ride to points that you think likely to be affected by a fox running for his life; in vain you "harden your heart," and sail away boldly over the line of gaps already established by your predecessors; you are only tiring your horse, and risking your neck in a wild-goose chase. You diverge to a distant halloo, and find it raised by a boy scaring crows. You succeed by extraordinary exertions in reaching the group of scarlet coats and bobbing hats you have been following so long, and learn that they have been "thrown out" like yourself, and the further you go, the further you are left behind; till you hate yourself, as much as your horse hates you for not having judiciously joined the band of second-horse riders, and so jogged contentedly along in ease and safety, sure to come up with the first flight at last.

On the other hand, we will suppose that you have tired your best hunter early in the day, or he has fallen lame on

K

that weak point where everybody said he *would* be lame when you bought him, or you have a hundred and fifty other reasons for wishing to sneak quietly home, out of the observation of your friends. Those plaguy hounds seem to follow you as if you were the Wild Huntsman himself, and you begin to appreciate the severity of the punishment inflicted on that wicked German Baron. They draw coverts that lie on your homeward way. They find, and hunt with provoking persistency alongside the very lane up which you would fain jog in solitude, crossing it more than once under your nose. There is sure to be a fair holding scent, not good enough to enable them to run clear out of your neighbourhood and have done with it, yet sufficient to afford plenty of enjoyment to such as are with them; these have, nevertheless, leisure to observe your movements, and to wonder why you are not amongst them. They are all your own particular friends, and you know you will be called upon, next hunting morning, to answer that difficult question—"What became of *you*, after we left you in the road at So-and-so?" Diana seems to delight in the rule of contrary. Like the rest of her sex, she takes you up and persecutes you, when you don't want her; and when you are most ardent and zealous in her pursuit, she rebuffs you and puts you down.

Nothing could be further from Mr. Sawyer's wishes than to find himself, on the present occasion, in a conspicuous position with the Quorn hounds. Had he wanted to be singled out in front of all that talent and beauty, Marathon was certainly the last animal he would have chosen on which to make an appearance in such choice company; nevertheless, the force of circumstances is beyond the control even of men like Mr. Sawyer, and however averse he might be to "achieve greatness," he found, most unwillingly, "greatness thrust upon him." For awhile he had lost sight of everybody, and was in the act of pulling out his cigar-case to enjoy one of his Laranagas in solitude and repose, proposing to hang on the line, keeping a little down wind, and as soon as he should spy the second-horses, mount the grey, and send Marathon straight home. Crasher, he thought, would buy the horse without asking any more questions.

Scarcely, however, had he got his weed fairly *under weigh*, than the music of a pack of hounds broke suddenly on his ear from behind a high impervious bullfinch that sheltered one side of the grass-lane along which he was proceeding so leisurely. "Confound the brutes!" said Sawyer to himself, "here they are again!" As he opened the gate through which the track led into a sixty-acre pasture, the whole pack swept under his horse's nose, running with sufficient energy to denote what sportsmen call a holding scent; they carried a capital head, and were forcing their fox at a pace which kept him going, but was not good enough to come up with him.

It was just the sort of gallop that enables people who ride to hounds to look about them, and enjoy not only the sport, but the accompanying humours of the scene.

In these days, a *real* quick thing is such an affair of hurry, that the lucky few who are in it cannot spare a moment's attention from anything but their horses' ears.

Had he been riding a donkey, it was not in Mr. Sawyer's nature to abstain from turning the animal's head towards the hounds under such temptation; moreover, he distinguished amongst the first flight his Harborough companions, including the pale face of the Honourable Crasher, who by "bucketing" Boadicea most unmercifully, had got there

K 2

somehow, and appeared quite satisfied with his situation. What could our friend do, but cut in, and go to work at once?

Marathon, excited by the turmoil, was fain to set his back up once more. He found, however, that the kicking was now all the other way. Taking him in a grasp that would have lifted a ton, Mr. Sawyer drove his spurs into the half-bred brute, and set him going close to the hounds at the best pace he could command. For a short distance, and when held well together, Marathon could stride away in a very imposing form. The sensation of having a lead is, in itself, provocative of emulation; behind our friend were four or five intimate companions, who were not likely to let him hear the last of any instance of "shirking" that should come under their notice. Close on their track were the flower of Leicestershire; and these again were succeeded, so to speak, by a whole army of camp-followers, "maddening in the rear." Had the Styx been in front of him, he must have charged it "in or over."

Instead of the waters of Acheron, however, there was nothing more formidable in his line than a straggling, overgrown bullfinch at the far end of the field; just such a fence, indeed, as Marathon was in the habit of declining, but yet which he hoped the turmoil behind, the general excitement, and the persuasive powers of his own spurs, would enable him to induce his horse to face. He had plenty of time to scan it as he approached. Half a mile or so of ridge and furrow, even at a hunter's best pace, gives leisure for consideration. Ere the hounds had strung through it in single file, he was aware of a wide ditch *to* him; on the further side was obviously a grass-field, *and* an uncertainty!

Marking with his eye the weakest place, through which,

nevertheless, he could not see daylight, Mr. Sawyer, crammed his hat on his head, and set his horse resolutely at the fence; Marathon, according to custom, when he expected anything out of the common, *shutting up* every stride he went. Had it not been rather downhill, even his master's consummate horsemanship would have failed to bring him close to it. The fall of the ground, however, and the pace he was going, forbade the bay to stop. *Crash!* he plunged into the very middle of the fence—broke through it from sheer velocity, to jerk both knees against a strong oak rail beyond—blundered on to his nose over *that*—slid half-a-dozen yards on his head—nearly recovered himself—stumbled once more, and finally got up again, with his curb-rein turned over his ears; the rider's feet out of both stirrups, hat off, a contusion on his left eyebrow, and the horse's nostrils full of mud, but *no fall!*

"By the powers, that's a *rum one!*" said Mr. Sawyer, as he cantered slowly up the opposite slope, repairing damages the while, and turned round to see the first flight charge the obstacle, which had so nearly disposed of his own chance.

Lusty as eagles, ravenous as wolves, jealous as girls, down came the four *gluttons* at the fence, each man having chosen his own place, and scorning to deviate one hair's breadth from his line. None, however, had made so judicious a selection as Mr. Sawyer. The rail, which had so nearly discomfited the latter, would neither bend nor break, but he had the luck of getting it where it was lowest and nearest to the fence; everywhere else it was not only high, but stood out a horse's length into the field, just the place which must catch the cleverest hunter in the world, if ridden to do it all in his stride.

The scene that met Mr. Sawyer's eyes was amusing,

though alarming. Four *imperial crowners* at one and the same instant—four loose horses galloping wildly away—four red coats rising simultaneously from Mother Earth—eight top-booted legs shuffling in ludicrous haste after the departing steeds. Had our friend been Briareus himself, he could not have caught *all* their horses. He was a man, however, who seldom lost an opportunity, and was not likely to miss such a chance as the present. Selecting Boadicea, he galloped after her, and succeeded in pinning her against a pound: notwithstanding that the mare lashed out at him more than once, he brought her back in triumph to her panting owner.

Meanwhile, the four dismounted sportsmen condoled breathlessly with each other, as they laboured up the grassy slope.

"I'm but a poor hand at *this* game," observed Struggles, who did not fancy carrying his own weight across country.

"I wish I'd gone faster at it," said Savage, who had been grinding his teeth and hardening his heart the whole way up the field.

"My chestnut mare would have jumped it!" exclaimed Major Brush, inwardly registering a vow to abstain from "oxers" for the future; whilst the Honourable, though he held his tongue, was thinking what a capital horse that was of Sawyer's, and dismally reflecting that if Boadicea hadn't kicked at him when he was down, he never would have been such a tailor as to let her go.

"Catch hold!" said Mr. Sawyer, throwing the mare's reins to her owner, whose gratitude he thereby earned for the rest of his life. "There's no hurry," he added, as the Honourable, in a coat plastered with mud and a hat stove in, dived wildly at his stirrup; "they've over-run it a mile back, and checked in the next field."

The latter part of the sentence was true enough. His quick eye had shown him the pack at fault, as he secured Boadicea in the corner where the pound stood; the former was a bit of what theatrical people call "gag." It was as much as to say, "Whilst you fellows are hustling and spurting, and tumbling about, I am so well mounted that I can observe matters as coolly as if I was hunting in a balloon."

It was not without its effect on his listener. As they rode through the hand-gate together into the enclosure where the hounds were at fault, the Honourable Crasher no longer scanned Marathon with the eye of a purchaser. He looked on the horse now as his own property. He was determined to have him.

By some mysterious law of nature, whenever one individual succeeds either in what is termed *pounding* a field, or in getting such a start of them that nobody shall have a chance of catching him whilst the pace holds—and this, be it observed, is no everyday occurrence in countries where the best riders in England congregate for the express purpose of riding as well as they can—it invariably happens that the immediate failure of scent, or some such untoward contingency, robs the lucky one of his anticipated triumph. On the present occasion, much to Mr. Sawyer's delight, they never hit off their fox again. By degrees, the tail of the field straggled up, having found their way by every available gate and gap; then came the second horses, carefully ridden, cool, and comparatively clean, not having turned a hair; lastly, arrived a man in a gig, by a convenient bridle-road, hotter than any one present, wiping his face on a coloured handkerchief, which he afterwards put in the crown of his hat.

Whilst sandwiches were being munched, and silver horns drained of their contents, ginger-cordial, orange-brandy V. O. P.,* and other enticing fluids, Mr. Sawyer was giving The Boy stringent orders about taking Marathon home. He could not feel thoroughly comfortable till that impostor was fairly out of sight, and he should find himself established on the unassuming little grey.

When he had made up his mind, the Honourable Crasher was a man of few words. Refreshed by a mouthful of sherry, not unacceptable after a rattling fall, and comfortably perched on the back of Confidence, a delightful animal that a child could ride, and perhaps the best and safest hunter in his stable, he ranged alongside of our friend, and plunged at once *in medias res.*

"So you want to sell the bay horse you have just sent home?" said he, with none of the hesitation and beating about the bush to which Mr. Sawyer had hitherto been accustomed in his horse-dealing operations. "If you do, and will name the price you ask for him, I should like to buy him."

The owner could not resist the impulse of enhancing the value of his horse, by affecting unwillingness to sell him, and, in so doing, nearly lost the chance of disposing of him, altogether.

"I don't think I ought to part with him," said he reflectively; "it strikes me he's about the best in my stable."

Crasher fell back apparently satisfied. It was evident he

---

* Very Old Pale—a tempting label attached to certain black bottles containing the best French brandy; an excellent liquor, doubtless, and wholesome, *provided* you don't drink too much of it. Opinions vary, however, as to what is *too much.* The modest quencher of 9 P.M. growing to a superfluous stimulant at the same hour the following morning.

did not attach so much importance to the act of "exchange or barter" as did our friend. Mr. Sawyer picked himself up without loss of time. "I shouldn't like to sell him to *everybody*," said he affectionately, "but if you fancy him very much, I wouldn't mind letting you have him," he added, after a pause, and in the tone of a man who makes a painful sacrifice in the cause of friendship.

"I'll give you two hundred and fifty for him," drawled out the Honourable, with apparently about as much interest as he would have felt in paying three-and-sixpence for a pair of gloves.

"Guineas!" stipulated Mr. Sawyer; "Guineas," was the answer; and in this simple manner the deal was concluded.

My readers will agree with Isaac and his master, in thinking that Marathon was not the only one of the party who was pretty well sold. The old groom laughed in his sleeve a week afterwards, when he heard that on giving him "a spin" with Chance, just to keep his pipes clear, the mare went away from him as if he was standing still.

Mr. Tiptop couldn't make it out at all.

CHAPTER XVII.

"TEMPTED TO BUY."

AND now for the well-pleased John Standish Sawyer, came in what may be called the "sweet of the day." His horse disposed of, two hundred and sixty-two pounds ten shillings in his pocket (for the Honourable Crasher's word was as good as a bank-bill), and the wiry little grey under him, an animal for which he had not given a fourth of the above sum, and yet in whose pace and fencing he had the utmost confidence, with the additional delight of a certain find for the second fox—all these influences combined, were enough to put a man in thorough good-humour with himself. To do our friend justice, he was not of a mercenary disposition; but having been kept exceedingly short of funds during his youth, and in those hard times hunted under considerable pecuniary difficulties, he had insensibly imbibed a horror of what he called "riding upon too much money." "A man must have good nerve," he used to say, "who is not afraid to risk a couple of hundred every time he jumps a fence;" and I really believe he would shove a forty-pound screw along with greater satisfaction than the winner of the Liverpool. The grey was a right good little nag, easy to turn, quick at his fences, and thoroughly accustomed to his master's hand. It is wonderful what a deal of time is saved by a horse that is pleasant to ride, and how rapidly a moderate galloper, with a fine mouth, and quick upon his legs, can slip over a country compared with an animal that may have the pace of a racehorse, but requires a segundo bridle, and a hundred-acre field to turn him in. Mr. Sawyer drew the curb-rein gently through his fingers, struck his heels down, and mingled in the crowd upon the best possible terms with himself.

As the smoking, laughing, chattering cavalcade trotted merrily along, he had an opportunity of scanning many well-known individuals whom his business avocations of the morning had prevented his hitherto recognizing. "The talent," as it is called, was present, from Melton,—Melton, once the very metropolis of the hunting world, now, thanks to railroads, rivalled, if not surpassed, by Leicester and Market Harborough; and yet, what a nice place it is!

Who that has ever spent a season in the cosy, cheerful, joyous little town, but would wish to turn the stream of time, and live those golden days and pleasant nights over again?—would wish to be galloping his covert-hack once more through the fragrant air and under the dappled sky of a February morning, with a good horse to ride from Ranksborough Gorse or Barkby Holt, as his day's amusement, and a choice of at least a couple of invitations, offering him the pleasantest society *and* the best dinner in England, for his evening's gratification?

It is not more than thirty years since Nimrod wrote his celebrated " Quarterly Review Run"—the best description of *fashionable hunting* that has ever yet been printed, though many a hand, as light upon the bridle as the pen, has portrayed the same subject since then—not more than thirty years, certainly, and the ways of Melton are but little changed, only, of the *dramatis personæ* there are not many left. Of those who charged the flooded Whissendine so boldly, the majority have already crossed the Styx. Nevertheless, a few of the old lot may still be seen ready, when the hounds run, to face "wood and water," as of yore.

Mr. Sawyer, for an unimaginative man, was the least thing in the world of a hero-worshipper. As he rode along, contemplating from behind them the fine powerful frame and the slim and graceful figure of two Meltonians, who for many years have shone, a couple of *lucida sidera*, in the front rank, and of whom, indeed, so fast have they always gone, it may almost be said that

" Panting Time toils after them in vain,"

he was accosted by the pleasant, gentlemanlike personage with whom he had spent an agreeable quarter of an hour in the hovel, on that memorable day when his ambition had so completely "cooked the goose" of Hotspur with the Pytchley.

"Good morning, sir," said this affable individual, bringing his horse alongside of our friend, with a bow such as nobody in the Old Country could ever have perpetrated. "I thought you'd be out to-day, so I've a couple here for you to look at."

When a nobleman not only touches his hat, but takes it off to you, at the same time offering you "a couple of horses to look at," as if he were about to make you a present of them, such politeness, thought Mr. Sawyer, is rather overwhelming than reassuring. He returned the greeting, however, with his best air, and took off his hat in return, somewhat disconcerted, however, by the rude behaviour of Struggles and Brush, who were riding beside him, and who both burst out laughing.

The illustrious stranger, too—who, by the way, though still in a black coat, was "got up" with the utmost splendour of which a hunting costume admits—looked rather surprised, and winked at the two irreverent laughers as they are certainly *not* in the habit of winking in the House of Peers.

"Is that a favourite one you are riding?" inquired Mr. Sawyer, who fancied he must say something, and could think, at the moment, of no more apposite remark.

"I don't know much of him," was the reply. "He's only a five-year-old; and I haven't had him a fortnight. A thundering well-bred one, though, and can jump like a deer! I gave a hat-full of money for him, without getting on his back; but we'll see what he's made of this afternoon, I hope. I should say, now, that he'd carry *you* alarming!"

Mr. Sawyer, whose conversational powers were soon exhausted, made no reply, but, more out of civility than curiosity, contented himself with scanning the five-year-old from his ears to his tail.

The illustrious unknown seemed to have no dislike to inspection: on the contrary, he courted further companionship, by producing the gorgeous cigar-case, and offering Mr. Sawyer a weed.

"You will find them pretty good," said he, striking a light from a little *bijou* of a *briquet* that hung to his watch-chain. "I import them myself: it's the only way to ensure getting them first-rate, and it certainly is the cheapest in the long-run."

The cigar was indeed excellent. Mr. Sawyer thought this would be a good opportunity to draw his noble friend for a box. He might perhaps make him a present of a couple of pounds or so. At all events (as he said, it was the cheapest plan) there was no harm in risking the chance of having to pay for them. He asked him, accordingly, with some little hesitation, if he could do him the favour of procuring him a few?

"Certainly, certainly," replied the other, in the most off-hand, good-humoured way possible. "You shall have them from my man. I'll write to him to-night. How much shall I order? You can't get anything like them at the money: they only stand us in *five guineas a pound!*"

Mr. Sawyer modestly opined "one pound would be quite sufficient for the present;" but he felt as if he had just lost a large double tooth. Without being stingy, it was not the custom in the Old Country thus to throw money away. He fell back upon Brush, sucking at the costly tobacco with considerable vehemence.

"Who is he?" said he, nodding towards the rider of the five-year-old, then cantering on ahead, and sitting well down in the saddle, as he prepared to "lark" over a large fence, to the admiration of the field, instead of defiling through the hand-gate.

"Why, you seem to know him very well," rejoined Major Brush, smiling (as well he might) at the query: "I thought you seemed very thick, and were going to give him your custom."

Mr. Sawyer had not the heart to repudiate the soft impeachment. He liked to be "very thick" with a peer, and to have the credit of "giving him his custom" as a visitor and intimate.

"Yes," he said, "I am; but, somehow, I cannot, for the life of me, remember his title. I've no 'Debrett' at Harborough; and I've such a bad memory for names. Lord— Lord—what the deuce is it? Some Irish peerage, if I remember right?"

Major Brush fairly burst out laughing. "No more a lord than *you* are, Sawyer," said he, "though, I grant you, he *ought* to be a Duke. I thought everybody knew Mr. Varnish, the horsedealer!" And the Major went off at score again, thinking what a capital story he had got against Sawyer for that day at dinner, and a good many days after. A joke, you see, lasts a long time in the hunting season, when the supply is by no means equal to the demand.

And Mr. Sawyer turned his horse's head out of the crowd, feeling a little humiliated, and not a little disgusted. The five guineas for the cigars stuck horribly in his throat. However, he and Mr. Varnish, as will presently be shown, had by no means closed accounts yet.

But where are the low spirits, blue devils, or uncomfortable reflections that can hold their own for an instant against the cheering sound of " Gone away !"? Three notes on the huntsman's horn, five or six couple of hounds streaming noiselessly across a field, the rest more clamorous, leaping and dashing through the gorse, a rush of horsemen towards the point at which the fox has broken; and the man who is really fond of hunting has not the vestige of an idea to spare for anything else in the world.

John Standish Sawyer could ride "above a bit." Even in a strange country, and with hounds running "like smoke," he was not a man to shrink from taking his own line; and scarcely valuing the grey, perhaps, according to its deserts, he had no scruple in risking that good little animal at whatever came in his way.

A quick turn to the five couple of leading hounds, that he spied racing down the side of a hedgerow, and the happy negotiation of a very nasty place, with a stake in it that would certainly have impaled a more costly nag, placed our friend on terms with the pack. A fine grass country lay spread out before him. The fox, evidently a good one, bore straight across the middle of the fields. The hounds, without forcing any extraordinary pace, appeared well settled to the scent, and not inclined to flash over it a yard. A large fence and a little brook had combined to afford them more room than usual. Everything seemed to look uncommonly like a run; and the Honourable Crasher, shooting by our friend, on Confidence, whom he rode with a shamefully loose rein, observed that "It was all right; and he shouldn't wonder if they were going to have a gallop."

Mr. Sawyer laid hold of the grey, and determined to assume a place in the front rank—of which the occupants would have been equally at home in the rows of stalls nearest the orchestra at the Opera. There was more than one lady riding as he never saw lady ride before—perfectly straight; turning aside from no obstacle; jumping a gate with extreme cordiality, if it should be locked; and taking it all in the earnest, yet off-hand, graceful manner, with which a woman sets about doing what she likes best. The Meltonians, stride for stride, and fence for fence, were sailing away with perfect ease, looking as if they were scarcely out of a canter; yet, do what he would—and it must be owned he was *very* hard upon the grey—Mr. Sawyer could not, for the life of him, decrease the distance between himself and these leading horsemen.

The Honourable Crasher, having got Confidence amongst some very intricate fences on the right, though a little wider than he liked of the hounds, was disporting himself therein with considerable gratification. Struggles and the Reverend Dove (to-day without the daughter) were forward with the flyers, though the former was already beginning to calculate on a check.

The double posts-and-rails about Norton-by-Galby were already visible: but the fox had evidently no intention of entering the gorse. Albeit much against the grain, and what he was totally unaccustomed to in the Old Country, when hounds were running, Mr. Sawyer found himself obliged to ride to a leader. That chestnut five-year-old was for ever in front of him, now doing an "in-and-out" cleverly, now topping a flight of rails gallantly, then creeping under a tree, with a discretion beyond his years, and anon facing and rasping through a bullfinch, in the successful temerity of youth, Mr. Varnish sitting very far back the while, with the graceful ease of a man who is playing a favourite instrument in an arm-chair.

Presently the hounds checked, under Houghton-on-the-Hill; and Mr. Varnish, turning round to our friend, and casting his eye pitifully on the grey's sobbing sides, consigned them to reprobation for so doing, "just as the crowd was shook off, and the horses getting settled to their work!"

Mr. Sawyer's *dander* was up. It had been rising for the last two or three fences. He vowed, in his wicked heart, that chestnut should be his own before nightfall; and the way in which the young one jumped out of the Billesdon Road, when they got to work again, only confirmed him in his determination.

Long before the crowd could come clattering up the high-road, the pack and the first flight had put a couple of grassy slopes once more between themselves and their pursuers. Considerable grief and discomfiture took place amongst the sportsmen, as must always be the case when hounds run straight, over Leicestershire. The holding pace at which they kept on, and the straight running of the fox, forbade the slightest chance of any but such as had got a good start at first, and stuck to them through thick and thin. Even these, well-mounted and skilful as they were, had enough to do. The fox never turned but once, under the Coplow; and five minutes afterwards he was in hand, held high above the huntsman's head, with the pack baying round him in expectation of their reward.

Those who were there to see, it would be invidious to name. Sufficient for me to say that Mr. Sawyer was *not*, though he came up whilst Warrior and Woldsman were disputing the last bit of a hind-leg.

Despite his judicious riding and undeniable nerve, he had not the material under him that was quite adapted for so severe a country. The grey had neither pace for the extensive fields, nor scope for the large fences, each of which, though he did them so gallantly, entailed too great an exertion to bear frequent repetition. Notwithstanding two falls, however, he struggled gamely to the end; and it speaks well both for man and horse, that they should have got there at all.

Mr. Sawyer, however, was now thoroughly bitten. He had never felt so keen in his life. He would never hunt anywhere else. He could ride with any of them, he thought: he was determined to be as well mounted. Mr. Varnish and he discussed the subject in all its bearings, as they rode home; and the result of their conversation was—the arrival of the chestnut five-year-old and a good-looking brown at Mr. Sawyer's stables, and the transference to Mr. Varnish, in lieu thereof, of the Honourable Crasher's cheque, and another signed in full with the perfectly solvent name of John Standish Sawyer.

CHAPTER XVIII.

THE DOVE-COTE.

LET us take a peep into Dove-cote Rectory, smiling in the wintry sun, as it lies snugly sheltered from the north winds by a thick plantation, and rejoicing in that most desirable advantage in our climate—a southern aspect. This house is one that would make any sportsman oblivious of the tenth commandment. Who could refrain from coveting possession of those cheerful rooms; that fine extensive view; above all, the excellent and commodious stables within reach of three packs of hounds, and situated in the best grass country in England?

It is however with the *inside* of the mansion that we have now to do, and with those gentle beings who constitute a home, without whom a palace is little better than a dungeon.

Breakfast has been over at the Dove-cote for an hour or so. Cissy and her mamma have established themselves in what they call "the little drawing-room"—a snug apartment of small dimensions, with windows opening to the ground, and "giving," as the French say, on a neatly laid-out garden, in spring and summer the peculiar care of the daughter of the house. To-day, however, flowers and blossoms are replaced by a million sparkling gems, formed by last night's white frost, which is melting rapidly under the noon-day sun. Inside, the furniture is of a rich and somewhat gaudy pattern, assorting well with the rose-tinted muslin curtains and multiplicity of looking-glasses, which are so characteristic of a lady's bower; whilst a thousand pretty knick-knacks, and a graceful litter of books, music, work, paper-lights, stray gloves, and gossamer handkerchiefs betray at once the sex of the occupants. A little statuette of a Cupid in tears, with nothing on but a quiver, occupies a niche between the windows, under a portrait of Miss Dove, depicted by the artist in a graceful attitude on the chestnut horse, attired in a blue riding-habit, with her hat off, and her hair falling about her shoulders, as, it is only right to observe, she is *not* in the habit of wearing it when taking equestrian exercise. Altogether the painter's idea seems to have been borrowed from a French print entitled "The Rendezvous," representing a disconsolate damsel waiting for a gentleman in a wood—not in the best of humours, as is natural under the circumstances,—and sitting her white horse in a listless, woe-begone attitude, unworthy of an Amazon. The laggard, however, is perceptible in the far distance, making up for lost time on an exceedingly bad goer, whose "form" must at once absolve him of intentional unpunctuality in the eyes of his ladye-love. As a *pendant* to this work of art, hangs a portrait in *crayons* of Mrs. Dove, done some years ago, when people wore bunches of ringlets and a high comb at the back of the head—a fashion by no means unbecoming to the original, who must have been a sufficiently handsome young woman when she sat for this likeness. Indeed, the Reverend, no mean judge of "make-and-shape," always declared (at least in his wife's presence) that Cissy could not hold a candle to what her mother had been in her best days.

That matron, though somewhat voluminous in person and too highly coloured, is by no means bad-looking even now. As she sits at the window, shaping a little child's shirt for a poor parishioner (Mrs. Dove is a managing, bustling person —prejudiced, it may be, and deaf to argument, as what woman is not? but overflowing with the milk of human kindness), a judicious artist might tone her down into a very picturesque study of "A lady in the prime of life."

She looks up from her work, and casts her eye across the trim garden over many a mile of undulating prairie, to where a dim smoke in the far distance denotes the locality of Harborough.

"Cissy," observes the matron, "wasn't that Papa going round to the stables?"

Cissy raises those killing eyelashes from her crochet, and dutifully replies—"Yes, Mamma. He's only going to smoke his cigar as usual. I'm glad it's not a hunting day: we shall have him all to ourselves till luncheon."

Miss Dove pets her papa immensely; and it is needless to remark that, although on occasion he runs rusty with his wife, his daughter can wind him round her little finger at will.

"That reminds me," continues Mrs. D., in the inconsequent manner in which ladies follow out the thread of their reflections—"that reminds me we haven't had any visitors lately from over there," nodding with her head in the direction of Market Harborough.

Cissy looks very innocent in reply, and observes that "Gentlemen seem to make hunting the one great business of life."

Mamma, whose rest for the last five-and-twenty years has been broken every winter whenever the nights have been symptomatic of frost, and who can scarcely be expected to share the anxiety which drives the Reverend at short intervals from the connubial couch to open the window and look out, is unable to controvert so self-evident a proposition; so she tries back on their Harborough friends.

"Mr. Crasher *never* comes except on Sundays, or when there is a hard frost; and the rest of the gang I would just as soon be without, for they *will* light their cigars in the hall—a thing I've quite broke your papa of doing, till the whole place smells like a public-house. But I do think that Mr. Sawbridge, or whatever his name is, might have called in common civility, if it was only to ask how you were after your long day."

Cissy was of the same opinion; but she adhered steadily to the crochet, and said nothing: perhaps she thought the more. She had confided to her mamma certain passages of the nocturnal ride into Market Harborough, and Mr. Sawyer's categorical answers to her very pertinent queries.

I do not think, however, she had quite made what is called "a clean breast of it."

The mother, as is often the case in these days of improvement, had scarcely so much force of character as the daughter. She never dared cross-question "Cissy" beyond a certain point. Not that the girl was rebellious, but she had a quiet way of setting her mamma down, which was as uncomfortable as it was irresistible.

Mrs. Dove, however, was not without her share of matronly cunning. She had been young herself, and had not forgotten it; nay, she felt quite young again sometimes, even now. It does not follow that because a lady increases in bulk she should decrease in susceptibility. Look at a German baroness—fifteen stone good, in her ball dress, and *æsthetic* to the tips of her plump fingers. Mamma got up to fetch her scissors; cut the little boy's shirt to the true *Corazza* pattern, and, holding up that ridiculous little garment as if to dry, went on with her argument.

"I don't think much of that Mr. Sawbridge after all, if you ask *me*," said she, looking over the collar full in her daughter's face. "He seems very shy, by no means good-looking, and I should say has not seen much of the world! Steadier perhaps than Brush, and not so stout as Struggles, but yet he don't give me the idea of a very gentlemanlike person—like Mr. Crasher, for instance."

The Honourable was one of the good lady's great favourites. She admired hugely, as country dames will, his languor, his *insouciance*, his recklessness and dandyism—above all, his tendency to become torpid at a moment's notice, which latter faculty frequently provoked the strong-minded "Cissy" beyond endurance.

The girl's colour, always high, rose perceptibly. Like a true woman, she stood up for her new friend.

"Indeed, Mamma," said she, "Mr. Sawyer is quite as gentleman-like as anybody we meet anywhere, and as for being shy, I confess I like people all the better for not being forward, like that rude Mr. Savage, who told me I should look hideous with my hair *à l'Impératrice*. Now, Mr. Sawyer at least *tries* to make himself agreeable."

"And seems to succeed, Cissy," rejoined Mamma, with an arch smile that deepened the young lady's colour still more, and consequently heightened her resemblance to her buxom parent. "Well, dear, I must remind Papa about asking some of them to dinner. Shall I tell him to send Mr. Sawbridge an invitation?"

"Really, I don't the least care," answered Miss Dove, with a toss of her shining black head. "I suppose you can't well leave him out. But, Mamma, I wish you would call the man by his right name. It isn't Sawbridge, but Sawyer."

"I'll try and remember, Cissy," answered her mother with another of those provoking smiles, which might have been too much for the young lady's equanimity, had not the entrance of the Reverend, bringing with him a strong perfume of tobacco, stables, and James's horse-blister, put an end to the *tête-à-tête*, and diverted Mrs. Dove's attack to her natural prey.

The Reverend was not in the best of humours. He had been feeling a horse's legs—the swelling of which no stimulant, however strong, seemed to be able to reduce. It *was* aggravating to make his hands smell like a chemist's shop, and at the same time to be aware that his favourite's legs were getting rounder and rounder under the application. It was *not* consolatory to be told by the groom that "the old 'oss was about wore out." Nor was it reassuring to reflect that he wanted for half-a-dozen other purposes the couple of hundred it would take to replace him. These, however, are the annoyances to which hunting men are subject; the metaphorical thorns that bristle round our rose, and make her all the dearer and the sweeter for their sharpness. As he returned to the house *viâ* the pigsties, he could scarcely raise sufficient interest to examine the lately-arrived litter of nine. Spotted black and white, they reminded him of foxhound puppies; and to the Reverend, short of horses as he was, the association was but suggestive of annoyance.

When he entered the little drawing-room, Mrs. Dove knew by his face that the moment was an unpropitious one at which to hazard a request for anything she wanted to obtain; but having managed him for a quarter of a century, it would have been odd if she had not known exactly how to get her own way with him now.

"My dear," she said, "I've a letter from that man at Brighton about the house we had last year. He wants to know if we would like to engage it for a couple of months in the spring. It would be a good opportunity to give Cissy a little sea-bathing, you know."

Now, the Reverend had the same horror of that, as of other watering-places, which is usually entertained by middle-aged gentlemen of settled habits, who do not choose to accept second-rate dissipation and salt-water as equivalents for the comforts of a home. He had indeed, during the previous summer, been seduced into spending two months at Brighton, under the erroneous impression that on those Sussex Downs the harriers hunted all the year round; but, having found out his mistake, had inwardly registered a vow never to be "let in" for such a benefit again. It was no wonder that he rose freely at the suggestion.

"Gracious Heavens! Mrs. Dove!" exclaimed the Reverend, plumping down into an arm-chair, and raising both hands in irritable deprecation, "knowing what you do, how can you ask such a question? Of course, if this house is too uncomfortable to live in, and it don't matter about the parish going to the d— to the dogs, and the Bishop is to be a nonentity, and *my* duties a farce, you are perfectly right to go gadding about from here to Brighton, and from Brighton to London, and from London to Halifax, if you like, and I shall be happy to indulge you. I only wish you would tell me where the money is to come from—where the money is to come from, Mrs. Dove—that's all!" And, having thus spoken, the Reverend took up the *Leicester Journal*, and looked over the top of it at his wife, as if he had indeed propounded *a poser*.

This was exactly what that dear artful woman wanted. She knew that when he had blown off his steam, her husband would settle down into his usual easy temper, and become perfectly malleable in about five minutes. So she folded the poor parishioner's little shirt with the nicest accuracy, and replied in the most perfect good-humour:—

"Well, dear, I'm sure I don't want to move from here till we go to London. You know I'm so fond of my garden in the spring, and I like you to get your hunting as long as you can: it does you so much good. My idea is, London about the time of the Derby; then Ascot for a week; and home again by the beginning of July. After all, we are wonderfully well situated here for the country as regards society, and Harborough never was so full as it seems this season. What should we do in this part of the world if it wasn't for hunting?"

Precious, in proportion to their rarity, opinions so orthodox sank like music in the Reverend's ear. Five-and-twenty years' experience had failed to teach him, that such congenial sentiments must necessarily be followed by a request, as a soft southerly wind is succeeded by rain. And this is the strangest feature in our subservience to the other sex. Though they deceive us ninety-nine times, we believe them the hundredth, and, more foolish than the feathered biped, though its meshes be spread in our very sight, rush open-eyed, neck-and-heels into the net of the fowler.

The Reverend glanced at the wife of his bosom, and thought her wonderfully like that picture done a score of years ago. He said as much: but the compliment by no means diverted Mrs. Dove from the object she had in view. "Cissy and I were just talking," said she simply, "of your friend Mr. Crasher, and the rest of them. By the bye, you really ought to ask some of them to dinner. There's a barrel of oysters come by rail last night, and our turkeys this year are finer than usual. Better say Tuesday, don't you think, Papa?" added she coaxingly.

But the Reverend was not so hospitably inclined as he would have been had the old horse been sound. "They can have plenty of oysters at Harborough," said he. "They won't care to drive all that way in the dark. Bad roads, wet nights, perhaps, and nobody to meet them. Better put it off, I think, Dottie, till the days get a little longer."

You or I would hardly have thought of calling so ample a lady as Mrs. Dove, whose baptismal name indeed was Dorothy, by the above diminutive. Nevertheless, when in his best humour, it was the Reverend's habit to address her by the old pet name, and she returned to the charge accordingly.

"Better do it at once, dear," she replied. "The end of the season comes upon us before we know where we are. And if frost should arrive, or anything, they are all off to London by the express train. As for not liking to come, they'll *jump* at it! Mr. Crasher says yours is the best claret within three counties, and I'm sure you all sit long enough at it to appreciate its merits. How you *will* talk about hunting: won't they, Cissy? Well, we can't wonder at it—gentlemen are so enthusiastic. Why, if I was a man, with such wine as *that*, I'd sell 'em every horse in my stable before coffee came in."

The Reverend burst out laughing. The last argument was irresistible. " Have it your own way, Dottie," said he: " I must be off to write my sermon." And he betook himself to his study accordingly, leaving his wife and daughter to issue the invitations.

Of these it is unnecessary for us to trace the delivery of more than one. Mr. Sawyer, eating devilled kidneys the following morning for breakfast, felt his heart leap into his mouth at the reception of a primrose-coloured, highly-scented billet, in a long narrow envelope, bearing on the reverse what is called a " monogram "—a thing not unlike the puzzle-wit lock on a gate—consisting of the letter D and others twisted into every variety of shape. Though his experience in ladies' letters was limited, being indeed confined to one from Miss Mexico at the conclusion of their intercourse, in which she " wished to have no further communication with him, but hoped always to remain *friends*," something told him that the delicate, neatly-written superscription must have been indited by a fair hand. For an instant, the delightful suggestion flashed across him, that Miss Dove, forgetting maidenly reserve in the ardour of her affection, had plunged into a correspondence with himself, and he turned hot and cold by turns. Opening the missive with a trembling hand, it proved to be, if not from the young lady, at least from her mamma, and as it lay open all that day on his table, it is no breach of confidence on my part to publish its contents for the reader's benefit. Thus it ran:—

"Dear Mr. Sawyer,

"Can you give us the pleasure of your company at dinner on Tuesday next, at half past seven o'clock? Mr. Dove desires me to say that as you will probably drive, you had better not attempt the short way, but come by the high-road. My daughter unites with me in hoping that your poor horse has recovered the hard day in which he carried you so well, and I remain,

"Dear Mr. Sawyer,
"Yours sincerely,
"Dorothy Dove.

"Dove-cote Rectory, Friday."

There is nothing ambiguous in the above. It seems a simple invitation to dinner enough; you or I can gather its drift at a glance. Why the man should have read it over at least half-a-dozen times is more than I can divine.

CHAPTER XIX.

"THE BOOT ON THE OTHER LEG."

Meanwhile in the stable of the Honourable Crasher is considerable consternation and bewilderment. The helpers look wise, and wink at each other, as they pass from stall to stall, in the execution of their duties. Mr. Tiptop is completely at his wits' end. Can he, the knowing Tiptop, looked up to as the great unerring authority on training, pace, weight for age, and other racing mysteries—Newmarket all over—can he have made a mistake? He begins to think, not only that he *can*, but that he *has*.

First of all they gave the hapless Marathon a spin with Chance, as a mere breather, and I have already said with what result.

Mr. Tiptop being determined to get at "the rights of it," then tried the horses a mile at even weights; the consequences admitted of less doubt than ever. Marathon's "form" was so obviously bad, that the groom concluded he must be amiss.

"Why, he can't go no faster than our mare can trot," soliloquized Mr. Tiptop, as he contemplated the bay grinding away at his afternoon's feed (to do Marathon justice, he was always good at this part of his day's work), and thought that the animal did by no means show to advantage amongst his stable companions. "Can he be one of those extraordinary horses as I've hear'd of, wot can scarcely wag without they're trained a'most to fiddle-strings, but as nothing mortal can touch if once you gets them fit?" He almost persuaded himself that the new purchase must indeed be such a phenomenon, and resolved on putting him through a severe course of physic, and into strong training forthwith. Before, however, resorting to such ulterior measures, he had the wisdom to think of applying to old Isaac for a solution of the mystery.

He found the senior busy in his little saddle-room, engaged in no less important an occupation than the improvement of The Boy's morals and general deportment, for which I grieve to observe, since his arrival at Harborough, there was sufficient room. The youth, though he worked hard, was seldom sober now, and never told the truth but by accident. Isaac's method of imparting ethical instruction was uncompromising, if not agreeable. With the lad's collar in one hand, and a spare stirrup-leather in the other, he insisted forcibly on those maxims which he considered most salutary to the tender mind, accompanying each with a stinging illustration from the strap; the dialogue between the sage and his disciple being conducted much in this wise:—

Isaac: "I've told you over and over again, ye young warmint, and I'll tell it ye every day I live, if I larrup the skin off ye." (Whack.)

The Boy: "Oh, please!"

Isaac: "You'll never rise in life, nor be fit to be called a stableman, without you can work them qualities which have made *me* what I am; that's what I am a teaching of ye." (Whack.)

The Boy: "Oh, please!"

Isaac: "First and foremost, sobriety."—(Whack, and "Oh, please!") "Secondly, honesty, coupled with early rising."—(Whack again, and a howling "Oh, please!" from the pupil.) "Thirdly and lastly, sobriety."—(Whack.) "I'll go over 'em again; them's the three cardinal virtues. You mind what I'm a tellin' ye—Sobriety, honesty, coupled with early rising, and sobriety." (Whack, whack, whack; and "Oh, please! oh, please! oh, please!")

At this juncture, Mr. Tiptop entered. Casting an approving glance at the mode of treatment adopted, he seated himself on an inverted stable-bucket, and professed his readiness to await old Isaac's leisure ere he asked to have "a word with him." The other let go of The Boy's collar—who darted from the place like a weasel—and put on his own coat and hat. Thus armed, he waited to hear what his guest had to say. Mr. Tiptop broached the subject at once.

"Rum go, this here!" said he, hoisting his hat on to his eyebrows. "Uncommon queer start it is, about your bay horse. Can't get him out, I can't, do what I will with him; the beggar seems well, too, and pretty fit, as far as I see, and I've trained a few of them! If I didn't *know* he was a smartish nag now, I should say he was as slow as an eight-day clock when it runs down. What am I to think of it?"

Isaac's little blue eyes twinkled for an instant, but turned to stone once more, as he replied slowly, "Think of it? Well, it seems to *me*, now, that he won't be much use to your governor if he can't win."

"Not he!" answered Mr. Tiptop, contemptuously. "I could have told *you* that. What I want to know is, why the beggar was so much better in your stable than in ours? Come, old chap! you and me has always been good friends, give us an *item* now; what would you do with him, if you was me?"

Isaac's face altered not a muscle, nor did the eyes twinkle now, while he replied gravely, "If I was in your shoes, Mr. Tiptop, *this* is what I'd do—I'd put him into this here race surclie, and *lay agin him for the very shirt on my back!*"

And like the Pythian of old, Isaac having thus delivered himself, could by no means be brought back to the subject. If Mr. Tiptop had looked puzzled when he entered the veteran's saddle-room, the expression of his countenance, as he emerged from it, was that of a man whom mystery has so completely enfolded in her web, that he has no energy left to make an effort for escape. That he was so utterly bamboozled as to have recourse to his own master, thus risking his authority over the Honourable for ever after, may be gathered from the conversation held between the latter and Mr. Sawyer over their last cigar, before separating for the night, about two P.M. The Honourable, with an air of cordial approval, as that of a man who is paying another a well-merited compliment, drawls out—.

"That's an awful brute you sold me, Sawyer,—that bay of yours. You were quite right to part with him. My fellow tells me he can't go a yard: wants me to ride him myself; told him I'd rather not, if I can *walk* as fast. Do you think there's anything wrong with him, or used he *always* to gallop as if his legs were tied?"

This is not a very easy question for the former owner to answer, asked, as it is, in the Honourable's off-hand careless manner. Mr. Sawyer thinks of trying the "virtuous indignation" tack; reflects that under the circumstances it would only make him ridiculous, and that thoroughly to carry it out, he ought to be prepared to take back the horse, a measure that in his wildest moments he has never contemplated, and finally subsides into a good-humoured smile, and affirms—

"We thought him a fair horse enough in the Old Country. Perhaps he don't shine so bright amongst your clippers. He's a sound, good-constitutioned beast, too, and *never* off his feed; that I can answer for, and you've seen him jump. I am sorry you don't like him; but if you wanted a racehorse, you know, that sort of thing is quite out of my line."

The Honourable, who is good-nature itself, laughs heartily. "I don't hate him as much as Tiptop does; and if worst comes to worst, he's good-looking enough for harness. By the bye, old fellow, do you dine over at Dove-cote to-morrow?"

"Well, I've been *asked*," replied our friend, as if he

hadn't set his heart upon going, and been thinking of it ever since. "Why?" he adds, smothering a blush, as he thinks his companion may have found out his secret, and is laughing in his sleeve.

"Only that we're all going," rejoins the Honourable: "I'm glad to hear you are not to be left in the lurch. It's a fearful road, and an infernal long way; but Dove gives you such '41 as is not to be got anywhere else, and a skinful of it, my boy, not forgetting to drink his own share. I like the mother Dove, too, and pretty Miss 'Cissy' is always good fun!"

Sawyer felt the blood tingling in his ears. Amongst the many annoyances that gird as with briars the man who is sufficiently ill-advised to take an interest in any one but himself, not the least is that ridiculous sensitiveness to remarks, hazarded by the most careless of bystanders on the "object" or its belongings. If it is praised, we are jealous; if censured, we are angry; and if not mentioned at all, we are disappointed. That Mr. Sawyer, who had no more "vested interest" in her than the Lord Chancellor, should feel annoyed at Miss Cissy being spoken of as "good fun," by so amiable a critic as the Honourable Crasher, only shows the absurd organization of the human mind, and how careful we should be never to put off that armour of selfishness and self-conceit, with which nature has provided us for our self-defence.

Mr. Sawyer made a move towards his bed-candle.

"Good-night, old fellow," said the Honourable. "By Jove! we'll go together to-morrow to the Dove-cote. I'll drive you there in my phaeton; and, by Jove! we'll put that bay horse of yours in, and see how he goes with a trap behind him—so we will."

The Honourable appeared so delighted with his own suggestion, that it was impossible to controvert it; but as Mr. Sawyer wound up his watch and deposited it on his dressing-table, it certainly occurred to him that there was such a thing as retribution even at Market Harborough.

CHAPTER XX.

DEEPER AND DEEPER.

To walk a horse twice round a grass-field, in a set of light harness, allowing him afterwards to stand for half an hour in the stable without taking it off, can scarcely be called a thorough breaking-in of the animal to the duties of a coach-horse. Such, nevertheless, was all the tuition vouchsafed by the Honourable Crasher to Marathon's inexperience, ere the bay found himself placed alongside of another, in that gentleman's phaeton, for the purpose of taking his former and present owner out to dinner.

His companion—no other than the redoubtable chestnut which Crasher had been riding to covert on his first introduction to our friend—would have been rated as an experienced break-horse by few persons less reckless than his master. He was what is called "a bad starter," but made up for that deficiency by being as difficult to stop, when once off, as he was at first to set in motion. He had a way, too, of hugging the pole when out of humour, most subversive of his companion's equanimity. Such tricks were, doubtless, against the progress of Marathon's education. Altogether a more unpleasant pair, for locomotive purposes, have seldom been "lapped in leather."

There is no proverb more true than that " Where there is no fear, there is no danger." The Honourable Crasher's nerves seemed not only totally unsusceptible to the unworthy sensation

"Which schoolboys denominate 'funk,'"

but he appeared utterly to ignore the possibility of anything like a casualty wherever horseflesh was concerned. The consequence was that, both in the saddle and on the coach-box, he came scatheless out of scrapes that must have been fatal to a man of a more nervous temperament.

I will not dwell on the drive from Market Harborough to the Dove-cote—on the tension of Mr. Sawyer's nerves, and corresponding rigidity of his muscles, whenever the wheel grazed a heap of stones or an ominous bang against the splash-board reminded him that Marathon had not forgotten how to kick. The Boy, indeed—selected for the office as being of light weight—spent most of the journey on the hind-step, prepared for the worst, but was not obliged to get down and run to their heads more than a dozen times in the course of as many minutes, after which they settled to their work and pulled like griffins. It is sufficient to say that, when they arrived at the Rectory door, close on the tracks of the ignominious fly that had preceded them at least half an hour, Mr. Sawyer's white tie was unrumpled, and the Honourable's whiskers still in tolerable curl.

There was but one stranger present. The Reverend knew how to give a dinner, or if *he* didn't his wife did, and had too much consideration for his Harborough friends to inundate them with a host of country neighbours with whom they were not acquainted. This exception was a widowed cousin of Mrs. Dove's—a voluble lady, not so young as she had been, wearing her shoulders very bare, her dress very full, and her fair hair puffed out with considerable ingenuity. She was a little rouged, a little made-up, but very good-looking notwithstanding, in a *blonde*, full-blown, boisterous style. A better foil for "Cissy" could scarcely be imagined. This buxom beauty answered to the name of Merrywether, and, to all appearance, would have had no objection to change it.

I pass over the drawing-room ceremonials, generally somewhat dreary before dinner, and only enlivened, in the present instance, by the personal daring of Major Brush, whose idiosyncrasy compelled him at once to constitute himself Mrs. Merrywether's devoted admirer, and will ask my reader to imagine the company fairly settled at table (circular, with a quantity of light, and flowers), the soup sipped, the first glass of sherry swallowed, turbot and lobster sauce travelling leisurely round—in short, to use a hunting metaphor, which most of the guests would understand, their fox found and run into, and broken up with much *gusto* and satisfaction. "Whoop! Worry! worry! worry! Tear him and eat him!"

Mr. Sawyer has got a good start and a good place. He did not succeed in taking the daughter of the house in to dinner; for Struggles's stout figure was in the way, and he could not get by till that jolly personage had unwittingly offered his arm. He secured the chair however on the other side, and thought he spied the least shade of disappointment, succeeded by one of the brightest looks, as he did so. He was consoled accordingly, and, after the sherry, not so shy as usual.

Crasher, of course, in virtue of his rank, took in their hostess, who was supported on her other hand by Savage.

Mrs. Merrywether sat between the Reverend and Brush. Everybody talked at once; and the champagne was beyond praise.

Miss Dove was very agreeable, sharing her attentions with great impartiality between Struggles and the agitated Sawyer; only, when she addressed the latter, she used a somewhat lower tone than to any one else. The dodge has a prodigious effect on a man who is not up to it; and our friend was honest and inexperienced enough, where women were concerned. He felt in the seventh heaven, and more inclined for drinking than eating; always a bad sign. What is left to fall back upon, when the stomach is affected by the maladies of the heart?

Not so Struggles. When she had seen the latter wholly engrossed in the merits of a "*vol-au-vent*," Miss Dove turned her pretty face and dangerous attention to her other cavalier.

"You've never asked me how I got home that dark night," said she. "A long drive in the wet is no joke, after such a hard day. I dare say you've forgotten all about it, Mr. Sawyer." And the eyelashes went down till they swept the delicate peach-like cheek.

Our friend *looked* unutterable things. He could think of nothing more appropriate to *say*, however, than that "He —he hoped she hadn't caught cold."

Cissy laughed outright as she replied, "You wrapped me up too well for any fear of that. Do I *look* as if I had?" she added, lifting the eyelashes, and fixing our friend with one of her killing looks, as you run a great cockchafer right through the body with a pin.

You see, Mr. Sawyer wanted a good deal of bringing on; and the little witch encouraged him accordingly.

"You look remarkably well," said he, mustering courage, and proceeding desperately, as, when once a shy man begins, he is always the boldest. "I never saw anything so becoming as that dress. The effect is perfectly lovely."

"Hush!" replied Cissy: "you mustn't say *that*. *There's* our beauty. If you talk of loveliness, I am sure you must be perfectly smitten with *that*," nodding towards Mrs. Merrywether as she spoke, and drawing his attention to the charms of that lady, who was *fair*, whereas Cissy herself was more of a brunette, and thus smoothing the way for another compliment.

"I don't admire such light hair," replied the gentleman, whose own *chevelure* was of the sandiest; "and she wants expression; and her eyes are too far apart; and people's skins should be even whiter than hers to admit of such *very* low dresses."

Why are ladies always pleased when *other* ladies' dresses are thought too low? Cissy was not above the prejudices of her sex. She gave him a bewitching smile, and called him "a ridiculous creature."

Even Mr. Sawyer could not misinterpret such signs of favour. Whatever Miss Mexico may have *thought*, she had never called him "a ridiculous creature" in her life.

"What I admire," he proceeded, stealing a look at Miss Cissy, as he enumerated her personal advantages, "is more colouring, darker hair, and arched eyebrows, and deeper eyes, long eyelashes, and altogether a fresher and brighter style of beauty; in short, I don't think she would look at all well in a white dress with cherry-coloured trimmings."

It was the very dress she wore herself. There was no mistake, thought the fair angler: she had *hooked* him. So she gave him another of the captivating glances, and changed the conversation by drawing his attention to her fan, of which the fragrant sandal-wood only added fuel to his flame, while she turned to Struggles, who, having made an excellent dinner, was vainly endeavouring to talk to her about the coming ball.

Meanwhile, Mrs. Merrywether, whose most prejudiced detractor could not have accused her, at this juncture, of wanting *expression*, was forcing the running with the agreeable Brush. She was shaking her head, and making eyes, and showing her teeth, and flourishing her shoulders at him, with a degree of energy that must have been fatal to a less experienced campaigner. The Major, however, was proof against all the usual weapons of the female armoury. A confirmed flirt, it was his habit just to stop short of love-making with every woman he sat next to; but, if truth must be told, he never yet had seen one whose attractions he could place in comparison with his cutlet, his champagne, his claret, and his after-dinner cigar. A good-humoured, brainless, easy-going *bon-vivant*, it was the Major's eventual destiny to marry a learned lady, with blue spectacles, under whose dynasty he faded away, and was lost to the world altogether. But with this, at present, we have nothing to do.

Mrs. Merrywether was quite willing to take him as he was. Before the cheese was off the table, he had settled an expedition to the Crystal Palace with her, the first time they were both in London, and secured a flower from her bouquet, which he placed, with much mock-devotion, in a glass of sherry-and-water. Also, on the departure of the ladies, he dived for, and brought to the surface, the following articles, the property of the efflorescent widow : One French fan—epoch, Louis-Quatorze; one pair of white gloves, bound with ribbon, and numbered six and three-quarters; one gold vinaigrette, with tiny chain complete; and one lace-edged handkerchief, with a square inch of cambric in the middle—it is presumed, in case of necessity, to dry the fair mourner's tears.

After this crowning feat, he threw himself back in his chair, and settled to his host's claret, like a man who is thoroughly well satisfied with himself.

Never was a dinner that went off better. Mrs. Dove had Savage to listen to, who was well-informed, and Crasher to look at, who was well dressed. Struggles and Dove were congenial souls, and, if once they could get together uninterrupted, would talk about hunting by the hour. Mrs. Merrywether was pleased with her dinner; pleased with her neighbour; also—for she knew, even before she went to the glass in the drawing-room, that she was looking her best—pleased with herself. Cissy was satisfied; Sawyer enchanted; and Crasher, looking forward with lazy gratification to a dangerous drive in the dark, was in higher spirits than usual.

We will leave the ladies to their tea and coffee, undisturbed. The gentlemen close up round their host. A dry biscuit and a magnum of the undeniable make their appearance. The parson fills out a bumper of the rosy fluid, and proposes his first and only toast—"Fox-hunting!"

Each man drinks it with thirsty satisfaction.

CHAPTER XXI.

THE MAGNUM BONUM.

WHEN the Reverend's butler came in the first time with a fresh supply of claret, he found the assembled guests making themselves happy each in his own way. His master and Struggles were crossing the Skeffington Lordship with great enthusiasm, in an imaginary run with Mr. Tailby's hounds. Brush was expatiating on the merits of the vintage to the Honourable Crasher, who, saying but little in reply, was smiling faintly, and denoting his approval by the regularity with which he charged and emptied his glass. Savage, who dabbled in science, was explaining to Sawyer with considerable perspicuity, a new discovery termed phonography, by which sounds or vibrations of air are to be taken down as they arise, upon the principle of the photograph, and which, when thoroughly perfected and carried out, will make it no longer an impertinence to request a bystander "not to look at you in that tone of voice," and flattered himself that so good a listener must be imbibing stores of valuable information from his remarks; Mr. Sawyer, however, was lost in delicious dreams, tinged, as the decanter waned, with rosier and rosier hues. He was, for the moment, unconscious of Savage, of Brush, of Crasher, and only recognized the Reverend as the purveyor of the best claret he had ever drunk, and the father of such an angel as all England could not match.

The second time the white-waistcoated functionary arrived with "another of the same," things wore a far different aspect. Everybody was talking at once on the same subject. Like a bag-fox before an unruly pack of hounds, the topic of steeple-chasing had been started for the general confusion, and each ran his own line and threw his tongue for his own especial encouragement; there seemed no doubt about the long-talked-of race coming off. Preliminaries were adjusted, weights discussed, and a country suggested. Even Struggles seemed to have got over his aversion to the mongrel sport. But on the stout Ganymede's third and last appearance with "the landlord's bottle," the storm was at its loudest, Mr. Sawyer laying down the law with the best. Betting-books were out: even the Reverend had produced what he called "some memorandums;" and the only intelligible sounds, amidst the clamour, were the ominous words "five-to-two"—current odds which everybody seemed to lay, and nobody to take. The discreet servant then whispered to his master that a second edition of coffee was ready to go into the drawing-room, and ere long a glass of brown sherry all round screwed our friend's courage up to face the ladies once more.

Each man accordingly composed his features into a vacant simper, pulled his neckcloth up, and his wristbands down, and straddled into the presence of those indulgent beings, with an abortive attempt to look as if he, individually, had been drinking little or no wine.

Cissy was at the pianoforte. If Mr. Sawyer had thought her charming before, what must have been his opinion of that sparkling young lady now, seen through the medium of a fair share of champagne at dinner, and the best part of two bottles of claret afterwards? Lights, dress, and a general atmosphere of luxury and refinement, have a wonderful effect in enhancing the attractions of the fair. Alas, that we should have lived to admit it! Though the poet may opine that "beauty unadorned is adorned the most," our hackneyed taste cannot but confess that it prefers the French maid's *coiffure* to the dishevelled tresses; the trim silk stocking, and neat satin shoe, to the slippers down at heel; and the shapely *corsage*, with its abundant *crinoline*, to the limp and unassuming dressing-gown. Mr. Sawyer was quite satisfied with Cissy as she was.

The musician was playing "The Swallows," or "The Humming Bird," or "The Spring Geese;" Sawyer had no ear for music, and neither knew nor cared which. She just glanced at him as he entered the room, but the encouragement was sufficient to lead him to the instrument.

"How *long* you have been!" said Miss Cissy in a low voice, without looking up, rattling away at the keys in the loudest of *finales*, with a vehemence that drowned her observations to all ears but her admirer's. Then she closed the instrument, whispered papa to order the whist-table, and went and sat on the sofa by Mrs. Merrywether in such a position that Mr. Sawyer couldn't possibly get at her.

They do not read Izaak Walton, these young women, and yet how well they know how to play their fish! Is it constant reflection and mutual discussion, I wonder, that makes the least experienced of them such skilful anglers? or is it not rather an intuitive sagacity, akin to that with which the kitten teases her ball of cotton as dexterously as the cat does a full-grown mouse? They suck it in, the science of man-taming, I am inclined to believe, with their mothers' milk. Mamma was just the same, doubtless; and grandmamma too, whom she can just remember, with a cough and crutches, and so on, up to Eve.

With the good-humoured Struggles for a partner, and so

much of his brains as the claret had left untouched, filled with the image of a dark-eyed young person in white muslin, it was Mr. Sawyer's lot to do battle at the noble game of whist, against two no less formidable antagonists than Savage and Parson Dove, both first-rate performers even after dinner.

To be successful at this pastime, a man's whole intellects should be engrossed by the cards, and this was by no means the case with our friend. In spite of his partner's good-humoured entreaties to "pay attention," he could not prevent his thoughts, and sometimes his eyes, from wandering to the sofa near the fire-place. He had never liked Brush quite as well as the rest of his companions, but on the present occasion he could not refrain from wishing him even in a hotter place than that which he had selected. The Major with devoted gallantry, having placed his back to a fire that would have roasted an ox, was holding forth in his most agreeable manner to Mrs. Merrywether and the laughing Cissy. Crasher, in the easiest of arm-chairs, was helping Mrs. Dove to make paper lights, and revolving in his own mind, while he listened amiably to the continuous discourse of his hostess, whether he wouldn't pole up Marathon a little shorter going home, and try the more direct road against which the Reverend was in the habit of warning his guests. They would save a mile, in distance, he thought, and there was sure to be more light on their return. The Honourable had a sort of vague idea, that there was always a moon about one or two o'clock.

Suddenly an explosion of laughter from the widow, under cover of which the unconscious Sawyer revoked, and was immediately found out, startled the whole assembly. "How absurd you are!" exclaimed that noisy dame, in answer to some proposition of the Major's which appeared highly amusing to the ladies on the sofa. "Now I appeal to 'Cissy' whether she agrees with you. Girls are the best judges. Cissy! *do* you think the Major as invincible as he says he is?"

Mr. Sawyer, on thorns to hear the answer, trumped his partner's best with considerable emphasis, and lost *another* trick.

"It's not fair to ask *me*," answered Miss Dove, laughing heartily. "He knows I admire him *immensely;* I've always told him so!" and the three went on with their conversation, which, I am bound to say, was great nonsense, but but amused them considerably all the same.

After this, Struggles thought the sooner they left off whist the better. There is scarcely a mistake, of which that intricate game admits, into which Mr. Sawyer did not rush, so to speak, as if with a suicidal purpose. "Hang the fellow!" thought Struggles, eyeing his partner with a kind of good-humoured astonishment : "if he was drunk, one could understand it; never saw such a thing! never saw such cards so thrown away! and yet the man's no fool. Oh! he *must* be drunk! *must* be! but carries his liquor with discretion!" and thereupon Struggles found himself looking upon his partner's features with a more indulgent eye, and contemplating his own losses with the resignation of a man who suffers in a good cause.

Three rubbers! one of them a bumper! How many points, for the sake of my hero, I am ashamed to confess. It was indeed, as Struggles pathetically remarked, "about the worst night he'd ever had, since he left Westminster."

Yet there was balm in Gilead, after all. The Honourable, resisting all entreaties to stay and have some supper, rang to order his phaeton round, and went fast asleep in his armchair after the exertion. Their host, exhilarated by his winnings, and in high good-humour, began about the steeplechase; and the ladies, who, I am convinced, patronize these exhibitions chiefly on account of the silk jackets, and connect them remotely in their own minds with a fancy dress ball, began to betray great curiosity on the subject of the "colours of the riders," "*gorge de pigeon*," the Major's selected hue, having decidedly the call. During the discussion which so favourite a topic was sure to engender, it came out, somehow, that Mr. Sawyer was going to take part in the hazardous amusement—an announcement which he made darkly, and with a sidelong glance at Cissy, that seemed to say he would rather break his neck than not. The young lady having teased him enough, was quite ready to meet him halfway. "Isn't it very dangerous?" said she, with clasped hands and a look of affectionate interest. "Are you *really* going to ride, Mr. Sawyer? Oh! how I *hope* you'll win!" And down went the eyelashes once more.

After that, what cared Mr. Sawyer for rubbers, bumpers, points, and losses? Everything was *couleur de rose* again. Whilst the others gathered round the wine-and-water tray, he sank down on the sofa by her side, and for a delicious five minutes had his enslaver all to himself. In that brief period, he managed to find out her favourite colour, and promised to adopt it in the coming steeple-chase. A few stars were twinkling dimly through the cloudy atmosphere when he lit his cigar and got into the phaeton by the Honourable's side. Why couldn't Mr. Sawyer look at them without thinking of Cissy Dove?

CHAPTER XXII.

A WET NIGHT.

"Sit tight, exclaimed the Honourable, as the phaeton bumped forcibly against the stone post of the Rectory entrance, and proceeded into the road with what sailors call "a considerable slue to port," consequent on that brute Marathon hugging the pole and setting his mouth with pigheaded obstinacy. "I *must* pitch into you!" added the driver, suiting the action to the word, and administering heavy punishment to the transgressing animal—a discipline which Marathon resented by kicking hard against the splashboard; whilst the chestnut, a sensitive, high-couraged five-year-old, was driven almost mad by the sounds of repeated flagellation. "Are you nervous on wheels?" added the charioteer quietly, as he felt his companion's leg stiffen against his own with the instinctive rigidity of apprehension. "Nervous!" forsooth! Ask Launcelot fresh from the presence of Guenevere, or Charles Brandon tilting before the young Dauphiness of France, or Bothwell with his armour buckled on by Mary Stuart, if those doughty champions were afraid; but forbear to put so ridiculous a question at a moment like the present to John Standish Sawyer. "*Nervous*, indeed!" Our friend pressed his hat firmly on his head, folded his arms across his chest, and laughed grimly in his questioner's face. "All right, old fellow!" said he; "drive on, if you like, to the devil!"

"He's a rare plucked one," thought the Honourable to himself, as he started the horses in a gallop, apparently with no other view than that of arriving at the destination proposed. The night was dark, and threatening rain as it clouded over rapidly; the way intricate, full of turns and difficulties; and The Boy, it is needless to observe, helplessly drunk in the rumble. He would have been a venturous speculator who had taken five to one that they arrived safe at Market Harborough.

The wheels flew round with frightful velocity, scattering the mud profusely over the occupants of the carriage. The horses with lowered heads laid themselves down to their work, pulling wildly. The Honourable's arms were extended, and his feet thrust forward. He would not have admitted it, but it looked very much as if they were running away with him.

"An't they getting a little out of your hand?" asked Mr. Sawyer, hazarding the question in its mildest form, as he recognized Marathon's well-known manner of putting down his head when he meant mischief; and calculated if anything *should* give way, whereabouts his own body would shoot to, at that pace.

"Only going free," answered Crasher with the utmost composure, though his cigar was burnt all the way down one side to his lips by the current of air created in the rapidity of their transit. "Remarkably free—but I like phaeton horses to run up to their bits."

"*Do you?*" thought Mr. Sawyer; but, despite the enthusiasm and the claret, and the romance of the whole evening, he wished himself anywhere else. Independent of the ignominious ending of being dashed to pieces out of a phaeton, it *would* be hard lines never to see Cissy Dove again. However, there was nothing for it but to sit still and trust to Crasher's coachmanship. Anything like expostulation with that gentleman he felt would be worse than useless.

I recollect to have seen or heard somewhere an anecdote of the celebrated "Hell-fire Dick," which exhibits such *sang-froid* in a dangerous predicament as to be worth repeating. Dick, then, who had attained his flaming *sobriquet* by the dashing pace and general recklessness with which he drove, was not only one of the most skilful of the old-fashioned Long coachmen, but was equally noted for the cool imperturbability of his demeanour and the suavity of his replies. One very dark night, whilst proceeding at his usual pace, he was so unfortunate as to get off the road on a common where several gravel-pits yawning on each side for his reception, made the mistake as dangerous as it was disagreeable. With a tremendous lurch the coach swung over one of these ready-made graves, and there was just light enough to perceive the fifteen feet or so of sheer descent yawning for its victims. "Where have you got to now, Dick?" exclaimed the box-passenger, in accents of pardonable irritation and alarm. "Can't say, sir," replied Dick, with the utmost politeness, while they were all turning over together—"Can't say, I'm sure—*never was here before!*"

Now, if the Honourable Crasher had been going to be shot the next minute, it is my firm conviction that impending destruction would not have ruffled his plumes, nor agitated the languor of his accustomed manner in the slightest degree. Whether such a temperament is entirely natural, or is not rather to a certain extent the result of education, enhanced by what we must call the affectation peculiar to a class, it is not our business to inquire; but we may fairly acknowledge to a respectful commiseration for a quiet respectable country gentleman who finds his neck committed to the keeping of one of these imperturbable, placid, yet utterly reckless adventurers.

The wind was getting up, and a heavy shower of mingled sleet and rain dashing in their faces, added considerably to the discomfort of the whole process.

"This can't last long," murmured Mr. Sawyer below his breath, and holding on vigorously to the side of the carriage the while, as they whirled fiercely through the obscurity, the rush of their career varied only by frequent jumps and bumps that threatened to jerk him clean out over the splash-board. He was not very far wrong in his calculations.

Their course lay along one of those field-roads so common in Leicestershire, where the track on a dark night is not easily distinguished from the adjacent ridge and furrow, and which, delightful to the equestrian for that very reason, as no jealous fence prevents him diverging for a canter on to the springy pasture, are less convenient for carriages owing to the number of gates that delay the passage of the vehicle. They were now approaching the first of these obstacles to their course, and Crasher had not yet got a pull at his horses.

"It's open, I think," remarked the Honourable, peering into the darkness ahead, and endeavouring to moderate the pace without effect.

"I think *not!*" replied Mr. Sawyer, setting his teeth for a catastrophe.

Right again! Three more strides and they were into it!

A crackling smashing noise of broken wood-work—one or two violent bangs against the splash-board—a faint expostulation of "*Gently*, my lads!" from the Honourable—a tremendous jolt against the post, which was torn up by the roots—and Mr. Sawyer found himself on his face and hands in an exceedingly wet furrow; a little stunned, a good deal confused, and feeling very much as if somebody had knocked him down, and he did not know whom to be angry with.

As he rose and shook himself to ascertain that no bones were broken, much struggling and groaning as of an animal in distress, mingled with weeping and lamentation from a human voice, smote on his ear. The former arose from Marathon, who couldn't get up, with the other horse and the pole and part of the carriage atop of him: the latter from The Boy, who, frightened for the moment into a spurious sobriety, thus gave vent to his feelings of utter despondency and desolation.

"I thought the brute *could* jump timber," said a calm voice in the surrounding darkness. "Let us see: *here's* the carriage—*there* are the horses—and *that* must be The Boy. Where are *you*, Sawyer?"

"Here!" answered our friend, coming forward, rubbing his elbows and knees, to discover if he was hurt; the Honourable, who had never abandoned his cigar, endeavouring to extricate the horses—a measure only to be accomplished by dint of cutting their harness—and to estimate the amount of damage, and the impossibility of putting in to refit.

Our friend set to work with a will. By their joint endeavours they succeeded at last in getting the hapless Marathon and his companion clear of the wreck. Both were obviously lamed and injured; the carriage, as far as could be made out in the darkness, broken all to pieces.

The Boy, after flickering up for a few minutes, had become again unconscious. As the old watchmen used to sing out, it was "Past one o'clock and a stormy morning!"

"Whereabouts are we?" asked Mr. Sawyer in dolorous accents, as he tried to persuade himself he ought to be thankful it was no worse. "Whereabouts are we, and what had we better do?"

"Over a hundred miles from London," answered the Honourable, "that's all I know about it. Holloaing, I suppose, would be no use—there can't be a house within hearing, and the fly has gone the other road. Have a cigar, old fellow! and, just to keep the fun going, perhaps you wouldn't mind singing us a song?"

It was only under a calamity like the present that the Honourable condescended to be facetious.

Mr. Sawyer was on the verge of making an angry reply, when the sound of a horse's hoofs advancing with considerable rapidity changed it into a vigorous call for assistance.

"Hilli-ho! ho!" shouted Mr. Sawyer. "Hilli-ho! ho!" answered a jolly voice, as the hoofs ceased, and came clattering on again, denoting that the rider had pulled up to listen and was coming speedily to help. "What's up now?" asked the jolly voice, in somewhat convivial accents, as an equestrian mass of drab and leggings, which was all that could be made out through the darkness, loomed indistinctly into the foreground. "What's up now, mates? got the wrong end uppermost this turn, sure-lie."

"Come to grief at the gate," explained the Honourable. "Didn't go *quite* fast enough at it, Sawyer," he added, half reflectively, half apologetically, to his friend.

"Why, it's Muster Crasher!" exclaimed the jolly voice, in delighted tones. "Well, *to be* sure! Not the *first* gate, neither, by a many—only to think of it, well, well! But come, let's see what's the damage done—dear! dear! you'll never get home to-night. You must come up to my place, 'tain't above a mile through the fields—we'll get you put up, nags and all, and send down for the trap first thing i' the morning. How lucky I was passing this way! Coming back from market, ye see, I'd just stopped to smoke a pipe

with neighbour Mark down at The Holt, and was maken'
for home in a hurry, 'cause it's rather past my time, you
know, when I hear this gentleman a hollerin' murder! Up
I comes and finds the ship overboard with a vengeance.
What a start it is, sure-lie!"

Thus moralizing, and never leaving off talking for an instant, the jolly yeoman jumped off his horse, and lent his powerful assistance to clear away the wreck; shaking The Boy into life again with considerable energy. In a few minutes the four men, leading the two damaged carriage-horses, were stumbling and groping their way across the fields towards the new arrival's farm.

Ere they reached their destination, the owner with considerable politeness introduced himself to our friend. "No offence, sir," said he, "my name's Trotter—Trotter of Trotter's Lodge, and that's my place where you see the lights a shinin'—Mr. Crasher, he knows me *well*—think I've met *you* out a huntin' more than once this season—allow me, sir, we'll have the missus up in no time, and a hearty welcome to you both."

As Mr. Trotter thus hospitably concluded, he ushered his guests into a comfortable kitchen, where a tallow candle was still glimmering in its accustomed place. The master was obviously in the habit of coming home late; but that the practice was contrary to the rules of domestic discipline Mr. Sawyer gathered from the accents of a shrill voice raised in tones of reproach from an upstairs dormitory.

"Trotter! Trotter!" exclaimed the voice, unconscious of visitors, and proceeding apparently from beneath a considerable weight of bed-clothes, "is that you at last? It's too bad! It's nigh upon two o'clock. Mind you rake out the fire, and don't go spilling the candle-grease all about as you come upstairs!"

Mr. Trotter, still perceptibly elevated, winked facetiously at his guests. "Get up, Margery!" he called out; "get up, I tell ye! make haste and come down. Never mind your night-cap. Here's two gentlemen come to see ye!" And with many apologies and repeated allusions to the substantive "keys," Mr. Trotter stirred up the fire, lit another candle, and proceeded upstairs to rouse his better-half.

In less time than you or I as a bachelor could believe it possible, a smiling dame made her appearance from above-stairs, with a neat morning cap over her comely head, and a bright rosy face, very different from the sallow hues of many a fine lady when first she wakes, blushing beneath it. That her petticoat was put on in a hurry, and her gown unfastened behind, was only what might be expected in such a rapid turn-out. These trifling drawbacks detracted not the least from the bustling hospitality with which she received her guests. It was only by the most pathetic entreaties that the Honourable dissuaded her from having a fire lighted in the best parlour, and extorted her permission for them to sit in the kitchen.

Dry slippers were soon provided for the guests. The horses, inspected by the stable lantern, were discovered not to be irremediably injured, though Marathon's chance was out for the steeple-chase, "if indeed," as his former and present owners remarked in a breath, though with different emphasis, "he ever had one." The Boy was put to bed, where he might be heard snoring all over the house. What Mr. Trotter called a "snack" was set on the table, consisting of a round of beef, a ham, some cold pork-pie, an Eddish cheese, and a few other trifles of a like nature, adapted for a late meal as being light and easy of digestion. Port and sherry were produced and declined in favour of huge steaming beakers of hot brandy-and-water. Arrangements were entered into for forwarding the two gentlemen to Harborough in the farmer's gig "first thing to-morrow morning." Mr. Trotter produced a box of cigars and announced his intention of "making a night of it!"

A faint scream from his wife promised to a certain extent to modify the conviviality of the meeting. "She couldn't abear the sight of blood," she said, with many excuses for her feminine susceptibility, and drew the company's attention to the personal appearance of Mr. Sawyer, which everybody had hitherto been too busy to observe, and which indeed presented a sufficiently ghastly aspect to excuse the good dame's reiterated assurances that it "had given her quite a turn."

A severe contusion on the eyebrow, accompanied by a cut extending to the cheek-bone, and which had covered one side of his face with dried blood, made him look much more damaged than he really was, and though kindly Mrs. Trotter quickly recovered her equanimity and brought him warm water and vinegar and balsam, and eventually plastered him up with about half a sheet of diachylon, she could not help shuddering during the operation, and seemed glad when it was over. Our farmers' wives of the present day are not quite as much accustomed to broken heads as bonny "Ailie," the helpmate of immortal Dandie Dinmont.

The borderer, however, could not have been more hospitably inclined than was the jovial Leicestershire farmer. Setting aside the difference of time and locality, they had indeed many qualities in common. The same love of hunting, the same daring in the saddle, the same open-hearted hospitality and tendency to push good-fellowship a little over the bounds of sobriety. The only difference perhaps was this, that Dandie Dinmont would have been getting up before Mr. Trotter was thinking of going to bed.

I am not going to recapitulate the sayings and doings of those jovial small-hours after Mrs. Trotter had betaken herself once more hopelessly to her couch. The Honourable Crasher, always a gentleman, though rather a torpid one, was equally at home with a duke and a drayman, perhaps more in his element with a hunting friend like Trotter than either. The good runs they recapitulated, the horses they remembered, the grey that was bought by Mr. G——, and the chestnut that had carried Lord W—— so well for years, the fences they had negotiated—nay, the very toasts they proposed and did justice to, would fill a chapter. It is sufficient to say that when Mr. Sawyer awoke in the best bedroom about sunrise the following morning, he had a racking head-ache, his mouth felt like the back of a Latin grammar, and the only distinct recollection with which he could charge his memory of the previous night's conversation was his host's recipe for making a young horse a safe fencer, which he certainly did not then feel in a condition to adopt.

"If you've got a green horse as you're not very confident on at strong timber," said Mr. Trotter, about the fourth glass of brandy-and-water, "you tackle him *my* way. You take him out o' Sundays or any afternoon as you've nothing particular to do, and pick him out some real *stiff* ones. Give him two or three *good heavy falls*, and I'll warrant you'll have very little trouble afterwards. That's the way to make 'em *rise!*—ain't it, Mr. Crasher?"

After such a night's amusement as I have described, gentlemen are apt to be later in the morning than they originally proposed.

Our belated travellers had intended getting back to their

quarters at Harborough by eight or nine o'clock, there to make their toilets, discuss their breakfasts, and so proceed to covert methodically as usual, in time to meet Mr. Tailby's clipping pack at Carlton Clump. It was nine, however, before either of them was stirring, and then the hospitable Trotter, who was himself going to hunt, and who came in from shepherding as rosy and fresh as if he had never seen brandy-and-water in his life, would not hear of their going away without breakfast. Altogether they did not get clear of Trotter's Lodge much before ten o'clock, and as they drove out of the farmyard they had the mortification of seeing their entertainer mounted on his four-year-old ("Fancy riding a four-year-old after such a night!" thought Mr. Sawyer) on his way to the meet. "And we've got to go home and dress, and then come all this way back again," moralized the Honourable. "I say, Sawyer, I wish I could make this beggar go as fast as we did last night," and Crasher smiled at the recollection, as a man smiles who recalls some peaceful scene of his youth, or some good action which he will never find cause to repent.

This beggar, however, though a good farmer's nag enough, knew quite well that it wasn't his day for Market Harborough, and displayed great unwillingness to improve upon seven miles an hour in that direction. The chance of being in time faded away momently. Already they had overtaken several grooms with hunters; worse still, one or two early men on their hacks had overtaken *them*, and they had not yet struck into the high-road. At last the sound of wheels behind them caused the old horse to quicken his pace: not sufficiently so, however, to prevent the pursuing carriage from gaining on them rapidly. Mr. Sawyer looked back. Oh for a gig umbrella! It was none other than

Parson Dove driving his daughter to the meet, that young lady's very becoming costume denoting that it was her intention to join in the pleasures of the chase. Here was a predicament! To be detected by the queen of his affections, with whom he had parted at midnight, in all the correct decorum of evening costume, still in the same dress, so inappropriate at 10.30 A.M., bearing obvious tokens of having been out all night, and worse than all, with an inflamed countenance, blood-shot eyes, and a face half-eclipsed in plaister! Perdition! It was not to be thought of!

With the energy of despair he snatched the whip from the Honourable's astonished grasp, and applied it with such good will to the old horse's ribs, that the animal broke incontinently into a gallop, and turned into the high-road some fifty yards ahead of its pursuers, who would cross that thoroughfare directly, whereas Mr. Sawyer and its driver would follow its broad track to Harborough. "Cover me up!" exclaimed our friend to his laughing companion, as he crouched in the bottom of the carriage, under the scanty gig-apron, and devoutly hoped he had escaped recognition— "cover me up! I wouldn't be seen in this plight by any of *that* family for a hundred pounds!" Nevertheless, he resolved, so to speak, to substantiate his *alibi* by swearing the Honourable to secrecy, and abstaining altogether for that day from the chase.

CHAPTER XXIII.

DOUGHTY DEEDS.

ABOUT this period there might have been—and indeed, by his intimates, there *was*—remarked an obvious change in the appearance, habits, and general demeanour of our friend. No longer dressed in the rough-and-ready style which had heretofore been at once his glory and his peculiarity, Mr. Sawyer now began to affect a strange refinement of costume, bordering on effeminacy. His boots were thinner and much tighter than of old: he turned his collars over his neckcloth, after the prevailing fashion, thereby imparting to his physiognomy an expression of romantic vacuity; anointed his head till it shone again; affected gloves on all occasions; and set up a ring. Altogether, his exterior was as symptomatic of his disorder as that of Benedict. Also he purchased, at a printseller's over the way, a representation of a young person washing her feet in a stream, and purporting to be a "Highland Lassie," but of a meretricious aspect which, it is only fair to state, is rarely to be observed amongst the Scottish mountaineers. It was one of those startling accidental likenesses to the lady of his affections, which a man must be as hard hit as Mr. Sawyer to detect. In the hunting-field, too, he adopted an ambitious style of riding, totally at variance with his previous quiet, straightforward form; and a considerable interval of bad-scenting weather enabled him to distinguish himself to his heart's content. When hounds run best pace, horses have not wind for extraordinary exertions in the matter of fencing; and, moreover, such saltatory exploits as are out of the common way can be witnessed but by few, and those are completely engrossed in their own doings; but when the pack checks in every field, a man who chooses to single himself out by charging the ugliest bullfinches and the stiffest rails, either because he wants to attract attention, or to sell his horse, has every opportunity of showing up the latter, and calling down upon himself the animadversions of all true sportsmen. Our friend, with the two horses he bought from Mr. Varnish—both capital leapers—in addition to Hotspur and the grey, had no lack of material on which to flourish away in too close proximity to the chase. Charles Payne, though with a strong fellow-feeling for "keenness," began to hate the sight of him, Mr. Tailby to dread his appearance as he would that of a black frost, and Lord Stamford to find that even *his* imperturbable good-humour might be exhausted at last.

What is to be expected, however, of a gentleman who has taken to repeating Montrose's well-known lines—

> "If doughty deeds my lady please,
> Right soon I'll mount my steed;
> And keen his lance, and strong his arm,
> That bears from me the meed;"

varied by the resolute sentiment—

> "He either fears his fate too much,
> Or his deserts are small,
> Who dares not put it to the touch
> To win or lose it all!"

One or other of these romantic stanzas was continually on Mr. Sawyer's lips. After their enunciation, he was used to sigh deeply, shake his head, and light a cigar, which he would smoke vehemently for a quarter of an hour or so, in a brown study.

Our friend's reflections, however, were not wholly dipped in the roseate hues of hope. Stern misgivings would come across him, as to the imprudence of the career on which he had embarked. He was spending a deal of money, that was the fact; and he had always, hitherto, been of a saving disposition, rather than otherwise. In the prosecution of his schemes against Miss Mexico, his outlay, indeed, had been principally in cheap jewellery and lavender-water—articles of fascination for the purchase of which he would have been handsomely reimbursed by that lady's thirty thousand pounds, *if he had got it*. But in the present case, not only was his extravagance much greater, but it is mere justice to state, that he had never weighed Miss Dove's fortune or the want of it in the balance with her attractions. The former flame had half a plum; the present might not have half-a-crown. Bah! what of that? Those eyelashes alone were worth all the money!

Nevertheless, a stud of horses, though consisting only of the modest number of four hunters and a hack, are not to be kept for nothing, more particularly when away from home. Independent of stable-rent, forage, subscriptions to hounds, and necessary *douceurs* to different individuals, any man who has ever paid a groom's book, will bear witness to the extraordinary rapidity with which its different items accumulate. *Naphtha* alone is as dear as claret, and consumed with equal liberality; sponges, rubbers, currycombs, and dandy-brushes require to be replaced with astonishing frequency; and, what with shoeing and removing, the blacksmith's bill is as long as his stalwart arm. When you add to all this an every-day dinner of the best, with champagne and claret *à discrétion*—if such a quality, indeed, can be said to exist in a bachelor party—you will not share Mr. Sawyer's surprise at discovering that his present expenditure far exceeded his calculations. The four hundred he had paid to Mr. Varnish for two horses completed a good round sum; and, for a minute or two, he thought he had better have remained at The Grange.

This last item, however, in his outlay, suggested to him a method by which he might combine fame with money-making, and, if Fortune stood his friend, have his season almost for nothing. The chestnut five-year-old, whom, out of compliment to Miss Dove, he had resolved to call " Wood-Pigeon," was really a good nag. He was a quick and fine fencer; could gallop fast, and *go on*. Altogether, Mr. Varnish was not beyond the mark, when he described him to the purchaser as adapted for " safety, punctuality, and dispatch." Why not put him into this steeple-chase they made such a fuss about, win a hatful of money in stakes, bets, etc., to say nothing of the " honour and glory," and then sell the whole stud, and retire upon his laurels? Should Fortune smile, and land him first past the post, it would be the proudest day of his life; and even in the event of failure, why, " If doughty deeds my lady please," etc.; and Miss Dove could not but look upon him with a more favourable eye, when he had worn her colours in the race.

Old Isaac must be taken into consultation. For the first time, his master rather shunned the glance of that keen, hard eye. He walked into the stable one evening, after hunting, and began to sound his servant on the important question.

" By the bye, Isaac," said he, in an off-hand tone, " they're talking of a steeple-chase here. Only amongst the gentlemen, you know: we shan't want much training. I think I should have a fair chance with Wood-Pigeon?"

Isaac shook his head. "Well, sir," said he, "*you* know best. Who's to ride?"

"Oh, I should ride him myself, of course," replied his master, with a toss of the head that as much as said, "With such a jockey, he's sure to win." "Ride him myself, and do all I *know*, you may depend," he added facetiously.

Old Isaac reflected. "Have you ever ridden a steeplechase?" he asked, after a moment's consideration.

Mr. Sawyer was obliged to admit that he never had.

"Well, then, *I have*," said the groom. "You don't know what it is. Such a blazin' pace through the fields! and such an owdacious scuffle at the fences! Nothin' but a professional can keep his head at that work; and *he* often gets it broke. Better not try it, master: better let it alone. They'll only make a fool of ye."

Mr. Sawyer waxed indignant. "That's my business," said he: "yours is to get the horse fit. I tell you I've entered him—Wood-Pigeon by Wapiti. He'll be first favourite the day of the race. Do you hear? I depend upon you to get him thoroughly fit."

Isaac scratched his head. "Fit!" he repeated. "Yes— I'll get the *horse* fit: you get the *rider*. If you *must* have a turn at it, take my advice, master. You get yourself in good wind; keep your head clear; jump off the moment the flag drops; never let his head go; and, above all, *sit still.*"

After this, Isaac could never again be brought to open his mouth on the subject.

CHAPTER XXIV.

THE BALL.

WHEN a man has not been provided by Nature with more than an average share of personal advantages, that same process of dressing for a ball *after* a bachelor's dinner-party is an affair of considerable trouble and dissatisfaction. To devote those minutes, that are wont to pass so pleasantly in the enjoyment of conviviality or repose to the cares of the toilet, is in itself a sufficient infliction; but the contrast is rendered all the more aggravating by abortive efforts to eradicate the effluvia of tobacco-smoke, to disguise the appearance of satiety, not to say repletion, attendant on four courses and a dessert, with champagne and claret at discretion, and to achieve that general aspect of light and airy gaiety which even middle-aged gentlemen of spherical proportions consider most captivating in the eyes of the fair.

All these difficulties had Mr. Sawyer to encounter on the night of the Harborough Ball.

Yes, the important event had arrived at last, after much discussion by stewards and lady patronesses, and general differences of opinion amongst all concerned. After protestations from some that they could by no means fill their houses, and assurances from others that nothing would induce them to travel such distances by night in bad weather, and declarations from all that, for their own part, they voted the whole thing a bore, the day was at length fixed, the musicians engaged, the supper ordered, and the room prepared.

"It was to be a capital ball," said one, "comprising the *élite* of three counties, and at least as many beautiful *débutantes*." "There would be nobody there," vowed another, "but the M.F.H., and the M.P., and old Mrs. Half-caste, with a bevy of the townspeople." The room would be cold, prophesied the malcontents; the supper scanty, the roads slippery, and the moon obscured. Miss Cecilia Dove, in talking the matter over with her mamma, inclined first to one, and then the other of these opinions; supporting each in turn with vigour and tenacity. Under any circumstances, however, she had determined to go.

Behold Mr. Sawyer then, in his little smoky bedroom, struggling into a white neckcloth, about ten P.M., and contemplating a pale face and heavy eyes; the unattractive appearance of which he could not wholly attribute to the bad glass which adorned his dressing-table. He was nervous, too, was our friend John Standish Sawyer; unquestionably nervous. Of all nights in his life this was the one when he would fain have borrowed, if he could, the exterior of another hunting-man, a very different-looking person, whom painters strive to represent as worthy to be the Queen of Beauty's choice, in their embodiment of the hapless loves of Venus and Adonis. Alas! Mr. S. could not conceal from himself that he was anything but a good-looking fellow.

Nevertheless, a plain exterior, like a bad farm, must equally be cultivated at the proper season. Dress works wonders, and the tailor, if you employ Poole, doubtless helps to make the man. Like Brummel, our friend spoilt a good many white neckcloths before he effected *the* desired tie. At last, however, he got it to his liking, swung himself into a roomy dress-coat—scarlet, with silk lining—and proceeded, not without trepidation, to the scene of action.

Is there any penalty or disgrace attached to the solecism of being earlier than one's neighbours at ball, concert, or other public occasion of festivity? It is wonderful what pains people will take to avoid this appearance of over-punctuality. I cannot call to mind any occasion on which I have thus had the room *entirely* to myself; nor did I ever meet any one who would confess that he had enjoyed this monopoly of vacuity. And yet somebody must arrive first! I wonder how that desolate one employs the long leaden moments. Does he wander about with his hands in his pockets, trying to look as if he expected something, and scanning the decorations with critical *sang froid!* Does he fraternize with the musicians, who, drawn up in a row, must present, indeed, a formidable array of eyes to a person of moderate apprehensions, and win their eternal goodwill by performing a *pas seul* to their voluntary strains? or does he give way to a cowardly despair, and, retreating in disorder, retire incontinently to bed? Probably not the latter, or the ball would never begin.

Mr. Sawyer had none of this to confront single-handed. Loitering about the cloak-room door, he came upon Struggles, Brush, Savage, and Co.; all equally averse with himself to plunge prematurely into the festive scene, and was greeted by the conclave, from whom he had parted about an hour previously, with a boisterous cordiality born of their potations.

"He's *meant!*" said one, talking of our friend as if he were a race-horse in strong training, whom each had backed heavily to win. "Got up to the nines!" exclaimed another, scanning him from top to toe, as an adjutant scans a recruit. "Hang it! Sawyer, you've done it to-night!" laughed a third; "they won't let *you* out of this alive!" And Mr. S., who rather flattered himself the general effect was favourable, did not quite know whether to be pleased with their approbation or to take huff at their familiarity. Meanwhile carriages were setting down with increasing frequency. The clatter was quite alarming in the paved streets of the little country town; the steam of horses almost obscured the carriage-lamps, and sweet little satin-slippered feet stepped daintily from inside, over an interregnum of wet straw, on to a soppy foot-cloth. When ankles are neatly turned, but not otherwise, it is surprising what a deal of holding-up is required by the compressible and expansive *crinoline*. Warm greetings and affectionate pressures of the hand were exchanged between such swains as were lucky enough to intercept them and their own peculiar damsels in the passage to the cloak-room, whither the ladies betook themselves forthwith, there to leave their becoming and coquettish little *burnouses* ere they shook out their canvas and got under sail in all the splendour of full dress.

Mammas looked approvingly at their bridling daughters, as the latter tripped into the ball-room before them; mammas, the very counterpart of those blooming beauties, had you rolled up two or three into one, but fair-shouldered, brown-haired, and comely yet, as English matrons are, up to a very uncertain period. Papas, with white gloves and red faces, slapped each others' backs, and talked about yesterday's gallop. The musicians struck up the prettiest waltz of the last season but one; Major Brush, with unexampled temerity, dashed into the enchanted ring with Lady Barbara Blazer in his arms; Bob Blazer followed suit with flirting Miss Tiptoes. A whirling maze of tulle, and wreaths, and sparkling gems, and perfumed floating tresses pervaded the magic circle; louder pealed the cornet-à-piston, brighter glanced the eyes, faster flew the dancers, the top of the room began to fill, and the ball might now be said to have fairly begun.

It is only your habitual ball-goer, however, who can thus, like some consummate swimmer, dash in with a header and strike out at once into the flood. Less experienced performers may be excused for shivering awhile on the brink. Shy gentlemen congregating round the doorway fitted their gloves on with tedious accuracy, looking over their collars meanwhile at their future partners, with an air of melancholy defiance; the weaker-minded ones informing each other confidentially that it was "going to be a capital ball!" The ranks of these waverers thinned perceptibly though, as the dance wore on, and Mr. Sawyer, who did not waltz, found himself ere long stranded high and dry at the top of the room amongst the grandees; a little bewildered, truly, and lost in such a crowd of strangers, but greatly sustained, nevertheless, by Hope and Bordeaux.

These stimulants, as might be expected, waned simultaneously. Fresh arrivals blocked the doorway; and still she didn't come! Not she, indeed! Catch Miss Cissy doing anything half so green as arriving early or staying late. No, no; if you want to be sought after, ladies, you must be sparing of your presence and economical of your smiles. There is no dog so obedient as the one you keep sitting up on his hind legs, to beg for a crumb of biscuit at a time.

Mr. Sawyer was in despair. As a stranger, however, he was presented to the grandees, and found himself, he scarcely knew how, engaged to dance "The Lancers" with Lady Barbara Blazer, a formidable beauty, of dashing, not to say, overwhelming manners, and who attributed to extraordinary forwardness, for which she rather liked him, our friend's confused and half-unconscious request that she would favour him with her hand.

Now dancing was not Mr. Sawyer's *forte*, and he had never before attempted "The Lancers." It is no wonder, then, that the intricacies of that measure should have utterly bamboozled him, or that he should have set to the wrong people, got in everybody's way, and made himself supremely ridiculous. Add to this, that in the midst of the most difficult manœuvre, when, hunting over the set for his own partner in vain, he caught Cissy Dove's eyes fixed upon him with an expression of malicious amusement; and it is needless to specify that his discomfiture was complete: Cissy Dove looking radiant as a Peri. Oh, after that, it was all magic and moonshine. Lady Barbara never alluded to him subsequently as anything but "the poor queer man I met at Harborough;" and that magnificent dame's opinion of his intellectual attainments I had rather not be compelled to declare.

Mr. Sawyer was no sooner released from his self-imposed penance than he flew to the side of his charmer, whom he found, as might be expected, hemmed in by Mamma and Papa, surrounded by a bevy of female acquaintances, and receiving the homage of one or two elaborate dandies of considerable calibre and pretension.

She shook hands with him, however, across young Vainhopes; after which he was forced to fall back upon Parson Dove, whom he accosted with great cordiality and affection.

A man never shows to such advantage as in the presence of his ladye-love. How many a Hercules have we not seen holding her silks for Omphale; his lion-front looking sheepish—not to say asinine; his strength degenerated to clumsiness; his whole exterior denoting helpless subjection and dismay! Mr. Sawyer was no exception to the general rule. He pulled at his neckcloth; twitched his gloves on and off; looked at his boots; listened to the Parson's platitudes, without hearing a word; finally, made a desperate plunge, and entreated Miss Dove to dance the next quadrille with him.

Miss Dove was engaged.

"Well, the one after that."

Miss Dove glanced at a tiny list of running horses, so to speak, that she held in her hand.

"Dear me; she was engaged for that too!"

Our friend was disgusted beyond measure: he fell back with a mortified bow, and resolved he would not speak to her for the rest of the night. It would be a poor pastime to watch the dancers from a remote corner without participating in their amusements; nevertheless he entered at once on the self-inflicted penance. The ball, however, went on none the less gaily for his abstinence. Lady Barbara nearly swept him off his legs in a whirlwind of crinoline as she waltzed by him at the rate of forty miles an hour. The Tiptoes and the Vainhopes and the rest seemed as unconscious of his presence as if he had never left The Grange, and Cissy Dove, herself dancing with a succession of dandies, each more resplendent and more taken up with himself than another, never glanced but once in the direction of her disappointed swain. That single look, however, had in it something of a pleading expression, that found its way through the embroidered plaits of Mr. Sawyer's best shirt-front, and mollified the stern heart beneath. It brought him out of his corner; it induced him to think more favourably of life in general, and of the Scotch quadrilles, now striking up merrily, in particular; it even prompted him to select the youngest Miss Hare, a blushing virgin making her first appearance in public, as his partner; and, lastly, tempted him to request Miss Dove and her cavalier, no less a swell than Bob Blazer, to be their *vis-à-vis*.

Cissy watched him pretty narrowly during the dance. Ladies, as we all know, have the abnormal faculty of seeing without looking. I am bound to confess that his dialogue with little Polly Hare was of so harmless a nature as could not have excited the ghost of an apprehension in the most jealous disposition. It proceeded something in this wise.

Mr. Sawyer, with his whole attention absorbed in the lady opposite: "Are you fond of dancing?"

The youngest Miss Hare: "Oh! very."

Mr. S.: "What a pretty room this is!"

Miss H.: "Yes, very."

Mr. S.: "The music is remarkably good for a country band."

Miss H.: "Oh! very."

[Grand Round strikes up, much to their joint relief, and promises to put a speedy termination to the solemnity.]

But in the revolutions of this highly-exciting pastime there is one figure which admits of the gentleman and lady opposite saying nearly three words to each other; and it is needless to insist on the necessity of condensing as much meaning as possible into so short a sentence.

"Why so cross?" said Miss Cissy, as she approached her adorer at this propitious moment; and, although Mr. Sawyer had neither presence of mind nor opportunity to make an appropriate reply, he looked like a different individual henceforth, and almost forgot to return his little partner, none the worse for her excursion, to the maternal wing.

Little did Mr. Sawyer dream, as she thanked him with

her demure curtsey, how that sly puss, who had been indeed the life and soul of the school-room she had just left, would act the whole scene over again that night in her dormitory, for the edification of three elder sisters and a Swiss maid; how she would mimic to the life his stiff shy manner and preoccupied demeanour; nay, make her very draperies stick out like the square tails of his coat. In virtue of her sex, the little minx detected his secret, and saw through him at a glance, though she was but sixteen. He thought it was very good of him to dance with her, and she was making a study and a character of him the whole time. Dear, dear! how little we know of them! Happy the man who wraps himself in a waterproof garment of vanity; who is determined to ignore the reflection, that the smile he resolves to accept as approval may be nothing better than derision after all; who leaves them to their own devices, and thanks his stars that he has served his apprenticeship and is " out of his time!"

A quadrille with Miss Dove put everything to rights. She seemed resolved to make amends, and she did it so prettily. She gave him her fan to hold, and her bouquet to smell, and asked his opinion of the different beauties, and smiled upon him and petted him, till her dancing-bear was in thorough subjection once more. He almost made up his mind he would propose to her in the tea-room. An eligible spot for the purpose, as it was likely to contain about fifty couples wedged together in the closest possible proximity. He could hardly be mistaken, he thought, this time; yet a cold shudder crept over him as he recollected Miss Mexico. If this business should have the same termination, he felt he had lived long enough. He would go and drown himself in the Whissendine, or retire to the mountain fastnesses of Wales, there to hunt with the Plinlimmon harriers and that united pack, the glory of three districts, whereof no mortal tongue can pronounce the names.

He drew her nervously with him towards the tea-room. Ere they reached its entrance they were intercepted by young Vainhopes—all gloves and studs and curls and chains and smiles.

"*Our* waltz at last, Miss Dove," said he, with a captivating grin; "thought you'd forgotten me; quite in despair, waited all the evening." And he carried her off, amidst a running fire of such complimentary phrases as constituted his usual conversations with the fair, and which they were quite willing to accept at their real value.

It needs little knowledge of chemistry to be aware that cold water poured on hot iron generates steam. I think Mr. Sawyer showed his sense in retiring to blow his off, with one or two convivial spirits, who finished the evening in the Honourable Crasher's rooms on cigars and brandy-and-water; the latter gentleman, who had asked Lady Barbara to dance, and then forgotten all about it, having made an early retreat to those comfortable quarters.

Here we may leave these choice spirits to their potations. Mr. Sawyer, as his friends remarked, was noisier than usual, and mixed his glass remarkably strong. He did not feel inclined to go to bed, but was quite determined not to return to the ball. Perhaps, without knowing it, he could not have adopted a more judicious resolution.

Cissy looked for him everywhere. She even excused herself from dancing, more than once, in expectation of his return—meaning, however, to pay him off to some purpose when he *did* come back. But even at the cloak-room door there was no Mr. Sawyer. Bob Blazer got her shawl, and

Savage called the carriage, and Vainhopes put her into it. Yet Cissy felt out of spirits and out of humour. Though she declared she had never enjoyed a ball so much, her mamma thought she was very silent all the way home; and she took her bed-room candle and retired upstairs the very moment they arrived at the Rectory.

It was a "new sensation" to Miss Dove not to have everything entirely her own way.

CHAPTER XXV.

THE RACE.

With many men, and those not the least dashing and brilliant horsemen, courage is apt to be very much a question of caloric: their pluck rises and falls with the thermometer. When the mercury stands at 45 or 50 deg. they negotiate with pleasure the largest and most dangerous of fences; at a few degrees above freezing they are content to seek humbly for the gaps or weak places, and a gate, instead of being jumped, is lifted off its hinges; whilst at 32 deg. the turnpike-road has invincible attractions, and is not to be deserted under any provocation.

Granting such meteorological affinities, it is needless to observe that a steeple-chase is usually contested in the bitterest possible weather, with a cutting east wind.

The great event at Market Harborough was no exception to this general rule, and the important day was ushered in by about as unpleasant a morning as any gentleman could desire for the purpose of exposing himself in a silk jacket and racing leathers about the thickness of kid gloves. Frequent storms swept across the sky, bearing with them heavy showers of mingled sleet and hail, which stung the unprotected face like pins and needles. It was a bad day to see; a bad day to hear; above all, a bad day to ride.

Struggles observed: "It was lucky they were not out hunting."

Behold, then, between the storms, under a delusive gleam of sunshine, about two P.M., half-a-dozen canvas booths erected in a large, sloppy grass-field, within a few miles of Market Harborough. Behold, congregated around the same, a motley group of tramps, list-sellers, vagrants of every description, gipsies, and card-sharpers. Behold a few jolly yeomen and farmers, pulling their wet collars over their mouths to concentrate the fumes of that last glass of brandy, and poking their horses about in the crowd, to stumble ever and anon over certain mysterious ropes, placed, for no apparent purpose, in everybody's way. Behold two or three carriages of the gentlefolks herding together, as if rather ashamed of their company, and a pretty face or two, amongst which you may recognize that of Miss Dove, a little paler than usual, peeping out from under a multiplicity of wrappers, with an air of vague astonishment, the owner having been on the ground for more than an hour, and nothing done yet. Behold also Mr. Tiptop, galloping his master's best hack as fast as the animal can lay legs to the ground, in the direction of a dripping marquee, near which there is a little knot of gentlemen in waterproof clothing, who seem to constitute an assemblage of their own. Let us lift the dank, heavy sailcloth, and peep in.

Mr. Sawyer, paper-booted, silk-capped, and clad in a gorgeous raiment of plum-colour, with a face, too, on which the cares of an empire seem to sit, is "spread-eagled" in a weighing machine, vainly trying to keep his spurs off the wet straw, and to nurse on his uncomfortable lap a saddle, a bridle, a breastplate, a martingale, five pounds of dead weight, and a whip, of which the top is ornamented with an elaborate and massive design. He is what he calls "weighing in;" and the process appears to be troublesome, not to say painful.

Behind him, and preparing for the same ordeal, is Major Brush, tucking himself and his under-garment, with considerable difficulty, into a pair of extremely tight leathers, he having selected this most inappropriate shelter as his dressing-room.

The Honourable Crasher, with a large cigar in his mouth, is watching the proceedings vacantly, having to go through them in his turn; and a quiet, clean-shaved man, with a keen eye, who is prepared for the fray, but has wisely wrapped himself up once more in a long great-coat, is busy with his betting-book. This worthy, who answers to the name of Stripes, has come a hundred miles to ride Mr. Savage's bay horse Luxury. Judging from the use he makes of his pencil, he seems to think he has a good chance of coming in first. Already there has been a wrangle as to whether he is qualified to ride as a gentleman; but the only argument against his pretensions to that title being the superiority of his horsemanship, the objection has been suffered to fall through.

The stewards will have an easier task than they expected. The race has not filled well, and will probably not produce half-a-dozen starters. As the Harborough tradespeople say, "It is a poor affair." Nevertheless, a deal of money has been wagered on it; and the devoted few are resolved to do their best.

Under the lee of an outhouse—the only one, by the way, within a mile—old Isaac is walking Wood-Pigeon carefully up and down, with his usual imperturbable demeanour. It is hard to make out what he thinks of the whole affair— whether he esteems it an unheard-of piece of tomfoolery, or looks upon it as a means of making an addition to his yearly wages. Under either contingency, he has done his duty by Wood-Pigeon. Beneath all that clothing, the horse is as fine as a star; and even Mr. Varnish could not find fault with his condition. That worthy, however, is gone to ride a horse of Napoleon the Third's, at Chantilly, and is supposed by his admirers to be staying with the Emperor at Compiègne, for the event.

Mr. Tiptop and old Isaac are barely on speaking terms.

Presently, a heavier shower than any of its predecessors sweeps across the scene; and the only steward who can be got to attend, not seeing the fun of waiting any longer, has given the gentlemen-riders a hint that, if they are not mounted and ready in ten minutes, he will go home to luncheon. The threat creates considerable confusion and dismay. "Lend me a fourteen-pound saddle!" exclaims one; "Where are my girths?" shouts another; "I can't ride him without a martingale!" groans a third; "Where's my whip? and has any one seen my horse?" asks a fourth: and, for a time, things look less like a start than before. Nevertheless, the steward is known to be a man of his word; and his announcement produces the desired effect at last.

Let us take advantage of Parson Dove's kind offer, and, placing ourselves on the box of his carriage, abstract our attention from his pretty daughter inside, and take a good view of the proceedings.

A preliminary gallop, in the wind's eye, with a sharp sleet driving in their faces, prepares the heroes for their agreeable task. Flags mark out the extent and the direction of "danger's dark career." Starting in this large grass-field, they jump a hedge and ditch into yonder less extensive pasture, fenced by double posts and rails, which, successfully negotiated, brings them, after a succession of fair hunting leaps, to The Brook. Fourteen feet of water is a tolerable effort for a horse, everywhere but in print; and as the weather will probably have wet the jockeys through before they arrive at this obstacle, it matters little whether they go in or over. After that, the fences are larger and more dangerous, an exceedingly awkward "double" enclosing the next field but one to the run-in.

The Parson thinks the ground injudiciously selected. As he had no voice in the matter, it is as well to agree with him. Mrs. Dove's attention is a little distracted by the hamper with the luncheon; and Cissy hopes fervently that "nobody will be hurt."

Let us count the starters. One, two, three, four, five, six. Mr. Crasher's Chance, blue, and white sleeves (owner); Major Brush's Down-upon-'em, "gorge de pigeon," crimson cap (owner); Mr. Savage's Luxury, scarlet, and black cap (Mr. Stripes); Mr. Brown's Egg-Flip, white (owner); Mr. Green's Comedy, by Comus, black and all black (Mr. Snooks); and lastly, Mr. Sawyer's Wood-Pigeon, plum-colour, and blue cap (owner).

The latter's appearance excites considerable admiration, as he takes his breathing canter. Wood-Pigeon is a remarkably handsome animal; and Mr. Sawyer, at a little distance, looks more like a jockey than any of them, with the exception of the redoubtable Stripes.

Old Isaac goes up to his master for a few last words before the flag drops. " You mind the double comin' in," says the wary old dodger. " Close under the tree's the best place, 'cause there's no holes in the bank; and, pray ye now, *do ye sit still !* "

A faint exclamation from Miss Dove proclaims they are off. Out with the double-glasses! From the carriage, we can see them the whole way round.

One, two, three! They fly the first fence in a string, Chance leading. The Honourable means to make running all through. Wood-Pigeon is a little rash; but Mr. Sawyer handles him to admiration. He goes in and out of the double posts and rails like a pony.

This difficulty disposes of Mr. Snooks, who lets Comedy by Comus out of his hand, falls, and never appears again.

The others increase the pace, as the lie of the ground takes them a little downhill towards the brook. As they near it, you might cover them with a sheet; but, while the whole increase their velocity, Chance and Wood-Pigeon, the latter followed closely by Mr. Stripes on Luxury, single themselves out from the rest. All three get over in their stride; and a faint shout rises from the crowd on the distant hill. Egg-Flip jumps short, and remains on the further bank, with his back broken, the centre of a knot of foot-people, who congregate round him in a moment, from no one knows where. Down-upon-'em struggles in and out again, striding over the adjacent water meadow as if full of running; but Brush is far more blown than his horse. His cap is off, his reins are entangled, he has lost a stirrup, and it is obvious that the Major's chance is out.

The race now lies between the leading three; and Crasher, who has great confidence in Chance's pedigree and stoutness, forces the running tremendously. He and Sawyer take their leaps abreast, the latter riding very quietly and carefully, mindful of old Isaac's advice, to "sit still." Luxury is waiting close upon them.

"That fellow has been at the game before," remarks Parson Dove, eyeing Mr. Stripes through his glasses, and struck with admiration at the artistic manner in which that gentleman pulls his horse together for the ridge-and-furrow.

The Parson is not far wrong. Few professionals would care to give Mr. Stripes the usual allowance of five pounds.

Thus they near the "double"—the last obstacle of any importance. It consists of two ditches, and a strong staked-and-bound fence on a bank. No horse can fly it all in his stride, after galloping nearly four miles. Perhaps that is the reason why Stripes, who knows he is on a *quick* one as well as fast one, shoots a little to the front, and comes at it at such an awful pace, seducing his two adversaries, by the force of example, into the same indiscretion. Crasher, who never "loses his stupidity," as he calls his presence of mind, diverges for a rail that he spies where the ditch is narrowest, takes the chance of breaking that or being killed, and going at it forty miles an hour, smashes it like paper, and succeeds, as Chance rises not an inch, in covering both ditches at a fly. He lands almost abreast of Luxury, who has struck back at the fence with the rapidity and activity of a cat.

Mr. Sawyer, though remembering the place under the tree, dare not pull his horse off enough, lest he should lose too much ground, and Wood-Pigeon, who is a little blown, attempting to do it all at once, lands with both fore-feet in the further ditch, chucks his rider into the field before him, and then rolls over the plum-coloured jacket in an extremely uncomfortable form. The horse rises, looking wild and

scared; not so the rider : " He's down!" exclaim the crowd;
but their attention is so taken up by a slashing race home
between Crasher and Stripes, in which the former is out-rid-
den by the latter, and beaten by half-a-length on the post,
that probably no one present but Miss Dove knew who it
was that was down. As the plum-colour still lay motionless, poor Cissy turned very pale and sick, and then began
to cry.

Our friend was not dead, however, very far from it—only
stunned, and his collar-bone broken. He recovered sufficiently to be taken past the Doves' carriage before Cissy
had done drying her eyes; and although he was not able to
join the dinner-party at his hotel, with which the day's sports
concluded, and at which an unheard-of quantity of champagne was consumed, I have been credibly informed that he
partook of luncheon within less than a fortnight at Dove-
cote Rectory, and was seen afterwards with his arm in a
sling, taking a tête-à-tête walk to look for violets with the
daughter of the house.

CHAPTER XXVI.

THE MATCH.

LOUNGING past Tattersall's one baking day in June, I had
the good fortune to encounter Mr. Savage, apparently as
busily employed as myself in the agreeable occupation of
doing nothing. If you have ever been addicted to the fascinating pursuit of fox-hunting, you will understand how,
even in London, the presence of a fellow-enthusiast is as a
draught of water to a pilgrim in the desert sand. Linking

P

arms, we turned unconsciously down the yard, and were soon mingling with the motley crowd who fill that locality on a sale-day.

"Any horses you know to be sold here?" I asked, as we stepped into the office for a list.

"None but Sawyer's," answered Mr. Savage; "pretty good nags, too. I shall bid for one of them myself."

Then we fell to talking of the grass countries and their delights, of the different rumours afloat as to this master and that, how one county was to change hands, and another to be hunted six days a week, how the young Squire was getting keen, and the old Lord was growing slack, and how, under all conditions, the foxes were not so stout nor the sport so brilliant as it used to be. Lastly, we got upon the doings of our Market Harborough friends. Struggles was as jolly as ever, nothing changed, putting on weight, and looking for weight-carriers every day. Brush? Oh, Brush had lost a "cracker" on the Derby, *would* back "Skittle-Sharper," though Savage warned him not, and had been obliged to go on full pay. What of the Honourable Crasher? He had appeared in London as usual, and was gone for a little change of air to New York! I pictured to myself how enchanted the "Broadway Swells" would be with Crasher's superfine languor and general debility; how they would worship him as the "real article" in dandyism; how they would quote his sayings and imitate his nonchalance, and how favourable a contrast such an imitation would offer to their normal state of hurry and confusion, particularly about dinner-time. But I wondered what could have taken Crasher there, of all places in the world. Then I mentioned that I had seen nothing of my old friend Sawyer for a considerable period, and indeed had received no intelligence of his doings since the steeple-chase, in which he got so bad a fall.

"Haven't you heard?" exclaimed Savage. "Why, Sawyer's married, poor fellow! Married pretty Cissy Dove, that flirting girl, who used to look so well on a chestnut horse. You must remember Cissy Dove. Why, there's the very horse going up to the hammer with Sawyer's lot. I suppose she's given up riding now—got something else to do."

Sure enough there was the late Miss Dove's exceedingly clever palfrey, looking fat and in good case, as horses always do when they are "to be sold without reserve." There was Wood-Pigeon, twice his hunting size. There was the brown and the grey, and one I didn't know, and Jack-a-Dandy himself, submitting, not very patiently, to the attentions of a villanous-looking man in dirty-white cords, who was coughing him and punching him, and feeling his legs, and narrowly escaped having his brains knocked out for his pains.

I turned to moralize with Savage, but he was gone. You never can speak to anybody in London for more than five minutes together, and I walked out of the yard musing upon man's weakness and woman's power, on the uncertain tenure by which a bachelor holds his freedom, on the common lot, and how nobody is safe. "I never would have believed it of Sawyer," methought, as I turned meditatively into Piccadilly; but then I did not know he had been out gathering violets in seductive company, with his arm in a sling.

Turning into Sam's Library, with intent to secure a stall at the French play for my niece, I politely awaited the leisure of a very smartly-dressed lady examining the plan of the Opera House, and bending studiously over the same at the counter. Her cavalier, a thick-set man, attired with considerable splendour, was engrossed in a volume which he had taken up, as it would appear, to wile away a long and tedious interval of consultation between his companion and the shopman. The lady looked up first, and under her little white bonnet with its innocent bride-like lilies-of-the-valley, I discovered a pretty dark-eyed face, such as ere this has tempted many a son of Adam, forgetful of his progenitor's mishaps, into the commission of matrimony.

"An't you ready yet?" she inquired, addressing her cavalier with just the slightest possible turn of asperity, to give piquancy, as it were, to the dregs of honey still remaining from the moon. "An't you ready?" she repeated in a sharper key, perceiving the student so engrossed as to be unconscious of her observation. This time there was more of the vinegar and less of the honey, and he started to "attention" forthwith.

"Quite ready, dearest," was the reply in the most submissive of tones, as he laid his book down upon the counter. and disclosed to my astonished view the features of my old friend John Standish Sawyer.

Our greeting was of the most cordial. I was presented in due form to the bride, who vouchsafed me so sweet a smile as made me wonder less than ever at Mr. Sawyer's subjugation. After putting her into the hired brougham that was in waiting for them, he lingered for a moment to tell me of his late-won happiness. "The horses go up to-day," said he, "and I cannot affirm that I am sorry for it. With such an attraction at home, a man don't want to go out hunting. I don't think somehow I shall ever care to ride to hounds again!"

As I turned back into the shop, the book my friend had been studying so assiduously lay upon the counter. I took it up with a pardonable curiosity. It was the 'Life of Thomas Assheton Smith, Esq.'

I shall expect to hear of Sawyer's buying two or three hunters yet, before November.

INSIDE THE BAR.

INSIDE THE BAR.

CHAPTER I.

"THE GENIUS LOCI."

"I HOPE you feel your arm a little easier, sir, this evening?" says Miss Lushington, reappearing in her own peculiar department, fresh and blooming from the revision of her toilet, which usually takes place about seven P.M. Miss Lushington's habits are peculiarly regular and methodical; her attractions of a dazzling, not to say gaudy, description; she is a thorough woman of business, if indeed such a designation be not a contradiction in terms; but when she *does* take a day's pleasure, there are few ladies who can produce a more satisfactory effect than Miss L.

I raise my eyes to reply with becoming gratitude. The object on which they rest is no everyday sight—a full-bodied, fresh-coloured, buxom damsel, with shining hair, dark and lustrous as ebony, suggestive of no small expenditure in pomatum; a pair of light-grey eyes, restless and vivacious, called black by courtesy, because fringed with lashes of jet, and surmounted by arching eyebrows of the same colour, swarthy and strong of growth; a straight well-cut nose; a wide mouth, with red lips and white teeth, large, regular, and wholesome; not forgetting those captivating manners which spring from habitual good-humour and perfect self-possession in mixed society, backed by a pair of ear-rings that would have looked *rich* even on the Queen of Sheba. All this I take in at a glance for the twentieth time, and catch myself confessing, also for the twentieth time, that the bar-maid of the Haycock Hotel and Posting-house, Soakington, is the most fascinating, as doubtless she is the most fastidious of her sex.

Miss Lushington, I need hardly observe, is no longer young. Barmaids of tender years, albeit extremely attractive to the usual frequenters of the snug locality over which they preside, cannot be expected to possess the *aplomb* with which mature experience and the rejection of many offers invest the lady of more autumnal charms. They are apt to be a little flurried by the attentions of the military, and somewhat over-excited by their anxiety for the commercial interest; also prone, if good-looking, to fly away and *better* themselves matrimonially and otherwise. But Miss L. is far above all such weaknesses as these. Not a red-coat in the whole British army could raise a corresponding hue in her cheek by the most ardent avowal of devotion; nay, even a cornet of Hussars (and I take an officer of that rank and service to be more at his ease in female society than other children of men) has been known to retire abashed and worsted from a little match at quiet *persiflage* with Miss Lushington. As for the commercial gents! why, though they worship the very keys she jingles, and the lemons in the nets above her head, they would no more think of proposing to her than to the mother of the Gracchi. I have often wondered what Miss Lushington's early history can have been. Was she ever a little girl with long tails and frills above her ankles, swinging a slate to a day-school? Had she a mother, who washed her face, and scolded her, and taught her to sew, and eventually launched her on the boards of a minor theatre; for surely those majestic manners must have been acquired before the foot-lights? Was there ever a time that she came home wearied and saddened, pressing some girlish treasure to her heart, with a thrill, half joy, half pain, and looking along an endless vista in the future, containing a house, a garden, a pig, some rosy children, a couple of bee-hives, and a fresh-coloured young man at his tea. Was she ever young? or did she descend from her attic some fine summer's day, this perfect and finished creature of for— well! of *between* thirty and forty, just as Minerva sprang ready-armed from the brain of Jove, or Venus wet and glowing, with nothing on but her shells, emerged from the blushing sea? I incline to the latter supposition. I believe that Caroline Lushington (of course, with that colour on her cheek, her name is sure to be Caroline; besides, I saw it on her workbox)—I say I believe that Caroline Lushington never was the least different from what she is now, and that I should always have been as much afraid of her as I am at this present moment. I am a shy man—not too shy to confess it. I blush to the lobes of my ears, in replying to her kind inquiries; but Miss L. does not laugh at me; for, womanlike, she has a prejudice in favour of shy men, and she pities my infirmities, and my arm in a black leather sling.

"Your tea will have drawn in five minutes, sir, and your toast is down at the fire now," says she, patting and smoothing the cushions of her own particular arm-chair in her own particular corner, that I may sit at ease, despite my injuries. How kind, how thoughtful she is! And heavens! what a *torso* the woman has! Though her dressmaker lives over the saddler's, in the High Street, at Waterborough, that black satin fits as if it came direct from Paris. Even now, mixing a glass of brandy-and-water for a customer, the turn of her waist and the cling of her corset would drive an artist into ecstasies. I am no artist, yet I cannot but think of Alfred de Musset's song about his Andalusian Marquesa, of which, as the language and the sentiments are both French, I need not write them down here.

Whilst the customer drinks and pays for his glass of brandy-and-water, it is high time that I should explain how I came to be domiciled in the bar of the Haycock Hotel and Posting-house, Soakington, with a contused shoulder, a broken collar-bone, and a black eye.

Since my earliest boyhood I have been enthusiastically fond of hunting. I am not a skilful horseman; I never was what is called a *fine* rider, perhaps not a forward one, though I have tried hard to think so; nor am I one of those who *know about hunting* (by the way, I have often wondered what it is they *do* know), but in ardent affection for the pursuit I yield to none. My godfather, one of the old Holderness lot, and not the worst of those hard-riding East-Riding *undeniables*, used to say of me, "The lad has a loose seat, and heavy hands, and not an over-quick eye, but his heart is in it. That's what gives me hopes of him —*his heart is in it!*" And my godfather was right; my heart *was* in it. As a boy at school, I kept a few beagles, and ran with them on foot, imitating, as far as a biped can, the actions and motions of a horse. At Oxford, I was a regular attendant on the far-famed drag, and to this day can remember vividly the merits of a certain game little chestnut called Jumping Jemmy, whom I used to ride unmercifully at a pecuniary consideration which must have cost me less than a shilling a leap. J. J. could jump like a cat, and had carried too many of us ever to allow an undergraduate to throw him down. That I never took my degree is the less to be wondered at, when I remember my favourite course of literature, in which, unfortunately, the examiner never thought of gauging my proficiency. I could have taken a "double-first" in all poor Nimrod's works, and could have repeated a page or two right on end from any part of the famous run in the 'Quarterly,' knowing the exact places in which Lord Gardner said, "A fig for the Whissendine!" and Lord Brudenel heard a cracking of rails behind him, and could not identify the man in the ditch because "the pace was too good to inquire!"

So they plucked me; but I persevered in my course of study notwithstanding. Do I not know and love Jorrocks? If I could find out Soapy Sponge in the flesh, would I not ask him to come and stay with me, and feed him and mount him, and let him smoke as much as he liked in his bedroom? Nay, I think I would even have bought the piebald pony of him as a cover hack; for to ride either Sir 'Ercles or Multum-in-Parvo would have been beyond my highest aspirations. Nay, with all his absurdities and affectations, I have a sneaking kindness for the dismounted sportsman in 'Ask Mamma,' who hung his wet towel out at window on doubtful nights, though he had not a horse to his name, and was no more likely to go out hunting than if he had been bed-ridden. Yes, I like the whole thing—the hounds, the horses, the servants, the second horsemen, the splashes on my top-boots, the golden drops on the gorse covert, and the wreath of cigar-smoke curling upward into the mild soft air.

People talk about hunting going out; being on its last legs; civilized away before the advance of railroads, the march of intellect, etc. All this is sheer nonsense. There are more men hunt to-day than hunted twenty years ago, twice as many as hunted thirty, and probably ten times as many as hunted fifty years ago. Hounds run harder than they did in the time of our fathers; horses are better bred, better kept, better bridled, and better ridden. The country is also more enclosed, and there is consequently a deal more jumping, and more occasion for skill and quickness, than when High Leicestershire was an open upland, and Naseby field an unfenced marsh. The best of the old ones could not have gone "a cracker" in higher form than the dozen or so of men who may be seen any morning in the week with any of our crack packs of hounds in a quick thing; and in the "days of Old Meynell" there was a good deal more room for those who liked to try. It really is by no means an easy matter to thread a crowd of a hundred horsemen in a narrow lane, all going racing pace, and then to jockey the best ten or a dozen of these for the easiest place in the first fence. The actual feat of keeping near hounds when they run hard requires skill and quickness; but the difficulty is much enhanced when it has to be performed by a score of men where there is only comfortable space for five. It is a pleasant sensation, too, when the first impediment has been disposed of, and a man feels what the fast ones of the present day call "landed," to sail away with the hounds, always supposing he is riding a hunter, and to feel that he will not now be interfered with till they check, but can do his own places at his own pace, without pulling his horse out of his stride, and gain all the advantages of seeing the hounds turn, while he has all the pleasure of watching them as they shoot across the fields, in swift, streaming line.

Great artists, indeed, boast that under such favourable circumstances, they can distinguish and criticize the performances of each individual of the pack; but for myself I confess that I never had either coolness or leisure for such details. By the time I have marked the best place in the next fence, chosen the soundest ridge, or the wettest furrow, by which to get there, given my hat a firm push down on my head, and arranged my four reins, which are apt to get confused together and entangled with the thong of my hunting-whip, in the manner I am accustomed to hold them, I have small attention to spare for anything else; and I have always been of opinion that the cheering to particular hounds in a rapid burst, from huntsmen and other professionals striving hopelessly to catch them, is the offspring of a vivid imagination, and a happy audacity in guess-work.

This forward riding, however, to a man who means to ride at all, is decidedly the best method of crossing a country, both on the considerations of pleasure and profit. Horses take their leaps in a more collected form when they see none of their own species in front of them; the hounds create quite excitement enough in a hunter to make him do his utmost; while the emulation he conceives of his own kind is apt to degenerate into a jealousy, that makes him foolhardy and careless. Also a great amount of unnecessary exertion is entailed upon him, by being pulled off and set going again, which must be done repeatedly in a run by a man who follows another, however straight and well his leader may ride. Also, the sportsman's nerves are spared much needless anxiety and misgiving. Can anything be more distressing, than to see our front-rank man fall, in the *uncertainty* he has attained on the further side of a thick fence, or cover it with an obvious effort and struggle? Caution whispers, we had better decline. Shame urges that "what one horse can do another can." Self-esteem implores us not to fall back into "the ruck" behind. So we first of all check our horse from hesitation, and then hurry him from nervousness. The probable result is a "cropper," with the additional disgrace of having been incurred at a place which the pioneer cleared easily, and an assumption, as unjust as it is unwelcome, that our horse is not so good as his. Now, in riding *for himself*, a man preserves his confidence till he is *in the air*. Should he be luckless enough to light in a chasm, he has at least the advantage of not being frightened to death in advance; and I am convinced that all the extraordinary leaps on record have thus been made by these forward horsemen, who, trusting dame Fortune implicitly, find that she nearly always pulls them through. With regard to the distance a horse can cover when going a fair pace and leaping from sound ground, even with thirteen or fourteen stone on his back, it is scarcely credible to those who have not witnessed it. Two- and three-and-thirty feet from footmark to footmark and on a dead level have often been measured off. There are few fences in any country that would let us in, if we could trust to such a bound as this; and the activity displayed by a good horse, when he finds the ditch on the landing side wider than he calculated, is perhaps the noblest effort of the bodily powers of the animal.*

* In the Black Forest in Germany there are two stones standing to this day, *sixty feet* apart, to commemorate the leap made across a chasm

Of course, we must fall sometimes. Of course, without that little spice of what we can hardly call *danger*, but which produces what we may safely call *funk*, it wouldn't be half the fun it is. Going down, indeed! Look at the column of advertisements, weather permitting, in the *Times;* look at the price of hay and corn; look at the collector's accounts of assessed taxes for saddle-horses (if you can get them); look at Poole's trade in coats, and Anderson's in breeches, and Peel's (not Sir Robert's) in boots. Why, the very shoemakers, though on foot, hunt regularly. So do the tradesmen and the farmers, and all the liberal professions; the army, the navy, the House of Commons, the Peers of the realm, her Majesty's Ministers, and the principal Commissioner of the Court of Bankruptcy; nay, the heir to the crown is an enthusiastic sportsman, and an excellent rider; and so *Floreat Diana!* and God save the Queen!

Talking of falls brings me back to my broken collar-bone, and the bar of the Haycock. I must explain, then, how I came to be established as the habitual inhabitant of that snuggery.

After so wet a summer as that of 1860, I confess I was sanguine as to an open winter: I have always supported the doctrine of compensation. If we don't get it in one way, we do in another. A deal of warmth was doubtless due on the year, and what was more natural than to anticipate an open season, and plenty of sport? With this conviction, I kept my eyes open all the summer, and raising my modest stud from the complement of three to five, was fortunate enough to purchase at Tattersall's two raw-boned, Roman-nosed animals, called respectively "Apple-Jack" and "Tipple-

by a hunted deer, attested by several sportsmen who were eye-witnesses of the wonderful and desperate effort.

Cider," who turned out to be sound, useful, and well-trained hunters. Lest I should delude the unwary into thinking it a good plan thus to put one's hand into "the Lucky-bag," let me observe, that I paid the full value for them, and esteem myself unusually fortunate not to have been "stuck," or, in plain English, cheated out of good money for a bad horse.

I then sent my stud down to the stables I had taken for them at Soakington, under the care of a steady old groom, who is as sagacious as he is obstinate, and engaging for myself the large parlour and the little blue bedroom at the Haycock, prepared for a comfortable five months' spell at hunting and nothing else. No society to distract me; no books that I couldn't go to sleep over, if I was tired; above all, no female influence to make one late in the mornings, restless in the day-time, and sleepless at night—an effect I have remarked as the usual consequence of a quiet bachelor suffering himself to be deluded into the company of that insidious creature, woman.

> "Beautiful she is,
> The serpent's voice less subtle than her kiss,
> The snake but vanquished dust; and she will draw
> Another host from heaven, to break heaven's law."

I did not then know of Miss Lushington's presidency at the board of control. I had not even pictured to myself the possibility of such a Siren in such a collection of satins; more innocent than Ulysses—who, I am convinced, was a finished profligate from the first, and only went to Troy to get away from Penelope—I did not even mistrust the cup of Circe. Ah! she made a pig of her admirer, that ancient enchantress; and in Miss Lushington's presence the admirer makes an ass of himself: that is all the difference. But I anticipate.

Soakington is a delightful situation for hunting; though perhaps for other purposes the extremely wet nature of the soil and dampness of the atmosphere might make it a less desirable locality. The village consists of a few buildings, of which the Haycock with its stables and out-houses forms far the largest part: there are half-a-dozen straggling cottages, a dilapidated barn, always open and always empty; a pair of stocks with no foot-hold, and a pound; the church is three-quarters of a mile off, and it always rains on a Sunday, except when it snows.

But the surrounding district for many miles would gladden a sportsman's heart. There are large wild pastures, all overgrown with rushes, and not half-drained, that cannot fail to carry a scent; the arable land is badly cultivated, and badly cared for; boys never combine the scaring of crows and heading of foxes in this favoured region, and when you do see a plough, it is generally lying stranded in an unfinished furrow, deserted by man and horse. Large woods, with deep clay ridings, holding no end of foxes, lie at intervening distances from each other, to afford a succession of famous gallops, and a certainty of hounds being left to work for themselves. Ay, and in the month of May, when the primroses are out, and the violets scenting the air, and other hounds have left off for the season, you may still follow up the chase, in these deep dark glades, with an ardour proportioned to the heat of the sun over your head. Large straggling ill-conditioned fences are the obstacles with which the hunter has to contend; and nothing but a good horse, with discretion as well as courage, is likely to see a run in safety; whilst for the latter quality there is no lack of occasion, inasmuch as the Sludge, a deep, wide, and treacherous brook, winds and doubles through the whole country, where it is least expected, and obtrudes itself in the most unwelcome manner, as one of the principal features, in every run that takes place. I have said enough to show that Soakington is no bad billet for a man who means to devote himself to the sport; and when I add that the field is usually small in number, consisting principally of hard-riding farmers, and the lords of the soil, whilst the hounds themselves are of the best blood in England, and established in the same kennels for half a century, it is no wonder that I looked forward to my season's amusement with considerable anticipations of delight.

I pass over my first fortnight's doings. It takes at least that period at the beginning of the season for a man to renew his familiarity with his old horses, and make acquaintance with his new ones. I have always envied the nerve and address of those who can jump on a strange hunter's back at a moment's notice, twist and turn him at will in any direction, and lark him over every description of fence, with a confidence as surprising as it is usually successful. This is a gift, however, that I do not myself enjoy. It takes me a week at least to feel really at home in boots and breeches; nor, until I have ridden each of my horses *twice* in his turn, do I consider that *he* is fit to go, or that *I* have acquired thorough confidence in his abilities. By the third week in November, when the ditches are beginning to get clear of tangled grass, and it is possible to see *through* a fence, that you cannot see *over*, I consider myself fairly embarked on the sport.

There were but three days without rain, to the best of my recollection, during the whole of the above-named month, in the year of grace 1860. Behold me, then, congratulating myself on the prospect of at last reaching the covert-side without being wet through, as I mounted my horse at the door of the Haycock, and caught a glimpse of Miss Lushington's black head above the window-blinds, not wholly uninterested in my departure. The fixture was at Claybridge, less than three miles from Soakington; and as the famous pack to which I almost exclusively confine my attentions meets at half past ten, I had ample time to breakfast comfortably, and ride my hunter on.

Although not sufficiently Spartan in my habits to do without a covert-hack for long distances, I have found out, in common with most men, I believe, that one's horse never carries one so pleasantly as when one has ridden him to covert oneself. Apple-Jack is a calm and deliberate animal enough, with none of the crotchets and fancies peculiar to so many superior hunters; and yet even he seems always a little less staid and careful than usual when he has carried my groom a dozen miles or so along the road. Few sensations are more enjoyable than to jog quietly to the meet, after a leisurely breakfast, with a good cigar in one's mouth, a horse that feels like a hunter under one, and the satisfactory conviction that one is in plenty of time.

It is not my province nor my intention to describe minutely the Castle-Cropper hounds. All the world knows that the Earl of Castle-Cropper is a thorough sportsman; that you might hunt with him from year's end to year's end, and, except to beg you civilly to "hold hard," never hear him open his lips; and that he is supposed to be as facetious and agreeable in private life as he is reserved and silent in his public capacity. The same world knows, too, that Will Hawk, who was with his father, the old Earl, in the famous days of Musters and Tom Smith, a sort of heroic period "*ante Agamemnona*," is the prince of huntsmen, and the flower of veterans; that the horses are undeniable, the servants respectable, well dressed, and trustworthy, though scarcely so quick as they might be; the whole thing goes like clockwork, and the hounds are beyond all praise. Well they may be; they have had that advantage which is so indispensable to the perfection of a pack, and, in these days of change, so often denied it, viz. time. In the best part of a century, a uniform height, an equal excellence, and a family likeness are to be attained, with constant perseverance and unlimited expense. From generation to generation the Earls of Castle-Cropper have devoted their leisure, their money, and their attention, to this favourite hobby. The present successor may well be satisfied with the result.

They are rather large, solemn-looking hounds, extremely rich in colour; the dark and tan, both in dogs and bitches, predominating. They have a strong family likeness in the depth of their girth, the width of their loins, and the quality of the timber on which they stand. You might seek through the kennels at the Castle for a summer's day without finding a pair of legs that were not as straight and square as a dray-horse's, with feet as round as a cat's. In hunting they run well together, without flashing to the front; and although other hounds may seem to make their way quicker across a field, the Castle-Croppers keep continuously on, over a country, seldom *hovering*, as it is called, for a moment, and carrying the scent with them, as it were, in defiance of all obstacles. Old Hawk assists them but little, and hollows to them not at all. These hounds are never seen with ears erect and heads up, waiting for information. If they want to know where their fox is gone, they put their noses down, and find out for themselves. Also, they come home with their sterns waving over their backs;

and finally, I cannot describe their uniformity of appearance
and general strength and efficiency better than by saying, that
the bitches are so like the dogs, you can hardly tell the one
pack from the other, but by the shriller music of its tones.

A dozen sportsmen, including the master, constituted our
field at Claybridge. There were half-a-dozen red-coats, one
belonging to an undergraduate, on for the first time; two
or three farmers; a horse-breaker, who kept at a most respectful distance from the pack, and a nondescript. The
latter might have been anything you please. I believe he
was a grocer. He wore a pair of low shoes, a grey frieze
shooting-jacket, a black satin waistcoat, and a hunting-cap!
His horse, a mealy bay, had a long coat, a long tail, a long
pedigree, and long legs. The man rode with one spur, an
ash stick, and a snaffle bridle. Nevertheless, I saw him
jump a locked gate just after they found, with considerable
address and determination.

Although I arrived at half past ten to a minute, ere I
could look about me a nod from the silent Earl motioned
Will Hawk to begin. Eagerly, yet under perfect control,
twenty couple of dog-hounds dashed into a wood of some
seventy or eighty acres, the noble master and his huntsman
accompanying them down a ride, that seemed to take them
up to their girths at every stride. The first whip galloped
off in another direction without a word; and the second,
before plunging into the obscurity of the forest, posted the
small and obedient field in a corner by a hand-gate, from
which we were forbidden to stir upon any provocation whatsoever.

Though you often wait several anxious minutes by the
side of a patch of gorse the size of a flower-garden, in these
large woods, you almost always find instantaneously; and we

had not occupied our station for many seconds, ere the note of a hound brought our hearts into our mouths. Another and another certified the truth of the declaration, and presently a grand crash and peal of deep-mouthed music proclaimed that there was a capital scent. Twice they forced their fox to the very gate at which we were standing. Twice huntsman and master came splashing and floundering up the deep ride, to go away with them; but the third time the fox made his point good, as these game woodland gentlemen will, and whisking his brush gallantly, put his head straight for the open within twenty yards of us.

I had just turned to holloa; nay, was opening my mouth for the purpose, when a low quiet voice in my ear whispered, "Don't make a noise;" and the Earl was close to me. How he got there I never knew; but he seemed to have an instinctive perception of my intentions, and a morbid fear lest I should "get their heads up."

In another moment the music, increasing in volume, reached the edge of the wood, and then the whole pack (not one missing, for I heard the Earl say so to the second whip) came pouring out over the fence, and proceeded to run in a steady business-like stream over the adjacent field.

"Give them a moment!" said the master; and away he went alongside of them—best pace.

"There was none of the usual hurry and confusion that may be witnessed in most fields, when a fox goes away. The red-coats dropped at once into their places, the undergraduate taking the lead gallantly, in a line of his own. The farmers caught hold of their horses, and proceeded as if they meant business. The nondescript charged the gate I have mentioned, in preference to a straggling hedge with an awkward bank, and seemed determined to see all the fun while he could; and I followed his Lordship, hoping to take advantage of his experience, although contrary to my usual principle. It was only the third time I had ridden Apple-Jack, and I had not yet acquired thorough confidence in my horse. Alas! my amusement was doomed to meet with an early termination. The first fence I negotiated most successfully; the second I avoided by making use of a friendly gate; the third landed me in a rushy pasture, over which the hounds were streaming, and whence I obtained an extensive view of the surrounding country, and the line we were likely to run. A black belt of wood crowned the horizon, and towards it the fox was obviously pointing. In the interval lay a fair flat country—green and pastoral; but a foot-bridge, a quarter of a mile to the right, and a stunted willow or two in the next field, denoted the vicinity of the omnipresent Sludge. I dreaded it even then. But I might have spared myself my apprehensions. Before I arrived at it, a low hedge and ditch were to be crossed, which I saw his Lordship accomplish with ease, and rode at myself in perfect confidence. Apple-Jack did it beautifully. Alas! he landed in a covered drain (I believe the only one in the country), and I remember nothing more, except a confused sensation of jolting in a post-chaise, till I felt the doctor's finger on my pulse, as I lay on my back in the own bed at the Haycock.

CHAPTER II.

TIPS, THE HORSE-BREAKER.

"It's a long business, a broken collar-bone," I observed to Miss Lushington, as I sipped my tea comfortably in the arm-chair she had vacated for my use. "I am only thankful to be in such good quarters, and—and—in such pleasant company," I added, with a little hesitation.

Miss Lushington smiled, showing all her white teeth, and shooting glances of consolation out of her bright eyes. "You must keep up your spirits, sir," said she (she pronounced it *sperits*). "Patience and water-gruel is a cure for most diseases, and a broken collar-bone is less painful than a broken heart, and easier cured than a broken neck!"

An observation like the above, involving the two fertile topics of physical and mental suffering, was an opening to further confidences, of which I should, doubtless, have availed myself, had our *tête-à-tête* not been interrupted at this interesting juncture by the arrival of two fresh customers, one of whom walked into the bar with the air of an *habitué* of the place, whilst his companion, evidently about to be treated to "something to drink," followed in a more diffident manner, and entered the snuggery, as it were, under protest.

"What shall it be, Tips?" said a cheery voice, in the loud frank tones of a man who 'stands treat,' but of which I could not see the owner, on account of a wooden screen interposing between his person and the corner where I sat. "What shall it be? Glass of sherry and bitters? Warm ale, with a stick in it? Brandy-and-water hot? Name the article, and Miss L. will measure it off for you, without a moment's delay."

"I'll take a little gin-and-water, Mr. Naggett," replied Tips, in a low hoarse voice. "Cold, if you please, Miss," he added, with the utmost deference, as he drew the back of his hand across his mouth, in anticipation of his favourite beverage; to my mind the most comfortless of all potations.

Whilst Miss Lushington, like a Hebe in maturity, was supplying the nectar, I had an opportunity of studying the exterior of Mr. Tips, the horse-breaker, a public functionary of whom I could not have been long in the neighbourhood without hearing, but whom I had as yet had no opportunity of meeting, so to speak, in private life.

Crippled as I was, I may here remark, once for all, that I was solely dependent for amusement on the perusal of such characters as I met in the bar at the Haycock. Deprived of my hunting, not overfond of reading, here was a book laid open, so to speak, before me, of which I had not even the trouble to turn the page, whilst the peculiarities of these different visitors furnished an inexhaustible fund of amusement; their rapid succession preserved me from the dangers of prolonged *têtes-à-têtes* with Miss Lushington— interviews that could but have resulted in my total subjection by that seductive being, herself cold and unimpressionable as marble, experienced in the falsehood of our sex, and superior to the weaknesses of her own.

Off his horse, Tips was, to say the least, a very singular-looking person. He was a low, strong, broad-shouldered man, a perfect Hercules down to his waist, and with a length of arm and depth of chest that would have made him an ugly customer in the ring, an appellation to which his physiognomy also fully entitled him. Not that he had what is termed a "fighting nob;"—far from it. High features, bushy eyebrows, an aquiline nose, and a long prominent chin, gave him a sort of resemblance to a dilapidated Henri Quatre; but the nose had been smashed and thickened by a fall, the chin knocked on one side by the kick of a horse, and one of the eyes, rent and lacerated by a thorn, was disfigured by a ghastly droop of the lid, and a perpetual crimson in what ought to have been the white of the eye; very large thick whiskers, of a rusty brown, framed this singular face, and a knowing wide-awake leer in the undamaged eye, would have told an observer, without the aid of the blue-spotted neckerchief, that its proprietor was a "party concerned about horses." Nevertheless, the man had a game, bold look about him, all the same,—that latent energy in his glance, which denotes physical courage, and without which a good judge of his species does not care to select one of the half-score he requires for the manning of a life-boat, the capturing of a gun, or the performance of any other dare-devil feat, that demands more boldness than brains. Had Tips been moulded in fair proportions, he would have been a heavy-weight; but below the waist, I must acknowledge, his limbs were more like those of a monkey than a man. His stomach seemed all to have gone up into his chest; and although his thighs were long, his thin shrivelled legs were absurdly short and small below the knee. He was made for a horseman and nothing else; nor, when you saw him at daybreak, exercising some lawless three-year-old, with its mouth full of "keys," and its dogged sullen eye, prepared to take the slightest advantage of its rider, either to jump, kick, rear, or go backwards, could you help acknowledging that here, at least, was the *right* man in the *right* place. Of his early history I gathered some particulars from himself. I give them as an additional proof, if indeed any such were wanting, that in every grade and situation,

"There's a sweet little cherub that sits up aloft,
  To take care of the life of poor Jack."

Tips, then, began his career as a chimney-sweeper's boy,

and to this appointment in tender years, may perhaps be attributed the physical development of his upper man, and the malformation of his lower limbs. His promotion, or rather I should perhaps say, his *descent* into the saddle, originated in a manner as alarming as it was unexpected. The master chimney-sweeper's wife was attacked with that malady which peoples this world and the next. The doctor lived three miles off, in the nearest market town. The pony that carried the soot was dead. Under such a concatenation of unfavourable circumstances, it is needless to observe that the master-sweep had taken refuge in inebriety. Beyond blessing the unborn, and cursing everything else above an inch high, he was incapable of any decided effort, and little Tips was started off in a hurry, on the back of a wellbred chestnut filly of the baker's, to go for the doctor. The boy was full of pluck, but deficient in practice. The filly full of corn, and quite well aware of the five stone of inexperience she carried on her back. It was not unnatural that her shambling trot should soon become a canter, which a desperate shy at a drove of pigs converted into a gallop under the most unfavourable circumstances. Little Tips, when she swerved, held on manfully by the bridle; the baker's tackle was old and frayed; the head-band broke, and the bit came out of the filly's mouth; no pleasant predicament for an urchin of nine years old, careering along a turnpike-road, on market-day, at top speed. He stuck to her, however, like a monkey, and devoutly hoped the gate at the town-end might not be shut.

Now it happened fortunately for Tips, that a certain old veterinary surgeon, the kindliest and best of sportsmen, was jogging into this very town on his thorough-bred mare, half a mile ahead of the runaway. The old man heard the clattering of hoofs, and looked back to see a child in imminent danger of its life. Quick-witted, cool, and sagacious, he bethought him at once of the winding streets, the slippery pavement, and the crowded vehicles. To enter the town at that pace would be certain death, and the child must be stopped somehow at all risks. There was a grass siding to the high-road, and nearly a mile further to go.

The old man was not long making up his mind. Putting his own mare into a gallop, he allowed the filly to come alongside of him, and encouraged her little rider with voice and gesture. The child gathered confidence immediately, and sat cool and collected, as if racing. Edging him by degrees off the road, the old man at last jostled his companion into the fence, where the filly attempting to take it sideways, of course remained, pitching little Tips over her head into a soft grass field.

"*Be'ant hurt a mossel!*" exclaimed the child in high glee, scrambling once more through the hedge, to assist his preserver in righting the filly, on whom, after properly securing the bridle, he again mounted to proceed on his errand, with unshaken nerve. The old man was so pleased with the coolness of the urchin that he begged him of his master, and took him into his own service, where Tips learned all of horses and horsemanship that he ever knew, and where he might have remained for life but that his employer died, and he was thrown upon the world once more, with nothing but his natural abilities to depend upon.

And here let me lift up my voice, to correct a very erroneous notion, rife amongst the unsporting portion of the community, to the effect that rough-riders and that class of persons are men of dissipated habits. Except in some rare instances, the very contrary is necessarily the case. No man can preserve that cool, clear-headed daring which we call nerve, if he addicts himself habitually to the use of stimulants. The sensitive fibres of the human interior, which when injured and irritated by alcohol, react upon the courage, spirits, and temper, exist equally in the rudest day-labourer as in the most delicate fine lady. When these are affected, the nerve begins to fail, and no man without that quality can pretend to tame unbroken, or to ride ungovernable horses. Practice will do much, and unquestionably the alarm created in the biped, by the hostility of the quadruped, is somewhat disproportioned to the real danger incurred; nevertheless, our own sensations and our daily observation of others cannot but prove to us, that there is much truth in the proverb which says, "He who would venture nothing, must not get on horseback!" However drunk some of these dare-devil equestrians may be willing to get on occasion, they are habitually men of temperate and abstemious habits; almost invariably early risers, and consequently sound sleepers during the night.

That a hardy, healthy habit of body is indispensable to such persons is obvious, when we consider the muscular exertion they have to go through, and the many hard knocks they are likely to sustain in their daily avocations. We all know that a prize-fighter, in training, is capable of receiving an amount of punishment without inconvenience, of which a tithe would knock the same man "out of time" were he not toughened and hardened against it by the severity of his preparation. The cutting blow that would raise a swelled and angry sore on the face or person of a man who had been indulging in gluttony and idleness, leaves but a slight red mark on the clear skin of the thoroughly purified athlete; and the latter rises rather refreshed than otherwise from a fall "over the ropes," that would have stunned and stupefied the former for an hour, and given him a bilious attack for a fortnight.

Now the same argument holds good with men who are liable to be thrown and kicked by horses, or exposed to the disagreeable contingency of being rolled over or laid upon by their pupils, in that early education at their fences, which all young hunters must go through. A rider in perfect training, with his muscles developed into the elasticity and toughness of *gutta-percha*, without a pound of superfluous flesh on his ribs or an ounce of undigested food in his stomach, not only rides with coolness, quickness, and confidence—the mental result of this physical condition—but rises uninjured from the severe falls and violent concussions to which his daring must occasionally subject him; and should he even be unfortunate enough in some more than usually complicated "cropper" to break a bone or strain a sinew, is cured by dame Nature in so short a space of time as to astonish the attending doctor, who has sufficient presence of mind, nevertheless, to take the whole credit of the recovery on himself. Tips seemed to be made of iron. According to his own account, he never was hurt but once, and that was out of a gig. The circumstances were a little singular, and I had them from his own lips on the first evening of my convalescence, whilst he sipped his gin-and-water, by permission of Miss Lushington, inside the bar.

Mr. Naggett, whom I gathered, from his order of "Port-wine-negus, with a scrape of nutmeg and a slice of lemon in it," to be of the genus "swell," was summoned away in a hurry to a "gent who wished to see him on business," as the waiter said, before he could put his own lips to the fragrant mixture or burst on my astonished sight from behind the wooden screen. Tips, accordingly, with the utmost diffidence, and at Miss Lushington's earnest entreaty, came alongside of my arm-chair, where he remained standing, with his glass in his hand, shifting from one leg to the other, and stirring his gin-and-water with an unnecessary tea-spoon the while. He was dressed in wide cord breeches, leather gaiters, a brown cut-away coat, the thickest worsted waistcoat I ever saw, and the blue spotted neckerchief, in which I believe he was born, and I am quite sure he will die.

"Sorry to see you laid on the shelf, sir," observed he, with a dab at his forehead as if to remove an imaginary hat, for men of all nations who are much concerned with horses acquire a sort of knowing politeness.

I answered feebly that "it was a tedious accident, but, I should think, nothing in *his* eyes, who had probably broken every bone in his body." And Miss Lushington smoothed the cushions while I spoke, and adjusted my arm in its sling.

The rough-rider shook his head, took a sip of his gin-and-water, and looked thoughtfully into his glass.

"Far from it, sir," said he. "Far from it. Bones isn't broke so easy as gentlemen think. Ask your pardon, sir; now how was it as *your* accident came about? Collar-bone, sir, warn't it? Well, sir, it wasn't a *young* horse as let you down that way, I'll take upon me to—" swear, he was going to say, but, looking respectfully at Miss Lushington, Tips put his broad hand over his mouth, and rounded off his sentence with the word "suppose."

I was forced to confess that the culprit Apple Jack was by no means a young horse. In fact, he "owned" to ten; and, like seven-and-twenty in a woman, that is an age at which a horse remains for an indefinite period.

"That's where it is, sir," answered Tips. "Now, a young one will spoil your face sometimes, and strain you in the groin, and kick at you when you're down; and I've even known of 'em breaking of a man's ribs. But a collar-bone? —no. If you'll excuse *me*, sir, I'll tell you the reason why. When a man breaks his collar-bone, 'tis because him and his horse comes to the ground all of a heap; and a young one never falls all of a heap without he's blown, and then he seldom gets to the far side of his fence at all."

"You've ridden a good many young ones?" I asked, not without some little admiration of a man who seemed to consider an inexperienced horse the *safest* mount.

"Here and there a one, sir," replied Tips, looking modestly downwards. "My old master, he bred a good sort; you don't see many such nowadays. And I mostly had the schooling of 'em, both with Sir 'Arry and the Squire. Bless ye, sir, the young ones isn't the most troublesome as we has to do with. A young horse is very *teachable*, as I call it; and the sooner you get him, the easier it is to show him what you mean. A little timorsome perhaps they are at first, and frightened at what they're about. I've seen the same with the women-folk.—[Here Miss Lushington coughed loudly, and frowned.]—But when they *do* go, they *mean* going, and no mistake.—[" Well, I'm sure!" said Miss L., gathering up her work, and preparing to draw some beer.]—I'd as leave ride a four-year-old, if he could have the *condition* in him, as a fourteen. If things don't go cross with him at first, to my thinking, he's the pleasanter mount of the two."

"But you don't mean to say a young horse can jump as well as an old one!" I exclaimed, completely aghast at such an upsetting of all my preconceived notions; and recollecting, not without a qualm, how my banker's book might testify to the value I placed on seasoned and experienced hunters. "Suppose you come to 'doubles'! Suppose you come to timber! Suppose you want to creep quietly through a gap by a tree!"

Tips indulged in a pitying smile. "Have you never had a violent *old* horse, sir?" said he. "How many nags have you owned that you could trust after half-a-dozen seasons to do a gate to a certainty, or land clear of the second ditch, when they knowed nothing beforehand, or to go by a post in a hurry without jamming of your leg against it? Now a young one *takes notice*, as the women say of their babies.—You'll excuse *me*, miss.—A young one is all for learning, for doing the best he can to please you—for going your way instead of his own. A young one may put you down quietly once or twice from ignorance, or because you won't let him alone; and he hasn't learnt yet to disregard your pulling him about, but he makes it up to you before the day's over. And if I was a going to ride for my life to-morrow over a country I'd never seen before, I'd ask for a four-year-old to do it on, if I was quite sure that he was a fast one, a bold one, and with a spice of the devil that he got from the mare that bred him!"

With this startling exposition of his theory, Tips swallowed his gin-and-water at a gulp, and then looked anxiously at the door, seemingly for the reappearance of Mr. Naggett.

As that worthy, however, did not return, I could but entreat the rough-rider to allow Miss Lushington to replenish his glass at my expense; and lighting a cigar myself, by that lady's permission, I begged Tips to take a chair, and proceeded with my inquiries.

"Is there no sort of horse then," I asked, "that you

consider dangerous? or do you believe that whenever an accident happens, collar-bones or otherwise, it *must* be the fault of the rider?"

"*Plenty* of dangerous horses about, sir," answered Tips, preparing to make himself comfortable—"*plenty* of 'em, more's the pity, even for horse-breakers and such-like, as I am myself. We never get no credit of them. Even if we get them pretty handy, and return them as quiet to ride or drive, why as soon as they're back in their own stable, they begin at their old tricks again. There was one as I had from Mr. Mohair, the draper in Waterborough; a grey he was, and up to all manner of games. Wouldn't go by the milliner's shop in the High Street, not at no price. Mrs. Mohair was just mad about it, sir, I can tell you. Well, they sent him over to me to break; and says the missus to me, says she, when I took him away, 'Break the spirit of him, Mr. Tips,' says she, 'if whip and spur will do it. And don't let me see of him backing and sidling into the windows of them bold hussies again,' says she, 'not if you cut him into ribbons for it!' You see the ladies is mostly for strong measures,—asking your pardon, Miss,—'specially when there's other ladies concerned. Well, I didn't cut him into ribbons, I didn't, because it's not my way; but I coaxed and humoured of him, and once or twice when we *did* have a tussle, I showed him pretty plainly who was master: and I rode him backwards and forwards into Waterborough and what not, and he passed the milliner's windows and took no more notice than if there hadn't been a pretty girl in the whole shop, front or back. So I takes him to Mr. Mohair, and says I, 'You may ride him any-wheres now, sir,' says I, 'for if you do but shake a whip at him, he goes as quiet as a lamb.' And I charged him for the horse's keep, and a sovereign besides, and so thought no more about it.

"Well, sir, in less than a fortnight, I happened to be in Waterborough on market-day; and as I came out of the horse-market, I see a crowd of foot-people running towards the High Street, and I hear a precious stamping and scuffling, and clattering of horses' feet just round the corner where the milliner's shop stands; so I walk on to see what the disturbance is. A precious shindy I found too. There was a donkey-cart drawed on to the pavement, and a hamper of greens upset on the door-step, and a old apple-woman cursing awful, and the foot-people flying into the middle of the street; and in the heart of them all, there was the grey horse right up against the milliner's front door, with his head going one way and his body another, and his tail tucked down in his quarters as if he meant mischief enough for a week; and Mr. Mohair (he's a timid gentleman, Mr. Mohair), sitting on his back as white as a sheet, pulling of him by the bridle, and kicking of him in the ribs, afraid to quilt him as he should have done by rights; afraid to stick to him handsome, and yet more afraid still to get off his back, for there stood Mrs. Mohair in her best black satin gown, with a shawl pulled over her head, a rowing of him tremendous, and all the pretty girls in the milliner's windows laughing fit to break their hearts. Well, I caught hold, and led him back to his own stable for pity's sake; and Mr. Mohair behaved quite like a gentleman; but he sold him to run in the 'bus, and never got on his back again."

"Very awkward for all parties," observed Miss Lushington, probably following out a train of ideas of her own.

Tips stared at her for a considerable period, winked solemnly with his damaged eye, and then subsided once more into his gin-and-water.

"Do you think these vicious horses, then," said I, "the most dangerous customers you have to do with?"

"No, sir, I don't," was the reply; "vice in a horse is the most troublesome fault of all to cure, because it's always breaking out again, and because a vicious beast is sure to be a sensible beast too. The horse-riders, you know, sir— them as teaches horses to fire pistols, and make tea, and dance on the tight-rope, and what not—they always give the preference to what they call a *restive* one, because you see it's the beast's sagacity that makes him to difficult to break, if so be the breaker has begun with him the wrong way. It's all *humbug*, sir, is horsemanship, that's what it is; and the easier a horse is humbugged, the pleasanter he is to ride and drive. Now a real knowing 'un won't be humbugged at no price, and so we come to forcing of him, which is always a difficult business, and then it's 'pull devil, pull baker,' and if the baker pulls hardest, why we call him vicious. But he's always got his wits about him, he has. He may be aggravating, *very:* but you can't call him *dangerous*. He won't put *himself* into a mess, not if he knows it, and so he's bound to take care of *you*, so long as you don't part company. I recollect of a nag, a very neat one, as belonged to a friend of mine, who says to me one evening, 'Tips,' says he, 'I'll sell you my bay Galloway,' says he, 'for seventeen sovereigns, there, and a glass of gin-hot, for I dursen't ride him, and that's the truth.' 'I'll give you three five-pun' notes and a bottle of French brandy,' says I, 'if it's all on the square.' 'Done!' says he. 'Done!' says I; 'and now what's his little game?' says I, when I'd ordered the brandy. 'Well,' says my friend, 'whenever I ride down wharf-side to my business, he makes a dash for the canal, and tries to plunge over head in the deep water.' 'Has he ever been *in* with you?' says I. 'Never!' says he, 'and I'll take care he never *shall*. I'm a family man, Mr. Tips, and plagued with the rheumatics besides.'"

"So I brought the little nag home: and next day I took a sharp pair of spurs, and an ash-plant, and rode him down wharf-side quite easy and confidential. Sure enough he takes the bit in his mouth, and away he goes best pace for the canal. We came at it so fast I thought we must both have been in; and he stopped so short on the edge, if I hadn't been ready for him, I must have gone clean over his head. Well, he fought and fought, but I couldn't force him into it, till at last I got his hind legs close to the brink, and I slipped off his back, and with a jerk of the bridle, tipped him over as neat as wax. He had to swim for a hundred yards and more alongside the towing-path afore he could get out, and he never tried on *that* game again, you may take your oath. He was a sweet cob as ever you see to carry fourteen stone, and I sold him to an old gentleman at Croydon for five-and-forty sovereigns, money down. But he didn't want to go into the canal, bless ye; though once he *was* in, he swam like an otter."

"I have always heard a frightened horse is worse than a vicious one," I observed, hazarding the remark with a certain hesitation in presence of so high an authority.

"That's *right*, sir," answered Tips with a smile, born of gin-and-water and approval. "It's a frightened horse that will face anything and go anywheres. He's a *mad* horse for the time, that's what *he* is. So long as you see your horse's eye standing out wild and red, you know that he's half out of his senses with excitement, and likely to astonish you above a bit; but still he keeps the other half pretty cleverly, and though he *might* jump a brick wall, he *won't* run his head against it. But when you see his eye *turn blue*, then look out! Nothing will stop him now, and he'll go overhead into the deep sea as soon as look at it. You saw that gentleman as came in just now, and went out again, sudden—Mr. Naggett? A very nice gentleman he is, and quite the sportsman: dogs, greyhounds, fancy rabbits, and game-fowl, Mr. Naggett he likes to have a turn at them all, and a kind friend he's been to me besides—we'll drink his health, sir, if you please. Well, sir, Mr. Naggett owned a well-bred, raking-looking sort of mare about two years ago, that he was uncommon sweet upon, but somehow he never could do much good with her. Tried her hunting, but she was a sight too rash and violent for that; then he thought he'd make a hack of her; beautiful action she had, stepped away like a cat on hot bricks; but she was so unaccountable nervous, he couldn't get her along the roads at all, if there was much traffic, on market-days and such-like. At last he comes to me in this very shop where we're sitting now. 'Tips,' says he, 'what'll you have to drink? I have been thinking about 'Fancy-Girl,'' says he. You see we called her Fancy-Girl on account of her skittish ways. 'I'm afraid I'll have to put her in harness.' 'Better not, master,' says I; 'them Fancy-Girls is bad enough without putting them in traces, a-purpose to kick over.' 'You're a old woman,' says he; 'you send for her first thing to-morrow morning, and break her nicely for me, single and double harness, teach her to be generally useful, make tea, and wait at table if required.' I didn't like the job, but trade's trade, and if your own brother's a undertaker, why he can't refuse to measure you for a coffin; so the mare came home, and we had her in the break alongside of a steady one afore the week was out.

"Well, sir, I took uncommon pains with 'The Girl' as we called her, uncommon to be sure! I drove her in double harness, and I drove her in single, and I was as gentle as a lady with her, and as quiet as a mouse. Somehow I knew she'd play me a trick afore we'd done, and I never let any one touch her but myself.

"One afternoon Mr. Naggett he comes up to my place and wants to see the Girl in harness, and to drive her himself. I told him it wouldn't be safe, not yet, at no price; but Mr. Naggett he'd been a-drinking, for things had gone cross at home, and he wouldn't be satisfied without a drive. Well, I got him set down to take a bit of dinner with me at my place (it's a poor place, sir, for gentlemen like you, but you're heartily welcome when you are passing that way), and he sent out for some brandy, and made himself quite comfortable. After he'd smoked a pipe or two, I tried to persuade him to go home. 'Home!' says he, 'I aint going home for a fortnight! while Mrs. Naggett's blowing off *her* steam, I'm a-getting *mine* up,' says he; 'and if I don't have a jolly good spree this week and the next, I'm a Scotchman!' says he, 'and that's all about it!'

"So we went into the stables, and had the Girl stripped; and at last, if it was only to content him, I was forced to put her into the trap, and take him out for a drive; but I got him to promise he wouldn't lay a finger on the reins, 'for,' says I, 'if anything *should* happen,' says I, 'without doubt Mrs. N. will cast it up to you, as you should have taken her advice and stayed at home.' He's not an obstinate gentleman, Mr. Naggett, and this convinced him at once.

"The Girl went kindly enough for the first half-mile, and

I wanted to turn back and go home afore worse came of it; but Mr. Naggett says, 'We'll just go down to the Silver Bells at Willow-tree, take a pint of purl, and come back to tea; so, as it's a good wide road and not much frequented, I put the whip in the bucket, and drove steadily on.

"Well, sir, as luck would have it, we hadn't gone a mile, before we came to some chaps at the roadside, cutting down a tree. There isn't many trees along that line, and I wished there was none, or else they'd leave them all standing. Them countrymen isn't over cute, and though I got by as quick as ever I could, the tree fell with a crash close behind us. The Girl gave a jump, that I thought would have taken her clean out of her harness, and away she bolted like a frightened stag. Bless ye! I'd no more power over her than a baby. There was a hill to go down a few rods ahead. I says to Mr. Naggett, says I, 'Hold on, master; when we get to the old Barn, the trap'll run on to the Girl, and we'll be kicked out, so look for a soft place!' Mr. Naggett didn't seem to care about arguing the point, but he swore awful.

"It soon came off, sir. The Girl wasn't going to keep us waiting. A shy at a heap of stones took us off the road, and the next stride brought us into the fence. At the pace we were going, Mr. Naggett shot clean over my head into a wheat-field, and got up quite sober and none the worse, but he had to destroy the Girl; and as for me, why the trap, you see, unfortunately turned on to me, and I broke three ribs and my collar-bone, put out my wrist, lost two-and-seven-pence out of my breeches-pocket, and had a concussion of the brain. But it might have been worse! Here's Mr. Naggett coming back to speak for himself, and I wish you good evening, sir."

CHAPTER III.

MR. NAGGETT.

As Tips took his departure, with a respectful inclination to myself, and a most polite bow to Miss Lushington, I observed that lady to adjust her shining locks, as it were mechanically, in obvious expectation of accustomed homage; and indeed ere I had sufficiently admired the attitude in which she performed this graceful movement, a fresh arrival swaggered into the bar, in as different a manner as possible from the modest entrance of his predecessor, Mr. Tips.

This gentleman, or perhaps the abbreviation *gent* would convey more distinctly the exterior of the individual thus designated—this *gent*, then, was a personage of dashing appearance, dressed in the style which the present age denominates "loud," and which presents, as far as the wearer's ingenuity will admit, a combination of extreme splendour, with a decided tendency to the sports of the field. I have remarked such a peculiarity of costume in several individuals, less distinguished for their general good sense and respectability than for a strong and somewhat perverted inclination in favour of dog-fighting, pigeon-shooting, excessive trotting against time, the pitting of game-fowl in deadly conflict armed with artificial spurs, and even the patronage of those human combats in which such profound secrecy is always preserved, and to witness which it is indispensable to be possessed of that mysterious passport termed by *Bell's Life* "the office."

Mr. Naggett, then, the well-known sporting butcher of the adjacent town of Waterborough, was turned out from top to toe exactly as a well-known sporting butcher ought to be. When he removed his low-crowned, close-shaved hat, and disclosed his abundance of crisp, short-curling flaxen hair, surmounting an extremely ruddy face with bright-blue eyes, good features, and the whitest of teeth, I could easily imagine that the respectful admiration of so well-looking an individual was an acceptable compliment even to Miss L. His fawn-coloured whiskers, of which he possessed a great abundance, were trained carefully to the very corners of his mouth, from which they descended in those seductive semi-circles that are seen to their highest advantage in the commercial-room. Scorning the delusion of moustaches, Mr. Naggett rested a stronger claim to admiration on the brilliancy of his blue-satin neckcloth, which, worn without shirt-collar, and ornamented by an enormous pin modelled to represent the head of the present Champion of England in massive mosaic gold, irresistibly attracted the eye of the beholder, while it dazzled alike his fancy and his judgment. From the buttons of his waistcoat, scarlet cloth with a binding of gold thread, not unlike those of Lord M——'s footmen, or indeed of the gallant officers on the staff of the British army, depended a massive watch-chain in the form of a curb, life-size, if I may use the expression, and hung with many ornaments, of which a death's head as big as a walnut, and a strike-a-light box, were perhaps the smallest and least conspicuous. Mr. Naggett's coat was light-blue, very much off his person, and very short in the tails; his trousers were of drab, considerably tighter than is customary in these days of easy fitting; and his Wellington boots were thick, clumsy, and badly cleaned. He wore rings, but no gloves, and his hands were hardly so well washed as might have been desired.

Such was the man who now swaggered, with a good deal of noisy assumption, into the bar. Removing his hat with easy familiarity to Miss Lushington, he nodded a patronizing "Servant, sir," to myself, and then producing what he was pleased to call "a weed" from a leathern case the size of a portmanteau, proceeded to smoke, and drink the port-wine negus that had been kept hot for him, with a great appearance of comfort and gratification. The man had an air of rude health and bodily vigour about him, that was especially provoking to a cripple like myself. Though short and fleshy, his figure was round-made and strong, whilst the clearness of his eye and the colour in his cheek denoted an unimpaired digestion, and a circulation, to which languor, blue-devils, and dyspepsia were unknown. There are some people in whose constitutions brandy-and-water and cigars seem to assimilate with the vital functions, and turn to health and strength. "They go all at once," says the valetudinarian, and this may be true enough; nevertheless, I have seen many of these enviable *bons-vivants* go for a very long time.

Notwithstanding the freedom of his manners, his brilliant attire and sporting exterior, I did not much admire Mr. Naggett. These instincts, prejudices—call them what you will—of likes and dislikes are oftener right than we suppose; and when I came to learn the antecedents of the sporting butcher, as in such a gossiping place as Soakington I was not long in doing, I was even less prepossessed in his favour than at first.

Mr. Naggett had begun life as the only son of a respectable tenant-farmer in the neighbourhood of Soakington. As a boy at a forty-pound school, he had distinguished himself less in mathematics, classics, and the use of the globes, than in such games of skill or chance as enabled him to get the better of his companions, to the increasing of his own stores in marbles, pocket-money, and what not. He smoked a short pipe in the playground, ate lollypops during school-hours, and smuggled shrub into the dormitory. When the master had him up for any of these offences, he was notorious for arguing the point, and comported himself on all disputed questions of discipline, like that troublesome mutineer who is called in the army and navy "a lawyer." Unlike this individual however, he took his punishment without wincing, and this Spartan quality made amends in the opinion of his schoolfellows for a good many shady tricks and unenviable qualities. The lad could use his fists too, an accomplishment he had learnt from an old poaching labourer who worked on his father's farm; and although he took care never to match himself with any boy whom he could not conquer pretty easily, his prowess in this line gained him immunity for a good many little peccadilloes and infringements of the schoolboy's code of honour, which is exceedingly stringent as far as it goes.

When young Naggett's education was supposed to be completed, and he came home to live with his father as a lad of sixteen, there was not probably a more finished young blackguard to be found within a circle of fifty miles. The old man tried hard to make him work, but it was hopeless; whilst at races, fairs, village feasts, anything in the shape of a junketing, he was safe to attend and safe to get into mischief. Then he always kept two or three greyhounds, much to the disgust of the Earl of Castle-Cropper, his father's landlord; and though he generally had a pretty good nag of the old man's to ride when he chose, he never won the Earl's respect by any display of daring in the field. Young Naggett's heart was not in the right place to ride well over a country, and although he liked the excitement and display of hunting, it was not for the sake of the sport that he attended at the covert-side.

His father died the year his son came of age, and the just old Earl, though much against the grain, on his usual principle let the latter continue the farm. Then began a career of extravagance that necessarily ran itself out in a brief space of time. Late breakfasts, silver forks, six-o'clock dinners, port, sherry, and punch till all the hours of the night, with three or four riding-horses in the stable, and a box of cigars always open in the hall, made Apple-tree Farm the most popular resort in the neighbourhood for every "good-for-nothing" in the country-side. This style of living went on for eighteen months. Then came a bad harvest, the failure of a county bank, and a sale at the farm, with Richard Naggett's name amongst the list of bankrupts, and a loss to the Earl of Castle-Cropper of more than he cared to think about. Nevertheless, his old landlord never quite turned his back on his tenant, and therefore we may fairly suppose that, beyond reckless imprudence, there was nothing tangible against the latter, and that in the main, and when confronted with a Waterborough lawyer, he acted what is called "on the square."

After this crisis, young Naggett was not much heard of, for some time. There *was* indeed an ugly poaching story in which the Earl was supposed to have dealt very leniently with the offender in consideration of certain old associations, and which, if possible, increased that nobleman's popularity, to the detriment of the culprit he had screened; and there was likewise a very disagreeable show-up on Waterborough race-course in regard to a horse called Cat's Cradle, who was entered, weighted, and described wrong for the Tally-ho Stakes, and then most indubitably pulled by young Naggett, riding as a tenant-farmer, without occupying one foot of land. There is a horse-pond at the end of the course, and it was only the good-nature of some of the townspeople, and the excitement created at the same moment by the detection of a *maladroit* pickpocket, that saved the adventurous jockey from involuntary immersion therein.

The next that was heard of our friend was his occupation of a stool as a copying clerk in an attorney's office, and from that stool he dated his subsequent rise in life. At first it was a gloomy change for the young farmer and sportsman, to sit at a desk copying law parchments, accustomed as he had hitherto been to the free open air and out-of-door pursuits, which, notwithstanding his occasional dissipations, had constituted his every-day life. Old Nobbler, too, was a pretty tight hand, and although he hugely respected the astute qualities of his pupil, that very good opinion made him look pretty sharply after him, and keep him very close to his work. Nevertheless Old Nobbler was not a bad fellow on the whole; and as he generally had a good horse in his stable, and was getting too short-winded to ride much himself, he would occasionally give his new pupil a mount with the hounds, enjoining him, somewhat unnecessarily, not to rush into needless danger, and if he *should* see any gentleman rather *sweet* upon the nag, why not to disappoint him, if he could help it.

Few men were better qualified to ride a horse *to sell* than Dick Naggett. He had good hands, great caution, and an instinctive knowledge of a customer. His excessive regard for his own neck ensured him from getting into needless difficulties; and as he was never forward in a run, but always conspicuous at a check, his horse obtained a reputation for stoutness and safety, which he had not earned by going fairly over a country in the line of hounds. There is a great art in riding hunters for sale, quite different from the straightforward science. It is not the boldest and most conspicuous horseman who can obtain the longest prices for the animals that carry him so brilliantly; the world is very suspicious. Men have an unaccountable objection to buying a horse they know anything about. Besides which, the hunter that has been ridden fairly, however good he may be, *must* occasionally have been seen in difficulties. It is impossible to cross a severe line of fences, at a good pace, and in the front rank, without an occasional mishap. A second Lottery may find an unexpected trap on the further side of a fence, which no exertion can clear, and another Eclipse might be blown in deep ground, if rattled along close to a pack of high-bred fox-hounds on a good scenting morning; then, when it comes to a question of buying, the purchaser is good-naturedly warned by half-a-dozen officious friends, each of whom has probably something of his own in the stall that he wants to get rid of, and that he thinks would suit him better. One considers the intended purchase very much over-rated; another saw him refuse some rails in a corner; a third heard he was down at the thick fence coming out of the wood; and a fourth has been informed that he was in *difficulties* when they killed their fox, and could not have gone on another half-mile. Like Cæsar's wife, a hunter must be above suspicion; so the alarmed purchaser goes and buys a soft bay horse from a dealer, of which mediocre animal nobody knows either good or evil—a beast that nobody has ever yet liked well enough either to "show him up," or to give him a chance of putting his rider down. But a wary salesman knows better than to keep a good place when he has got it. Whilst his horse is fresh he flourishes away over a few fences, the larger the better, for all England to look on and admire, knowing quite well that, in the hurry and confusion of a run, he can decline when he pleases, and turn up again at the first check in a conspicuous position, as if he had been in front the whole time. The very few that could tell anything about it have probably been so much occupied, and so full of their own performances, that they do not know whether he was in their neighbourhood or not; whilst the general public in the hunting-field, like the general public everywhere else, are quite satisfied, if he is only loud enough and positive enough, to take a man's assurances about himself on trust.

Now, Dick Naggett could do the selling business, especially the *talking* part of it, to admiration. Turning out in extremely neat attire, and with some article of dress, either coat, neckcloth, or hat, peculiarly conspicuous, he could not be overlooked, and whilst careful never to ask his horse to do more than the animal could handsomely accomplish, he at the same time gave a customer such glowing descriptions of its prowess, that he sold more than one very moderate hunter of Old Nobbler's for about twice its value, and three times what the lawyer had given for it.

On these emergencies, too, Dick thought proper to affect the townsman, and sink the agriculturist altogether—a propensity which elicited on one occasion from Lord Castle-Cropper the only joke that reserved nobleman was ever known to perpetrate. Dick was holding forth, as usual at the covert-side, on the merits of the horse he was riding, and the silent Earl emerging from the recesses of Deepdale Wood, which had just been drawn blank, and followed by old Potiphar, a solemn badger-pied hound, not entirely unlike his Lordship in the face, paused to listen to the conversation.

"I'm only asking a hundred and seventy for him," said Dick; "he's the cheapest horse out to-day. I'll appeal to my Lord if he isn't."

Lord Castle-Cropper ran his eye over the animal. "I could have bought him this time last year for that money exactly," replied he, "barring the hundred."

"Oh! but all stock has risen since then," retorted Dick, loud and unabashed, "cent. per cent. I should say—sheep, cows, poultry, guinea-pigs, and fancy rabbits!"

The silent Earl was one of those provoking people who, always sticking to facts, always seem to have them, so to speak, at their fingers' ends.

"I can only tell you, Mr. Naggett," said his Lordship, "that I am glad to take now two-thirds of the price I paid six months back for all kinds of stock. I am a farmer myself, as perhaps you know."

Dick was impudence personified. "Then you use us townspeople precious hard, my Lord," said he. "A nice price you farmers make us pay for our mutton."

"I think you lawyers make us pay a good deal dearer *for the skins*," retorted his Lordship; and although he never moved a muscle of his own countenance, the bystanders raised such a shout of laughter as made old Potiphar erect his ears and bristles, thinking a fox must have been viewed away, and as shut up Dick Naggett for the next ten minutes at least, after which he recovered himself completely, and sold his horse for a trifle less than he asked, before the day was out.

Now, Old Nobbler had a daughter, like Shylock, and Jephthah, and Virginius, and many other doting old gentlemen. Of course he was very fond of the girl, and she did with him pretty much as she liked. Well, "'tis an old tale and often told;" it was not likely that Barbara Nobbler, in all the flush of eighteen summers, could abide constantly under the same roof with Dick Naggett, and remain insensible to his attractions. The lady was a swarthy bouncing *brunette*, cherry-lipped, bright-eyed, heavy-handed, and with a foot and ankle of the mill-post order, such as seldom belong to a good mover. Nevertheless, she was a healthy vigorous girl, with a quick temper, and a good heart. It was natural that she should plunge at once chin-deep in love with rosy, trim, curly-headed, flaxen-haired Dick Naggett. Old Nobbler would not *hear* of the match, shut Barbara up in her room, and turned Dick off the stool in the office, and worse than that, out of the pig-skin in the saddle-room. There was a dreadful blow-up in the house. The father had a fit of the gout; the daughter was seen dissolved in tears; and the lover, looking trimmer, rosier, and saucier than ever, was observed to take tea, two days running, with Mrs. Furbelow, the dress-maker, a widow of a certain calibre, over the way.

Flirtations, however, in all classes of life, may have been carried on so far that it is better for all parties that they should not be interrupted. Old Nobbler, a man not without legal experience, was prevailed on to listen to reason, and an early wedding was the result, which placed Mr. Naggett's head once more above water, and indeed put him in immediate possession of a little capital, with the prospective reversion of a little more.

It was in consequence of this windfall that Mr. Naggett embarked on the very flourishing business that he had conducted for some years, at the period when I made his acquaintance,—a business that, somehow or another, led him into all sorts of places where you would have supposed there was neither time nor opportunity for the purchase and sale of meat. It conducted him to Epsom annually, at the Metropolitan Spring Meeting, and required his punctual return, for the Derby and Oaks. It released him from Ascot, probably in consequence of the hot weather, and swarms of flies prevalent in the month of June, but imperatively demanded his attendance in Yorkshire, and twice or thrice within a reasonable distance of Cambridge during the autumn months. In its prosecution he was compelled, at great personal risk and inconvenience, to take an expensive ticket by the very identical train that bore the invincible Tom Sayers down the line to battle with his gallant antagonist; and in order to do it thorough justice, he has often been detained from his own home till the small hours of the morning, and compelled to return fragrant with the combined odours of alcohol and tobacco; nor does it appear that this mysterious business can remain established on a secure basis, apart from the assistance of those agreeable stimulants.

Why it should necessitate, as it seems to do, the proprietorship of a half-bred stallion, three pointers, an Angola cat, the smallest terrier, and the largest mastiff I ever saw, one cockatoo, and a dozen Cochin-China fowls, is more than I can take upon me to expound. Probably Mrs. Naggett knows; for she has repeatedly demanded, not without high words, an explanation of its mysterious intricacies.

I should not say, from all I have heard, that Mr. Naggett is a domestic man. The habitual wearing of top-boots, combined with fancy waistcoats, I believe to be inimical to the fireside qualities. Although there are two or three

Naggetts, with dark eyes like their mother, and flaxen curls like their father, to be seen playing at hide-and-seek amongst the grove of dead pigs and sheep that pervade the premises, and Mr. N. seems to notice and be fond of the urchins, yet loud altercations are often to be heard in his private residence behind the slaughter-house, and Mrs. N.'s dark eyes are not always undimmed by tears. Fame, however, whose hundred tongues are no less ubiquitous at Waterborough than elsewhere, does not scruple to intimate that the butcher's lady is quite able to "hold her own;" and gossips have been heard to affirm, with dark and threatening glances at their own liege lords the while, that "though she has been so put upon, poor dear, she can give him as good as he brings, and quite right too." The inference is obvious, the moral doubtless not without its effect.

It was not in my nature to fraternize very cordially with a gentleman of Mr. Naggett's superior qualities. I am bound, nevertheless, to admit, that his advances towards myself were cordial, not to say familiar in the extreme. The undisguised admiration, however, with which Miss Lushington regarded his every movement, and the terms of intimacy on which he obviously stood with that decorous lady, may have prejudiced me somewhat against him There is a class of men, however, I have often observed, and I say it in justice to Miss Lushington, with whom the genus Barmaid seems to possess some mysterious affinity. As Eastern poets feign that there is a certain bird to which the tree involuntarily bends its branches, and the flower opens its petals, so I am convinced there is a description of individual who is looked on with peculiar favour by actresses, barmaids, hostesses, and other ladies whose avocations bring them much into the presence of a discerning public. These favourites of the sex are generally remarkable for exuberance of spirits, command of language, a vivid freshness of complexion, and general freedom of manner. They are loud in assumption, and great on all topics of political or public interest; also prone to plunge into quarrels, from which they invariably extricate themselves without recourse to ulterior measures. His female admirers, in describing such a one, generally sum up their catalogue of his merits by vowing that he is "very free in company, and *quite the gentleman.*"

Mr. Naggett, stirring the fire with his boot, and winking facetiously on Miss Lushington, as he drank her health in his hot negus, and asked her whether she had ordered her wedding-bonnet yet, obligingly remarked, that "it was a cold night, and he was sorry to see my arm in a sling;" also "that he had heard of my accident, and hoped it wouldn't be long before I *over-got* it," with which friendly wish, expressed in a compound verb, he finished his negus, and ordered some more, calling Miss L. "my dear," unblushingly, to my excessive disgust. He then drew his chair to the fire, expressed his astonishment that Tips had gone to "perch," as he called it, and proceeded to make himself agreeable.

"A nasty fall, sir, yours must have been, as I understand," said he, "and it's well as it wasn't worse. You've a nice-ish team standing here, but you'll excuse *me*, sir, they're not exactly the *class* of horse for a gentleman like you to ride. I've been fond of horses all my life, from a boy, I may say, and I'm forty years of age now : forty years of age, though perhaps you wouldn't think it, and in that time I've learnt to keep my eyes open. Now, sir, you don't ride so very light, I'll be bound to say."

I am a little touchy about my weight, I confess. I believe

most men are, the heavy ones liking to be thought lighter, and the light ones heavier than they really are. " I ride thirteen stone," I replied. " Thirteen stone, to a pound ; I weigh every day of my life, and I haven't varied since I was five-and-twenty."

" Thirteen stone ! indeed, sir !" replied Mr. Naggett, running his eye, as I thought, in a very free-and-easy manner over my proportions. " Well, I shouldn't have thought it. But you're thick, sir ; thick and a *little* fleshy. Now, your nags is hardly thirteen-stoners, sir—not in a country like this ; I'm sure you must agree with me ? "

Speechless with indignation, I seized the poker and split —not Mr. Naggett's head, but a burning coal in the very centre of the grate, without further reply. This coolest of butchers proceeded unhesitatingly :—

" It's a pity to see a gentleman undermounted, 'specially in a country like this : so dangerous too ! Why, sir, all the worst falls as I've known take place down here in our Soakington district, have been entirely owing to gentlemen riding horses below their weight. There was Squire Overend, only last season, got a little thorough-bred weed he called Happy Joe, as he swore nothing could touch. No more they couldn't when the ground was light ; but look what happened. There came a splash of wet, and the ground up to our girths, just as we've got it now, and likely to have it for the next six months ; and Happy Joe, he turns a complete somersault over a stile the Squire puts him at, and falls on to his rider with a squelch, breaking the cantle of his own saddle into shivers, and inflicting such severe internal injuries on Squire Overend, that he has never been out hunting since, and all from obstinacy—sheer obstinacy, I call it ; for I told the Squire myself how it would be, from the first."

Somewhat discouraged, I admit, by the ghastly catastrophe of Mr. Overend, I began to think it was just possible that Apple Jack might not be so good as he looked, and that perhaps it might be wise to purchase a horse or two more accustomed to the country, and with a little more power.

Mr. Naggett, who never took his clear blue eyes off my face, seemed to read my thoughts intuitively, and proceeded with more than usual volubility:—

"There's a friend of mine, sir, got a horse, that I should say was just about your mark, and would carry you as I can see you *like* to be carried. I had him in price all last season myself, but money couldn't buy him then; for my friend he was an out-and-out sporting chap, and could *ride* too! But he's been and got married since, and gone to live in Drury Lane for good and all; so he's no more use for a hunter now, than a cow has for a side-pocket, or a pig for a frilled-shirt. What a horse he is, to be sure!—dark brown, tan muzzle, not a speck of white about him; up to fourteen stone; by Ratcatcher, out of Sly Puss by Mousetrap, and Mousetrap, you remember, was by Grimalkin, and the sire of Whittington, Cat's-cradle, and a many good ones. I know all about him, and have done since he was a foal. My friend he bought him off of the farmer that bred him."

"Why, Ratcatcher has been covering at the Castle for years," I replied, rather congratulating myself upon having Mr. Naggett "out;" "and Sly Puss never belonged to anybody but the Earl!"

"Well, sir," retorted he, "and that's exactly the farmer I mean. A very respectable farmer I call him too, and one that farms *his own land*, which is more than can be said for a good many of them. Talk of jumping, I wish you could only see this nag jump!"

There is something about the discussion of horseflesh in front of a good fire, with a cigar in his mouth, that disposes a man unaccountably *to buy*. Knowing I couldn't hunt for six weeks, what did I want with another horse?

"Why should I not?" I rashly inquired. "I might look at him, at any rate. Where is he to be seen?"

"Well, sir, he's at my place now," replied Mr. Naggett, adding, with an air of charming frankness, "The fact is, I've got him to keep for my friend, who is a cousin of my wife's, and I've got the riding of him for his corn. If it wasn't that my business won't allow me to hunt as much as I should like, I'd buy him myself, particularly considering the price."

"What does he ask?" I inquired, walking as it were open-eyed into the pitfall prepared for me.

Mr. Naggett looked me over from top to toe, as if I had been a prize ox. Probably he was making a mental computation of my soft-headedness. I am afraid I looked very much like a fool, for he replied boldly—

"One hundred and twenty sovereigns; take him as he stands; no questions asked; and dirt-cheap at the money."

"How old is he?" was naturally my next inquiry. "Is he quiet to ride?" I added; "and thoroughly temperate with hounds? Also, is he fit to go at present? and does your wife's cousin warrant him sound?"

"Come up and see him, sir! Come up and see him!" was the only reply Mr. Naggett could be brought to give. "My business will take me away all to-morrow and the next day; but say Saturday, sir. You know my little place. Any time on Saturday I shall be at your service, and the horse too. Ride him, lark him, have him galloped, see him jump! If you can get him into a difficulty, I'll *give* him to you—at least my wife's cousin will. You may take my word for it, that if once you lay your leg over him, he'll never go out of your stable again!"

And Mr. Naggett, suddenly remembering a very particular engagement, vanished incontinently, after wishing me an exceedingly civil "good-night."

CHAPTER IV

TOM TURNBULL.

THE hasty departure of Mr. Naggett seemed to produce a corresponding effect of drowsiness on Miss Lushington— an unusual weakness, to which I am bound to admit she was by no means subject. Like the Roman vestals, she never seemed tempted to quit her post, nor desirous of flinching from the duty of keeping alive the sacred fire, represented in her sanctuary by a blazing heap of coals through the day, and a jet of gas continually flaring from a pipe above the tap during the small hours towards morning. Now, however, she yawned most unreservedly, and hinted freely on the propriety of "shutting up for the night." Perhaps, after the departure of the flash butcher, everything seemed by comparison tame and insipid. As I shall not have occasion to refer to Mr. Naggett again, I may here mention that as soon as I was able to move about, I *did* go to inspect the famous horse by Ratcatcher, out of Sly Puss by Mousetrap, and found him a good-looking animal enough,—large, strong, well-bred, and a fine goer, with many hunting-like qualities about him; but, on the other hand, by no means likely to emerge blameless from the ordeal of a veterinary surgeon's examination, being indeed a little suspicious in one eye, very queer about the hocks, and with a curious catch in his windpipe, which Mr. Nagget triumphantly quoted as a proof of the excellence of his lungs, but which to my fancy seemed uncommonly like the respiration of a prospective whistler.

I need hardly observe that I declined the proprietorship of this high-bred animal upon any terms whatever, although I was offered him as a *swap*, as a contingent reversion, and as a temporary investment: nay, so anxious was Mr. Naggett to accommodate me, and so liberal in his professions, that I was compelled to decline very strenuously the purchase of him at a considerable reduction on his original price, with half the money down, and my bill at three months for the remainder.

Though I have often seen Mr. Naggett in the hunting-field, and have partaken of many excellent joints, both prime beef and Southdown mutton, of his purveying, this was the conclusion of my dealings with him in horseflesh, and the termination of our somewhat unexpected intimacy.

"Drat it!" exclaimed Miss Lushington, as I lit a bedroom candle, and she herself prepared to collect her different effects, such as keys, scissors, workbox, and thimble, preparatory to retiring for the night, "it's never over here, it isn't! One down, t'other come on! I did think I'd have had my hair in curl-papers to-night before one o'clock," she added coquettishly, smoothing down the glossy bands that encircled her fair forehead; "but goodness gracious me! Old friends is welcome in season and out of season! If it isn't Mr. Turnbull!"

So warm a greeting, from a lady of Miss Lushington's self-control, impelled me to put down my chamber-candlestick and study with some curiosity the manners and appearance of the new arrival. On his first entrance he was so completely enshrouded and enveloped in a top-coat, a shawl handkerchief, and a round low-crowned hat, that I could perceive nothing of him but his boots. These, however, were sufficiently characteristic. Strong, round-toed, and with deep mahogany tops, fastened up round the knee with the old-fashioned string, they harmonized well with the double-Bedford-cord breeches, of which they formed the appropriate termination. As their owner, unwinding himself gradually from the coils of his shawl, and emerging from his drab top-coat, stood at last conspicuous in the full glare of the gas-light, I could not help thinking that a man might travel through a long summer's day, without meeting so fine a specimen of the real British yeoman as Mr. Turnbull.

I like the round-cropped bullet-head that you never see out of our own little island. I like the fresh healthy colour, that deepens, instead of fading, with age, and the burly thick-set form, square and substantial as a tower, deriving its solid proportions from a good English ancestry, " men of mould," since the days of Robin Hood, and its vigour from good English beef and floods of nut-brown ale. These are the sort of men that kept the green wood in merry Nottinghamshire, and bore back the chivalry of Europe at Agincourt, Crecy, and Poitiers. These are the sort of men that would turn the tide of an invasion to-day, shoulder to shoulder in their dim grey ranks, handling the rifle as deftly as their fathers did the bow, yet impatient somewhat of long-bowls at five or six hundred yards, and longing withal to get to close quarters and try conclusions with the bayonet. When it comes to clash of steel, depend upon it "the weakest will go to the wall."

Five foot ten in his stockings; fourteen stone, without an ounce of superfluous flesh upon his ribs; built in the mould of a Hercules, with a ruddy-brown complexion and dark crisp hair, short, close curling and grizzled about the temples, for our friend is nearer fifty than forty, Tom Turnbull, as he is called at every fair, market, and cattle-show in three counties, nods good-humouredly to Miss Lushington, and gives a backward scrape of his foot in deference to myself.

"Glass of strong ale, if you please, Miss," says he, in cordial cheery tones, and holding it up to the light, tosses off the clear sparkling beverage, with a sigh of intense satisfaction. No wonder. Since a market dinner at one o'clock, Tom Turnbull has ridden the best part of thirty miles. He has nine more to go before he reaches Apple-tree Farm, where he has succeeded Mr. Naggett (what a contrast!), and he will be out to-morrow morning at daybreak, looking after the ploughs, and taking perhaps a vigorous spell between the stilts himself. There is a good animal, however, waiting for him at the door, submitting impatiently to the caresses of the admiring ostler, and having had her own suck of gruel, looking wistfully round for her master, who she knows is never very long having a suck of *his*.

If you want to be thoroughly acquainted with your horse, to inspire him with that unreserved confidence which the animal is certainly capable of feeling in his master, ride him at night. An hour in the dark draws the bond of partnership tighter than a day in the sunshine. When you have made a journey or two together over bad roads, without a moon, you learn to depend upon each other thoroughly, and the animal will answer your hand and bend to your caresses with a willing promptitude he would never acquire by daylight. Tom Turnbull spends many an hour of darkness in the saddle, and except on one occasion when he took a short cut over some low fences, and tumbled neck-and-crop into an open culvert, breaking his own head and his horse's neck, has never met with what he calls an accident.

I fancy the old-fashioned highwaymen knew more about the sagacity and powers of their horses than any more respectable sportsmen of the modern times. They rode, as their business obliged them, continually by night; and the distances they accomplished were so marvellous as to be incredible, had they not been attested by the most unimpeachable of evidence in the witness-box. Horses can see wonderfully well in the dark, and no doubt a man who was riding against time for an *alibi*, with so heavy a stake as his own life depending on his success, would be tolerably venturesome in his efforts to "get forward;" but yet, under the most favourable circumstances, it cannot but have proved haphazard work, jumping fences by moonlight; and what a good mare must poor Black Bess have been, when she started fresh on the North road for her journey to York!

In this one respect Tom Turnbull resembles Dick Turpin; the former, too, has a mare he rides long journeys by night, and for whose merits and reputation he entertains the profoundest respect. She is a lengthy, low, wiry, bay mare, with short flat legs, clean and hard as iron. She rejoices in a lean, game head, with a curl not unlike a sneer above her nostrils, and a wild eye; also, the long, fine, and rather lop ears, which belong to her high-born family. In the breeding of all stock Mr. Turnbull knows what he is about. If he wants a promising foal that shall grow into a couple of hundred pounds at five years old, he does not put an old worn-out mare, whose constitution and physical qualities are exhausted by hard work, to a fashionable stallion, and calmly expect the produce to excel the united excellencies of sire and dam in the best days of both. On the contrary, he begins, as we humbly opine, at the right end. He gets a foal or two out of the young fresh mare before she commences work, instead of after she is incapable of it. The dam's functions are then in their highest state of vigour and redundance; nor is it possible but that this must materially enhance the value of her offspring. The infant is all the better, and the mother none the worse.

The Arabs, who are by no means behind-hand in their knowledge of horses, and whose every-day wants necessitate their bringing the animal to its highest state of perfection, at least as regards their own purposes, have established, as an incontestable maxim, that while the colt inherits "make and shape" from his sire, his inner qualities—if we may so call them—his mettle, speed, temper, and powers of endurance, come from his dam. None of us who have taken an interest in the rearing of young horses can have failed to observe the strong outward resemblance they usually bear to their sires. "How like the old horse!" is a remark one hears every day when looking at some dark-brown flyer by The Dutchman, or some commanding animal with extraordinary power and substance by Cotherstone; but we seldom see any striking resemblance to the dam, although, when some veteran sportsman is relating the feats of the "best he ever had in his life," whether hunter, hack, or trotter, he generally winds up with the observation, "He was as good as the old mare!" Now, the Arab ought to be a capital judge, and though by no means despising speed, endurance is the quality which he most values in his horse, and puts most frequently to the test. It is no unusual feat for an Arab to ride a hundred miles a day for four days together, through the desert, carrying with him (no trifling addition to his own weight) the water that is to last him throughout his journeys, also the forage that must supply his steed, and the handful or two of pressed dates that shall serve to keep the rider alive till he reaches his destination. Now we have nothing of this sort in England, and, since the introduction of railroads, have indeed small occasion to prove the lasting qualities of our horses. The covert-hack of the present day is the animal that is required to prove his superiority to his stable companions, for he *may* be asked, by a master who likes to get his beauty-sleep after eight A.M., to do his fifteen miles, with as many stone on his back, in five minutes over the hour; and this is exceedingly good going. Still, a summer's day's journey of eighty or ninety miles, with only one stoppage to bait for an hour or two, such as used to be frequently accomplished by jockeys and other locomotive individuals on the old-fashioned hackney of the last century, was a very different matter, and required in the performer not only perfect soundness of limbs and constitution, but a a very true and even style of going, that gave every point and articulation fair play, and no excess of work above its due share. Such a fault in a horse as *hitting his legs* of course would have rendered him utterly useless before two-thirds of his task was accomplished.

It is feared that we shall lose altogether the breed of animal that is capable of such performances. For many years we have been studying to acquire increased *power*, and consequently *pace*, to the disregard of *stamina*. It stands to reason that the *larger* a horse is, *cæteris paribus*, the *faster* he can go; but it does not the least follow that his size should enable him to *go on*. Doubtless the object for which we get into the saddle is *dispatch*, and ".the slows" is the worst disease our horse can be troubled with; nevertheless, there is a good old rule in mechanics which affirms "*nil violentum est perpetuum;*" and if your engine is to go with the weight and *momentum* of an express train, you must calculate on a considerable expenditure of fuel, and great wear and tear on the nuts, screws, and fittings of the whole. Now, Nature, although the neatest and most finished of workers, will not submit herself to the laws of commensuration. She will not make you a model in *inches*, and supply you with a work on a corresponding scale in *feet*. It would seem as if she only issued a certain amount of stores in the aggregate, and if you are to get more iron, she gives you less steel; you shall have plenty of coke, but in return she stints you in oil. So, if the living creature she turns out for you on your estimate is to be very magnificent in its proportions, the chances are that it will either fail in activity, or be deficient in endurance.

We have now established half-mile races for our two-year-olds, as, with some few exceptions, the most important events of our English turf—our very Derbys and St. Legers —are but a scramble of a dozen furlongs, with little more than the weight of a child on a *very* young horse's back. With all the forcing by which art strives to expel nature, it returns, in this instance, as Horace says, literally with a stablefork,* we cannot get an animal to its prime at three years old, who ought not to arrive at maturity till twice that age. Still we continue to breed more and more for a "turn of speed," utterly regardless of endurance, till our famous

* "Naturam expellas *furcâ*, tamen usque recurret."

English race-horses have degenerated into such galloping "weeds," that I myself heard an excellent sportsman and high authority on such matters affirm, in discussing the hounds-and-horses match, which was to have come off last October, that " he did not believe there was a horse at Newmarket that could get four miles *at all;* no, not if you trotted him every yard of the way!"

This, of course, was a jest; but, like many a random shaft pointed with a sarcasm and winged with a laugh, it struck not very far off the centre of the target. Even our hunters, too (and surely, if you want endurance in any animal alive, it is in a hunter), we are *improving*, year by year, into a sort of jumping cameleopard. Where are the strong, deep-girthed horses on short legs of thirty years ago? horses that stood just under sixteen hands, and could carry sixteen stone. Look at what people call a first-class hunter now! (and it must be admitted that, for the high price he commands in the market, he ought to be as near perfection as possible.) Look at him, as you may see him in fifty different specimens with the Pytchley or Quorn hounds, any hunting-day throughout the winter! He is a bay or a brown—if the latter, more of a chocolate than a mottled, with white about his legs and nose. He stands sixteen two at least, with much daylight underneath him. He has either a very long weak neck, with a neat head; or more often a good deal of front and throat, with a general bull-headed appearance, that conveys the idea of what sailors term "by the bows," and argues a tendency to hard pulling, which, to do him justice, he generally possesses. He has fine sloping shoulders, and can stride away in excellent form over a grass field, reaching out famously with his fore legs, which, though long, are flat, clean, and good. Somehow you are rather

T 2

disappointed with him when you get on his back. With no positive fault to find, you have yet an uncomfortable conviction that he does *not feel like it;* and, for all his commanding height, you are subjected to no irresistible temptation to "lark" him. When Mr. Coper asks you three hundred and takes "two fifty," as he calls it, alleging the scarcity of horses, the excellence of this particular specimen, his own unbounded liberality, intense respect for yourself, and every other inducement that can mitigate the painful process of affixing your name to a cheque, you seem to give him your money without exactly knowing why; but when the new purchase *stops* with you in deep ground the first good scenting day, after you have bustled him along honestly for two-and-twenty minutes, you think you *do* know why exactly; and, although you may be, and probably *are* disgusted, you cannot conscientiously admit that you are surprised.

I have not seen these sort of nags, though, in the Soakington country; I presume they all go to "The Shires;" and this brings me back, after a long digression, to Tom Turnbull and Apple-tree Farm.

There never was such a farm for coziness and comfort as that. Surrounded by an ugly though sporting-looking country, it possesses the only undulating fields for many miles round, and consequently boasts a view from a certain eminence called Ripley Rise, that commands half-a-dozen of the Earl's best fox-coverts, the distant towers of Castle-Cropper itself, and no less than seventeen church-steeples. There are stately old elms close to the dwelling-house, and a rich and plentiful orchard, from which it takes its name, adjoins a snug little walled garden, celebrated for the earliest summer fruit, and the best plums in the district—thanks to the late Mr. Naggett, a far-seeing, shrewd old agriculturist. Apple-tree Farm is a good deal better drained than most of the adjoining lands; consequently its acres of arable return a heavier produce, and its upland fields are more calculated for rearing young horses than any in the country.

Nothing gives a colt such a chance as a fine high and dry pasture, on a slope, where he can exercise himself in the practice of going up and down hill, unconsciously strengthening his hocks and acquiring liberty in his shoulders whilst he is at play.

Horses bred on uplands, too, have a far harder and sounder description of hoof than those that have been accustomed in youth to splash about in rank, marshy meadows; and, strange to say, their very coats are finer, and their whole appearance denotes higher blood than can be boasted by their own brothers, reared on lower grounds. Those who profess to be acquainted with the physiology of the horse, affirm that the produce of Arab stallions and mares, if suffered to breed in the rich wet marshes of Flanders, would, in half-a-dozen generations, without any sort of cross, and from the sheer influence of keep and climate, lose every trace of their noble origin. The Prophet himself would not recognize the dull-eyed, coarse-shaped, heavy-actioned progeny, for the lithe and fiery children of the Desert.

Here, then, Tom Turnbull breeds and rears many a good nag, taking care never to have above one or two at a time, so that sufficient attention may be devoted to the yearling, and, above all, that it may have plenty of keep.

The Arabs, to go eastward once more for our proverbs on this subject, have a saying, that "the goodness of a horse goes in at his mouth," and it is incredible by those who have not watched the result, what improvement may be made in the animal by the very simple recipe of old oats and exercise, plenty of both; indeed, of the latter, in contradistinction to *work*, a young horse can hardly have too much. It is exercise that forms his shape, strengthens his joints, hardens his limbs, produces action, and clears his wind. All the time a young one is out, he is acquiring something— either how to use his legs, or to obey his bit, or to conform his inclinations to those of his master; whilst, even should he be standing still and unemployed, he is at least learning to see and hear, accustoming himself to sights and sounds with which it is of the greatest advantage both to himself and his rider that he should be familiar. Also, it is far better for him to be breathing the cold outward air than the more luxurious atmosphere of his stable; and it is not too much to say, that a horse of three or four years old cannot be brought out too often, so long as you take care that he shall never go home the least bit fatigued.

Tom Turnbull begins handling the foals as soon as they are born. By the time they are weaned, he has accustomed them thoroughly to the halter; and although he never backs them till three years old, they have been bridled and saddled long before that period, and are so accustomed to the human form and face, and so confident no evil is intended them, that you may do almost anything you please with such willing and good-tempered pupils.

Consequently, there is none of that rearing, and plunging, and buck-jumping, which usually make the mounting of an unbroken colt such an affair of discomfort, not to say danger, to the two parties immediately concerned. By the time Tom Turnbull has hoisted his fourteen stone of manhood on to his colt's back, the pupil is quite satisfied of the *bonâ fide* nature of the whole performance, and walks away with him as quietly as any elderly gentleman's cob who comes round to the door regularly every afternoon, for the sober and digestive exercise which elderly gentlemen are apt to affect.

Tom Turnbull, though he puts a strong bridle in his mouth, then takes his young friend lightly by the head, and proceeds to ride him leisurely about, as he overlooks his farm. There are, of course, many gates to open, and the horse in learning this very essential accomplishment, receives at the same time a valuable lesson in the *moral* virtues of patience and obedience. If he sees anything to alarm him, a scarecrow, an old man pulling turnips, or a sheep-trough on its beam ends (the latter, like all inverted objects, being much dreaded by the animal), he is not whipped, and spurred, and hurried by it in a matter that agitates his nerves for the rest of the day, but is coaxed and re-assured, and persuaded gently and by degrees to examine it for himself, and so discover its innocuous nature. The next time he observes the same bugbear, he probably shies for fun, but that is a very different thing from shying for fear; and the same practice repeated will make him pass it the third or fourth time with no more notice than he would take of his own currycomb. He is by this time getting accustomed to his rider's hand, has learned to put his head down, and toss the bit about his mouth, and is beginning to feel some confidence in his own activity, and a certain pleasure in doing what he is bid.

There are short cuts on Apple-tree Farm, like every other, which lead from field to field without going round by the gate. These entail the necessity of crossing certain gaps, which are periodically made up, and gradually destroyed again as the year goes round. Here the colt takes his first lesson in fencing. He is permitted to do the job exactly in his own way, without interference from his rider, except so far as a continual pressure of his legs warns the young one that it must be done somehow. Generally, after poking his nose all over it, and smelling every twig of the adjoining hedge, he walks solemnly into the very bottom of the ditch, and emerges somewhat precipitately on the further side: then his rider pats and makes much of him, as if he had done his work in the most scientific form possible. Thus encouraged, he tries next time to improve for himself, and soon jumps it standing, without an effort. Ere he has been ridden half-a-dozen times he will trot up to any ditch about the farm, and, breaking into a canter the last stride, bound over it like a deer, perhaps giving his head a shake and his hind-quarters a hoist on landing, in sheer exuberance of spirits at the fun. In this manner he soon learns to do the fences equally well; Tom Turnbull's plan being, in his own words, as follows:—" First, little places at a walk, then at a trot, then at a canter, and then bustling of them off their legs to make them *quick*. After that, fair hunting fences the same way. To my mind, a hunter ought to jump upright places, such as walls and timber, at a slow trot; but he ought to be *able* to do them if required, at speed, not that I, for one, would ask him for that, except as a lesson. All fair fences he should do with a loose rein, at an easy canter."

But he is no theorist, my friend Mr. Turnbull. It is a treat to see him get away with the Castle-Cropper hounds on a good scenting day and in a stiff country, say for instance the Soakington Lordship. Though there is hard upon fifteen stone on his back, his horse seems to make no extra exertion, and though the rider keeps very close to the hounds, and follows no man, not even the Earl himself, he never appears to be out of a canter. How well he brings his horse (probably a five-year-old, who has done very little hunting, but has had plenty of practice, "shepherding," and consequently jumping over the farm) up to his leaps! How he screws him through the thick place under the tree, and hands him in and out of the blind double, as you would hand a lady into an outside car! When you come to the rails in the corner, which he trotted up to so quietly, and seemed to rise at with such deliberate ease, you are surprised to find a dip in front of them, a bad take-off, a ditch beyond, and a general uncompromising appearance about the timber, that makes you wish you were halfway across the next field, and "all were well."

If you mean to see the run to your own satisfaction, and belong to that numerous and respectable class of sportsmen who are unable to ride for themselves, you cannot do better than follow Tom Turnbull; and should you cross the Sludge, which in that district you will probably do more than once, you will acknowledge that it is a treat to see him get triumphantly over that obstacle where its sluggish waters are deepest, and its banks most treacherous and rotten.

But it is not for a man with a broken collar-bone and his arm in a sling, to call up such dreams of enjoyment as a quick thing across the Vale with the Castle-Cropper hounds; so I took my chamber-candlestick once more, and wishing Miss Lushington a courteous "good-night," which she returned with a gracious politeness, that would drive sleep for many an hour from the pillow of a younger and more inflammable swain, I shook Mr. Turnbull by the hand, and paused on my way to my dormitory to see him get into the saddle for his homeward ride.

"It's a very dark night," I remarked, as I watched him stuffing a well-filled note-case, the produce of his sale at to-day's market, into his breast-pocket. "I wonder you like to travel these bye-roads with all that money about you, and such a lot of 'roughs' hereabouts, always on the tramp."

Turnbull grinned, and taking me by the sound arm, pointed to the mare's head—"They've tried that on, once before, sir," said he; "and within half a mile of the Haycock. Look ye here, sir! that's the way I done 'em that time: that's the way I'll do 'em again."

Following the direction of his glance, I saw that he had run his bridle (a single snaffle) through his throat-lash, so that no part of it when he mounted would hang below the mare's neck.

"There, sir," said he; "that's the way to keep 'em at out-fighting. When they tried it on, last winter, there was a pair on 'em. One chap he run out o' the hedge on the near side, and makes a grab at the reins. He didn't catch 'em though, but he caught something else, I expect, as he wasn't looking for, right across his wrist, fit to break his arm. He sung out, I can tell you, and bolted right off without waiting for his mate. T'other had gripped my right ankle at the same time, to give me a hoist out of the saddle; but you see, sir, I knowed the trick of it, and just let my leg double up at the knee quite easy, and came down upon his head with a back-hander, from a bit of stick I had in my fist, that felled him like a bullock in the road. So I took him easy, and by that means we got the other one in a day or two, and they were both transported. So that's the reason, whenever I travel this way, I always run my reins through my throat-lash. I wish you good-night, sir, and pleasant dreams, if so be as your arm will let you sleep!"

With these words Mr. Turnbull trotted off, and I betook myself leisurely to the privacy of my own room, and the tedium of a somewhat restless couch.

CHAPTER V.

OLD IKE, THE EARTH-STOPPER.

In a day or two, with the constant attendance of my medical man, himself rather a character in his way, and the considerate cares of Miss Lushington, I was sufficiently recovered from the effects of my accident to crawl to the stable and visit those now useless animals which I had reviewed with such pride and pleasure on the first Sunday afternoon that I had taken up my quarters at Soakington. In my opinion, there are few more unsatisfactory performances than these inspections of a stud thus thrown out of work. The horses all look so blooming in their coats, so high in their condition, and altogether so fit to go, that it seems a pity that they should be disappointed of *their* hunting, and compelled to limit their energies to that exploit which is called "eating their heads off"—a feat never performed with such an appetite as during a course of enforced idleness either from frost or any other cause that stops the fascinating pursuit for which they have been bought, and summered, and got into condition. Also, on these occasions, partly from their actual fullness and vigour consequent upon losing a turn, partly from that peculiarity in the human mind which enhances the value of everything out of reach, we cannot help fancying the nags a good deal better than they are, and ourselves much more enthusiastic and skilful than we know ourselves to be, in our cooler moments, say, for instance, when mounted and at the covert-side, a fine country before us, every probability of a run, a north-east wind rather keener than agreeable, bathing our uncovered face like cold water, and a chill misgiving that last week's frost is not thoroughly out of the ground, particularly just under the fences, and that the thaw which rejoiced us so exceedingly after dinner, has only succeeded in making the surface greasy, and not in rendering it soft. Ah! if we could always feel as we do for that glorious hour from about seven to eight P.M., when we stretch our napkin-covered legs towards the cheerful fire, blazing and crackling, and sparkling into rubies, as it reflects itself in our brimming glass of Bordeaux, what good fellows we should all be! how generous, how open-hearted, and how successful in our avocations and pursuits! The process of digestion, that highly important function, when properly performed, seems to endow us with all the most admirable qualities of manhood. We become conscious that we are possessed of sagacity, courage, humour, and general benevolence. We could lend a friend a hundred pounds willingly, *if we had it*. We could go the best run that ever was seen, on the very backs of the hounds, if that was only an actual existing country, which we trace in the glowing embers, instead of a dream of fairyland, the offspring of Newcastle coal and Château Lafitte. Then how we can converse on the inexhaustible topic, of "The Horse and how to ride him!" We are never tired of laying down the law "what to jump, creep, and avoid." We do not believe we are deceiving ourselves, or our listeners, when we profess our partiality for high timber, or our proficiency and personal experience in water-jumping. We combine, in our heated imaginations, the "science of Meynell," with the courage and dexterity of the late Mr. Assheton Smith. We believe, for the nonce, in many fallacies that our better judgment has so often proved to be such by the testimony of sad experience; to wit, that "if a horse can only gallop, he is sure to jump;" that, "what one hunter can clear, another can;" that, "if a man's heart is in the right place, his horse is sure to carry him well with hounds:" and that, "large fences are the safest to ride at"—established positions which nobody thinks it worth while to dispute, laid down as they are by retired sportsmen, confirmed valetudinarians, and other non-hunting members of the community, but which to-morrow morning too clearly demonstrates to be mere after-dinner sentiments, unsafe to act upon, and in practice but a delusion and a snare.

If we were to pin our faith on what we hear, and what we read, concerning the engrossing theme of horsemanship, we should ere long be led to believe that nothing was so easy as to keep alongside of a clipping pack of fox-hounds running hard over a grass country intersected with those formidable impediments which defend such verdant districts. Poor Nimrod tells us how to get our horses into condition; Beckford, Cooke, Delmé Radcliffe, Grantley Berkeley, Smith (not Assheton), and a host of others, instruct us patiently and at considerable length, in the scientific details of our favourite amusements. The author of "Soapy Sponge" presents to our delighted view the humours and ridiculous side of the question, conveying, by means of Mr. Jorrocks's inimitable vein of absurdity, many home-truths and incontrovertible reflections; whilst last of all comes Sir Francis Head, with the brilliancy of his reputation, and the weight of his personal experience, to give the finishing touches to our education. He tells us in the simplest language, and as if it were the easiest thing in the world to do it as well as himself, how we are to saddle our horse and bridle our horse, how to dress and how to feed, how to go out in the morning and how to come at night, how to transform our hack into a hunter, and, when so metamorphosed, how to ride the astonished animal over the highest gates and the widest brooks than can be found in the midland counties of merry England; the whole performance to be achieved in a jovial off-hand style, as if it were the simplest and safest thing in the world. Now this is all very well in theory, but becomes a more complicated question when reduced to a matter of practice. It seems to me that to achieve excellence in riding to hounds, something more is required than a hard heart and a light pair of hands; that with all the advantages of courage, strength, and activity, being good horsemen, and with excellent hunters to ride, many men go out day after day, and season after season, without ever seeing a run to their own satisfaction; nay, with a certainty, unless they are piloted by some more gifted sportsman, of losing the hounds in the first three fields: A man may be as bold as Alexander, and as well mounted too, never giving less than "three figures" for his Bucephalus, and yet unless he be possessed of a peculiar knack of finding his way over a country which it is almost impossible to explain, he will invariably be left behind in a quick thing.

This knack is a sort of instinct rather than an acquirement, an intuitive sagacity, akin to that faculty by which the Red Indian, in common with other savages, takes the right direction through the pathless woods, and over the monotonous prairies of the West. We will suppose a man to be riding his own line, fairly with a pack of fox-hounds, in a country he has never seen before, with a good scent, and a fox's head set up-wind. He jumps into a field from which there are but two possible egresses, a quarter of a mile apart, the one to the right, the other to the left; he goes unhesitatingly to the former, and the hounds bend towards him almost as soon as he is clear of the obstacle which has obliged him to diverge from his line. He could not, probably, explain why he thus acted; yet he *did* it, and he was right. All through a run you will see some men gaining every turn upon the hounds, just as others lose them. This happy facility is but a modification of that which makes the difference between a bad huntsman and a good one. The latter seems to possess an intuitive knowledge of the run of a fox, independent of all extraneous accidents, such as wind, sheep, dogs, people ready to head him at every turn, and the thousand obstacles that are always present to destroy the chance of a good run—nay, even of country, for such men exhibit it in districts with which they have no acquaintance. I begin to think people are *born* sportsmen, just as they are born poets, painters, and peers of the realm. We see them in every class of life; and there is many an honest fellow who loses half a day's work, and wears out his shoe-leather, to make the best he can of his fox-hunting on foot, who, in a higher position, would have achieved a brilliant reputation in the eyes of the sporting world.

What leads me to this reflection is the glimpse I had of Miss Lushington, at the window of her sanctuary commanding the stable-yard, pouring out a wineglassful of a fluid that *looked* like water, but *smelt* like gin, and handing the same to one of the most dilapidated individuals it has ever been my fortune to encounter.

As I entered the back-door of the Haycock, he touched an extremely damaged hunting-cap, and greeted me with much cordiality. I then recognized a character with whom I could not fail to have made acquaintance, even during my short stay in the Soakington country, and whom I never heard called by any other name than "Old Ike, the Earth-stopper." As an example of what I have above alluded to —the creature in whom the sporting instinct seems fully developed, the man who must obviously have been intended by Nature for a sportsman—Old Ike deserves to have his portrait taken, more especially as the office he fills so well is the only one in which he could have found his appropriate place in the world.

He is a tough, spare old man, very lean and very wrinkled, who looks as if all the juices had been exuded from his body by severe and unremitting exercise, till nothing has been left but sinew, gristle, and a pair of keen, dark eyes, like those of a hawk. It is as if the original Isaac had been boiled down to what chemists call a *residuum*, and "Ike" was the result. He must have been a tall fellow in his youth, although he is now so bent, and twisted, and knotted, that he carries his head at a much lower elevation than was intended by Nature, and his light wiry form still denotes the possession of considerable strength. To look at him, you could swear he was the sort of fellow who was the best runner, leaper, cricketer, and fisherman of his parish; who could throw a stone further, and consequently hit harder, than any of his brother-yokels, and who was sure to be at the core of all the merry-making, and half the mischief that angered the squire and made the parson grieve. There is always one such scape-grace in every hamlet. As a boy at the village school, he climbs the tallest elms, takes the earliest birds' nests, and is constantly prowling about the belfry, to curry favour with the ringers, and interfere, with unspeakable interest, when anything is done to the church clock. As a lad, he turns out a swift bowler, a dead hand at skittles, and a very useful fellow at all odd jobs; yet somehow, continually out of work. By degrees, he becomes an irregular attendant at church, and is always hankering about the stream, partly to make love to the miller's daughter, and partly (as the squire's keeper—a wary old bird, who began in exactly the same way himself—has found out) to set night-lines, trimmers, and such abominations, thereby entering unfailingly on the downward career of the poacher, to which "the contemplative man's recreation" is apt to be the first step. After that, he gets thoroughly inoculated with the fatal passion. Then come the "shiny nights," the slaughtered pheasants, and the netted hares; the sleep by day; the pot-house rendezvous; the covered cart driven to a poulterer's, who ought to know better, in the neighbouring market-town; the general laxity of principle, and utter demoralization consequent on a life of habitual crime —perhaps the irresistible temptation of too heavy a sweep, the conflict with the keepers, fought out fiercely and unsparingly on both sides, to result in a verdict of manslaughter, and transportation for life.

Old Ike's beginning, however, although sufficiently unpromising as regarded steadiness of habits, or the prospect of ever doing well in some settled trade or profession, was not destined to end in so fatal a catastrophe. Moreover, his was one of those characters so often met with, of which it is difficult to reconcile the apparent contradictions. With a tendency amounting to a passion for every pastime that could possibly come under the category of the term "sport," he was yet the gentlest and most amiable of created beings, where his fellow-man was concerned. Although as a boy he would risk his neck with the greatest delight to get a bird's nest, and when obtained seemed utterly pitiless of the poor parents' anxiety for their offspring, the same reckless lad

U

would sit still for hours to rock the cradle of a suffering child, or run any number of miles in the wet and the dark to bring home the medicine for itself or its mother.

Though he could handle a game-fowl with remarkable coolness in the pit, and, what is a far more brutal and debasing amusement, look on with excited interest whilst two faithful and high-couraged dogs tore and worried each other for a five-shilling stake, he could not bear to see a fellow-creature in pain, and would soothe any of the village urchins, with whom he was a prime favourite, under the infliction of a bruised knee and cut finger, as gently and tenderly as a woman. " Ike " was made up of contradictions, both within and without, nor was his moral being less twisted, and toughened, and knotted, than his frame.

Like a good many other persons in a higher sphere, "Ike" was ruined by the agreeable process of having a small fortune left him. This legacy acting on a temperament in which the love of approbation largely predominated, made him for a time an exceedingly conspicuous and remarkably popular individual in his own humble circle. He was not an idle man—far from it; but his habits were desultory,—a much more dangerous characteristic. In fact, an idle man seldom does himself great positive harm. Like a vegetable, he may run to seed, or he may be trampled down; but he will not seek misfortune, and that unwelcome visitor is often a long time before she finds a tranquil person out.

Now Isaac must always be doing something; only, unluckily, it was the profitable work that ever seemed to him the most laborious. To set-to with a will, and earn a shilling by six hours' labour, would have been the most unwelcome proposal you could have made him; yet he would readily have paid you the same money, if he had it, to carry a game-bag for fourteen or fifteen hours, over the roughest country you could choose. You see the game-bag was *unproductive*, and therefore attracted him irresistibly.

Ike's fortune was not a large one. It consisted of two hundred pounds, and this he spent in about fourteen months, during which period he constantly treated some of the worst characters in the parish, and lived almost entirely in the open air, undergoing great hardship, both of work and weather, in the pursuit of that sport which to him was certainly synonymous with pleasure.

Just as he arrived at the last five-pound note of his two hundred, an Irish gentleman who was staying at Castle-Cropper, and delighted the whole neighbourhood with the breadth of his brogue, the daring of his horsemanship, and the vivacity of his manners, took a great fancy to Ike, from the masterly way in which he saw the latter fishing a pool below the Mill, and easily persuaded him to accompany him back to Ireland, as a sort of humble sporting companion. There being no profit and nothing definite to do, the situation was exactly suited to our friend; and as he could neither read nor write, it is needless to state that his patron called him his private secretary forthwith.

Most men have some period in their lives—not always the happiest while it was actually present—on which they are continually looking back, and to which they lose no opportunity of reverting, as a sort of Utopian existence, rendering everything else tame and desolate by comparison. Such, it would appear, was Ike's residence in the county Galway. Whenever the old man's heart was warmed and his nose reddened by his usual potation, "a little gin and cloves," he would enlarge upon his favourite theme. He was never tired of detailing the glories of Bally-Blazer, the improvidence of the housekeeping, the liberality and general recklessness of "The Master." The latter, by Ike's account (although the narrator, it must be admitted, varied a little in his statistics), seems to have kept more young horses and old servants, drank more claret, and betted more freely on the Curragh, than any other gentleman in the West of Ireland. Here Ike acquired his principal knowledge of hunting, and a taste, which rapidly grew into a passion, for that amusement. Mounted by The Master upon what he was pleased to call "the pick of the stable," Ike, by his own account, distinguished himself for his daring feats of horsemanship as well as by his scientific knowledge of the chase.

It is difficult to make out whether the aborigines of the country believed him to be an English relative of The Master's, or a foreigner of distinction on a special mission from his Holiness the Pope. Isaac rather leads us to infer that the latter supposition was the favourite theory in and about the demesne. Be this as it may, under the auspices of his patron he soon became, in every sense of the word, a leading characteristic with "The Flamers," that celebrated hunt, which has so often been immortalized in song and story. "Mr. Isaacs," as he vows he was always called, drank, talked, and rode with the boldest, the loudest, and the thirstiest of them. He seems to have ridden in and out of the celebrated Pound at Ballinasloe, on an average, once every half-hour, during the two days and nights that well-known horse-fair is supposed to last; and it was here that Ike distinguished himself by the great and crowning exploit of his life.

It was in the old fighting, roistering days. Captain Bounceable quarrelled with Major O'Toole, upon the merits of a "harse," as each of the belligerents was pleased to term the noble animal that originated their differences. The lie which had been *told* pretty frequently during the dispute, was at length *given* with offensive directness; and nothing but "thunder an' turf!" pistols and coffee, could be the result. The time was hard upon midnight; the next morning was Sunday; the principals, men of the strictest orthodoxy and the soundest Protestantism. The quarrel could not possibly keep till Monday morning. Major O'Toole was impatient for action: Captain Bounceable thirsted for blood. They must have it out then and there, in the inn-garden, without waiting for daylight.

Except at the two ends of a handkerchief, however, even Irishmen cannot conveniently fight a duel in the dark. It was proposed, therefore, and agreed to with considerable cordiality, that each combatant should hold a lighted torch in his left hand, to direct his adversary's fire; a loaded pistol in his right, to return it. But here arose an unexpected difficulty. Major O'Toole had but one arm; and, although Captain Bounceable had but one eye, the advantage was obviously on the side of the latter, in a case of steady pistol practice.

The duel might now have been postponed—perhaps even prevented altogether—had it not been for the self-devotion of Mr. Isaacs.

"The gentlemen shall not be disappointed," said Ike—"*I'll* see fair, and hold the candle for both of 'em."

"Where will you stand?" asked Major O'Toole.

"Halfway between ye," replied the daring Englishman, "and take the chance of both of ye missing me. Give us a lantern, though, he added; "for the wind's rising from the south-west."

"Faith, if it's a bull's-eye," quoth Bounceable, "I'll be safe to snuff it out; and we'll be worse in the dark than ever, for a second shot."

So Mr. Isaacs placed himself in a cross-fire, at five paces' distance from the muzzle of each pistol; and it is not surprising that one bullet should have gone through the tail of his coat, and the other grazed his elbow, so as to incapacitate him for ever for that hard work to which he had always shown such a profound disinclination.

After this truly Hibernian satisfaction had been given and received, the party all sat down again, and drank claret till church-time.

But these days could not last for ever. One rainy morning, Ike's good-humoured patron sent for his old nurse, his huntsman, his trainer, and the parish priest, bid the three first an affectionate farewell, and took his own departure very peaceably under the offices of the last. He left a handsome amount of debt, accumulated during many years, but no ready money, except a crooked sixpence on his watchchain. Mr. Isaacs, returning to England without a shilling, became plain "Ike" once more.

He tried life in towns, under many different characters. As a billiard-marker, a light porter, an assistant-ostler, and a penny-postman; but the temptation to the copses and hedgerows was too strong for him, and the receipt of regular wages so unnatural as to be almost unpleasant. Even the tinker's nomadic profession, which he adopted for a time, was of too settled and business-like a nature; and he gave it up ere long, in a fit of impatience and disgust.

This wandering trade, however, brought him one winter into the neighbourhood of Soakington; and a day with the Castle-Cropper Hounds, beginning on the old pony that drew his cart, and ended on his own active and enduring feet, revived all his smouldering passion for the chase.

From that time, he took up his residence in one of the

tumble-down cottages near The Haycock, of which he rented a little apartment like a dog-kennel. Hence he hunted as regularly as any other sportsman with half-a-dozen horses and a covert-hack. No distance was too great for him in the morning; indeed he generally travelled to the meet with the hounds, stayed out all day, and came home in the same good company. Whatever might be the pace, he contrived to live with them, even before he became thoroughly familiar with the country, and would face the large Soakington fences—ay, and clear them, too—in his stride, as gallantly as a thorough-bred horse sixteen hands high, and up to fourteen stone.

"Old Ike," as he began in the lapse of time to be called throughout the Hunt, must have made a good thing of it during the winter season, in the many half-crowns and shillings with which he was presented by his riding friends, to whom he was often useful, in the way of pulling up girths, tightening curb-chains, and catching loose horses. Nay, on one occasion he is reported to have ridden a young one over the Sludge, on behalf of a cautious sportsman following his property on foot, but who, not calculating on the difficulty of clearing some fourteen feet in boots and breeches, *landed* (if we may use the expression) up to his chin in water, and was extricated, at great personal inconvenience, by the daring pedestrian to whom he had entrusted his horse. Old red coats, too, were amongst the perquisites freely bestowed on Ike. At one time, I have been informed, he had no less than forty of these cast-off garments in his wardrobe—the origin of many jests and much amusement, at the expense of their previous wearers.

It may be supposed that Ike's Irish experience had not failed to sharpen his powers of repartee; and many anecdotes were current anent the "retorts courteous" with which, on several occasions, he had turned the laugh against those who thought either to brow-beat or what is vulgarly termed "chaff" him.

One frosty morning, at the covert-side, bidding a cordial "Good-morrow" to a certain patron not distinguished for sweetness of temper, the gentleman, who seemed to have forgotten the universal courtesy which alone gives a man a title to the name, replied by telling him to "go to ———" a place not mentioned in good company.

"Faith," says Ike, "it's warmer there than here, at any rate; for I'm just come from it."

Struck by so strange an answer, the mounted sportsman asked the one on foot "How things were going on in those lower regions?"

"Much as usual," replied Ike, with a sly twinkle in his eye, and a glance at his interrogator, who had lately inherited a large fortune—"much as usual, and terribly crowded about the doorway. The poor all coming out, and *the rich all going in!*"

The wealthy man struck spurs into his horse, and forbore to ask Ike any further questions.

But Time, which, as the poet tells us, will "rust the keenest blade," did not fail to leave the marks of his progress upon old Ike. Hard work, hard fare, and the lapse of years eventually disqualified him for such severe exertion as that of following foxhounds on foot; and the Earl of Castle-Cropper, with that consideration which, under his calm exterior, has always attested the warmth of his heart, gave him the appointment of earth-stopper in his establishment—an office which the old man fills thoroughly *con amore*, and for which his exceedingly active habits, his utter disregard of all conventional hours or customs, and his extraordinary familiarity with the habits of wild animals, render him peculiarly fitted.

It is not often he indulges, as I saw him at the bar-window, in the use of stimulants; but when he does "take a drop of anything, it is always a glass of gin-and-cloves." In this fragrant compound he invariably drinks the same toast—an old-world sentiment almost forgotten—

> "Horses stout, and hounds healthy;
> Earths well stopped, and foxes plenty!"

CHAPTER VI.

MISS MERLIN.

I ALWAYS think convalescence is a more tedious process than actual illness. A man of active habits, who has lived a great deal out-of-doors, pines to be at work in the open air again; and although intellectual pleasures are doubtless very delightful, there is something in the sense of rapid motion, and strong physical exertion, which "leavens the blood" far more effectually than the richest mental food the Bodleian itself can afford. Before I had been confined to the inside of The Haycock for a week, or had digested a tenth of the contents of such new books as I had brought down with me in anticipation of occasional frosts, I had begun to loathe the very sight of the dust-coloured curtains in my bedroom, the staring paper in my sitting apartment, the smell of coffee that prevades the passages of an inn at all hours of the day and night—none the less because that beverage is seldom consumed within its precincts—and the general features of the prison I had chosen of my own accord. Nay, I almost caught myself, on more than one occasion, doubtful of my loyalty to Miss Lushington herself, censorious as to her appearance, sceptical on her excellence, and even insensible to her charms.

In this frame of mind I descended the stairs about ten days after my accident, with a strong feeling in favour of any novelty that might accidentally turn up, to divert the current of my thoughts.

During my late and protracted toilette, no whit accelerated by the difficulty of shaving in my crippled state (for I am no Volunteer, bearded like the pard, and hold that a smooth chin denotes a respectable man), I had been disturbed and a little irritated by sundry bumpings and thumpings on the stairs and passages, which I attributed on reflection to the awkwardness of a new chambermaid. Expecting to meet, in my descent, nothing more formidable than this red-armed personage, I was surprised, not to say startled, to encounter on the landing one of the smartest ladies'-maids I have ever seen, who started—as ladies'-maids always do, at the unprecedented apparition of a stranger in the principal thoroughfare of an edifice erected for the accommodation of travellers —screamed faintly, placed her hand on her side, and turned away in an attitude of graceful and elaborate confusion.

Such a functionary, with the trimmest of figures, the most voluminous of crinolines, the neatest of boots, and a silver-spangled net gathering "the wandering tresses of her sun-bright air," was sufficiently in character with a couple of wide imperials, an enormous wicker basket covered with black oilcloth, looking like a trunk of a considerable weight and substance, but which, instead of containing family jewels, plate, and valuables to a high amount, enclosed huge volumes of some cloudlike fabric, and when lifted, proved as light as a feather; two or more cap-boxes, a writing-case, a dressing-ditto, a leather bag, a square portfolio, several wraps, rugs, and shawls fastened together by a strap, and a bundle of parasols, *en-tout-cas*, and attenuated umbrellas, from the midst of which peeped an unaccountable but suggestive apparition in the shape of the sweetest little apology for a hunting-whip I have ever set eyes on.

I am not a curious man—far from it; but it was to be expected that I should be at least *interested* in so extraordinary an arrival at a place like The Haycock: nor was it entirely unnatural that I should come to a halt on the landing with such a strategical disposition as brought me face to face with the well-dressed attendant, and satisfied me that the countenance over against mine own was an exceedingly pretty one. Ere I had half scanned it, however, a voice from an adjacent bedroom calling "Justine! Justine!" prompted me to identify its owner at once as a foreigner; but the accent in which Justine replied, "Coming in a minute, ma'am!" was so undoubtedly English, that my speculations were again completely at a loss; neither was the maid inclined to hurry herself, till she had given me an opportunity of perusing an extremely pretty face, with sparkling black eyes and an expression of determined coquetry, scarcely modified by dark hair dressed "*à l'Impératrice*," and two little curls, something like those in a mallard's tail, plastered down to her cheek-bones in a mode that I am given to understand is termed the "*accroche cœur*," or "heart-hooker" —not at all an inappropriate title.

"Justine! Justine!" repeated the same lady-like and pleasing voice, this time in accents of command rather than entreaty; and Justine, after thanking me with great sweetness for stopping up the way, was compelled to obey the summons of her invisible lady.

Completely mystified, I descended to the bar, there to find Miss Lushington for the first time in the worst of humours, or what that lady herself was pleased to call "*uncommonly put about.*" She ordered the waiter to and fro like a drill-sergeant, rang the ostler's bell with vindictive vehemence, and mixed a glass of brandy-and-water for a customer that must have knocked his head off. Also she tossed her curls so haughtily, and carried herself so uprightly, as to denote she was prepared at any moment, if I may use the expression, to run her guns out and clear for action.

Without being a deep student in natural history, I have not failed to observe, that when a cow begins to put her muzzle to the ground, and throw the earth about with her feet, she is prepared to toss and gore. Also, that when a woman cocks her nose in the air, giving at the same time an occasional sniff through that elevated organ, while a perceptible rise and fall heaves the snowy cambric that veils her bosom, it is the forerunner of a breeze. In either case it is advisable to change the locality as rapidly as is practicable, and without reference to the ordinary forms of politeness.

Under these circumstances, I made my way forthwith into the stableyard, and had scarcely weathered the pump which commands its entrance, ere I came face to face with a very important-looking personage, whom I could not call to mind as having ever before seen within the precincts of the Haycock. There was no mistaking his profession, which was that of stud-groom. Not one of your working servants, who strips to his shirt on occasion, and straps like a helper; but a real swell groom, always in review order, just as I saw him now, and rejoicing in the only costume of the present century which has not varied the least in my recollection. These men have all the same figure—plump, dapper, and short-legged: clad in the same attire, to wit—a straight-brimmed hat, rather high in the crown; a pepper-and-salt cut-away coat, single-breasted, and of a length in the back only equalled by the shortness of its skirts; a blue-spotted neckcloth, with a horse-shoe pin; a waistcoat of the most extensive dimensions; drab breeches, with gaiters to match; and the old fashioned watch-ribbon with a key at the end. Like the Phœnix, the race is immortal and unchangeable. It possesses its own language, its own customs, its own traditions. As Napoleon the First said of the Bourbons, it learns nothing, and forgets nothing. It is reflective, sagacious, sober, and methodical; but on the other hand, it is opiniate, obstinate, wilful, and deaf to the voice of reason. You may leave one of the order, with perfect confidence, in charge of twenty horses, and be sure that everything will go on like clockwork, and that you will not be robbed of a shilling more than what he considers the due perquisites of his office; but if you want to arrange about your nags for yourself, to move them here and there, to enjoy for a day the pleasure of doing what you like with your own, be sure that you will reap only vexation and disappointment, confessing at length, in the bitterness of your heart, that the most accomplished of servants is but one degree removed from the most tyrannical of masters.

The man touched his hat to me with respectful politeness. Vanity whispered: "He acknowledges you at once for a gentleman, and perhaps you even look *a little Crimean* with your arm in that sling." I replied to his salutation by a remark on the weather and the sport; and having informed him I was staying at the hotel, and detailed to him somewhat circumstantially the particulars of my accident and progress of my recovery, to all of which he listened with grave courtesy, I asked him, "Whose horses occupied that range of stabling?" which I now perceived by the straw around the door-sills, and hermetically sealed appearance of the windows, were inhabited by some valuable stud.

"They're *ours*, sir;" answered the man, as if I must necessarily know who "*we*" were. "I shall be happy to show them to you before they are shut up;" and producing the ring-key from his pocket, he called a very neat light-weight pad-groom to his assistance, and ushered me, without further parley, into the *sanctum* of his stud.

Four better-looking animals, even as they showed then and there, with their clothes on, and littered up to their hocks in straw, it has seldom been my lot to set eyes on. They were much of the same pattern and calibre: small heads, large bodies, short flat legs, great power behind the saddle, and the best shoulders I ever saw. Two of them had been just run over with the irons, but not sufficiently to create an eyesore; the others had not a speck or blemish about them. What struck me most was, that while their appearance denoted they must be quite thorough-bred, they had none of the wincing, swishing, lifting ways that usually distinguish these high-born creatures when you approach them in the stable. On the contrary, they seemed as tame and docile as so many pet-lambs.

The first that was stripped, a flea-bitten grey, of extraordinary beauty and symmetry, may serve as a specimen of the rest. His head, when turned round in the stall, showed like that of an Arab, so square was it in the forehead, and so tapering at the delicate velvet-like muzzle. The small silken ears, too, might have listened for the bells of the caravan in the glowing Syrian air, so pointed and symmetrical was their form, so restlessly they quivered at the slightest noise; and the mild black eye, with its latent fire, might have belonged equally to a gazelle in the rose groves of El-Gulbaz, or an Arab maid at the door of her father's tent in the heart of the Buyuk-Sahar.

I have often thought that in the eye of no other animal is there so *reflective* an expression, as in that of a horse. There is a depth of honesty and *goodness* in that full shining glance, that vouches for the instrinsic worth of his character—that seems to denote courage, generosity, gratitude, all the nobler qualities which man would fain arrogate to himself, and a sensitive disposition, which is hurt, rather than angered, by an injury. When irritated, nay even maddened, by ill-usage, how soon he is soothed and appeased by a little judicious kindness! How he appreciates approbation! How willing he is to expend his force, his energies, his very life, for the sake of a kind word, or a well-timed caress from the hand he is so proud to obey! It seems to me that his is the brute nature which most resembles that of the best and bravest of the human race—true, loving, and courageous; writhing under injury, but giving all, freely and generously still; springing to the kind word or gesture, and always ready at the call of the voice he loves; game to the back-bone, and staunch to the last drop of his blood. This may seem a far-fetched parallel, and my reader may smile at me for a hot-brained enthusiast; but I love a good horse from my heart, and that's the truth!

Nevertheless, although the grey's head and neck may have seemed to argue an Eastern origin, the size and power of his lengthy frame were as far removed as possible from the attenuated proportions, the spare lean quarters of the indigenous Arab. He looked like getting through deep ground, and *shooting* well into the next field, whatever might be the size or nature of the fence that opposed his progress. I thought, on *such* a horse as that, there was no obstacle should stop me in the Soakington country; and I felt a momentary disgust while I compared his noble beauty with the more plebeian appearance of Tipple-Cider and Apple-Jack.

"He looks a right good one," said I, "and as fit to go as a man can get him. What is his name?"

"We calls him the 'King of Diamonds,'" replied the groom, modestly accepting, and passing over, my compliment to his own skill, as implied in approval of the horse's condition. "Next to him is 'Prince Charming;' and the chestnut mare's name is 'Beller Donner;' and the bay in the far stall, he's 'Lady-killer;' that's all our stud, sir," he added, touching his hat. "We don't keep any hack; they're no use to *us*, hacks ain't."

"I suppose the grey's the best of them," I observed, reverting to the beautiful animal who was now being covered up once more.

"Neatest fencer of the lot," answered the man, "and they can all go middling straight for that matter; but the Prince, he pounded of 'em all that heavy day last week in the Vale; and Beller Donner, she was the only one as got over the Bumperley Brook, down by Heel Tappington, last Thursday was a fortnight. Ah! we beat 'em all that day, we did. If it hadn't been for a man hoeing turnips, we'd have had to take the fox from the hounds ourselves. We did go owdacious, to be sure! 'The Beller,' as I calls her, had had pretty nigh enough, I can tell you, sir. But when we *do* get a start, of a fine scenting morning, I'll tell you what it is, sir—we takes no denial, and we stands for no repairs!"

Amused with the manner in which my new friend seemed to indentify himself with his proprietor, I proceeded to question him further about the horses, eliciting from him their various qualifications and merits, to which he was obviously willing to do ample justice.

"You see, sir," said he, "we rides 'em all alike; that's where it is. We doesn't go picking a horse for this here country, and a horse for that there; but we brings 'em out each in their turn, as regular as clockwork. Wery particular, we are; and when they are out, go they must, or we'll know the reason why. We haven't had Prince Charming, now, so long as the others; and the first day we rode him he seemed unaccountable shifty at large places; uneasy like, and prevaricating, and wanting to go anywhere but where we put him. Now some folks would have said, 'This horse won't suit at no price,' and been *dashed* a little, as was natural, and so perhaps sent him back again and lost of him altogether. But that's not our way, that isn't. We just laid him alongside of the hounds as soon as ever they began to run, sat down upon him, catched a good hold of his head, and *sailed* him at his places so as he might go in or over, which he pleased; but he *must* do one or the t'other. The Prince seemed to take to it all at once like. When we gets off him, we just gives a quiet little smile—we *never* laughs; and, says we, 'I know'd he could gallop and go on, and now I've found out he can jump. I think we'll keep him, John,' says we,—My name's John, sir," (with a touch of his hat,)— "'so put him in along with the others;' and up we goes to a cup o' tea, and a book till bed-time."

x

"That's the way to make a hunter!" I exclaimed enthusiastically; for I confess I felt my blood stir at John's description; "and to ride in that form, no doubt you require the very best, such as you seem to have got here."

"We doesn't grudge price, you see, sir," answered John confidentially. "When we hears of what we think likely to suit, at Tattersall's or elsewhere, we comes down with the money at once: two hundred, three hundred—no matter what, so long as they are *real* good ones. Now there's Lady-killer, (Here! Tom, take and strip that bay horse,) we bought him at The Corner, with never a character, for two hundred and fifty guineas. Know'd nothing at all about him, except that we'd seen him out, and seen him gallop. Well, Mason would have had him if we hadn't. First day as we rode him, and first fence as we put him at, blessed if it wasn't the park pales, up in Deersley Chase. My Lord's hounds, they found their fox like winking, and away right over the park and amongst the fallow-deer, as if they was tied to him. What a scent there was, to be sure! Never checked nor hovered, nor seemed to take no notice of the riot; but away, with their heads up-wind, as straight and as even as the crop of my whip. Well, there was an awful scrimmage, to be sure; such a rush among the fast ones! and we was a-going slap in front of the whole on 'em, with our hands down, I can tell you. It was a pleasure to see us, sir. Three-quarters of a mile of grass had just got the horses into their swing, when the hounds came to the park pales, and over, like a stream of water across a mill-dam. No time to think about it. While two or three of the tail hounds were falling back from the top, the others were rising the opposite hill, running *alarming*. It was a regular case of 'jump, or else go home.' Some of the gentlemen pulls up, and some goes shying away to look for a gate; and one —a young gent he was, from college—takes and rides at it; but his horse turns round and kicks. So there was plenty of room, you see, for anybody who wanted to go and try. We catches hold of the bay horse, very steady and determined, and we rides him at it, so that he could not have refused, if it had been ever so. I don't think, myself, he knowed anything about timber, for he just took it with his knees, and turned completely over on the top of us. 'Killed! by jingo!' says my Lord, turning as white as ashes, for he had waited to see us have a drive at it afore he galloped away to the gate. 'Worth a dozen dead ones yet, my Lord!' says we, jumping into the saddle again as light as a feather, and away after the hounds. So from that time we called the bay horse 'Lady-killer,' although I never knowed him touch a rail since, and now he's as safe a timber-jumper as we've got in the stable!"

"Your master must have extraordinary nerve," said I, somewhat aghast, I must confess, at this stirring narrative of escape and daring. "There are few men who would care to ride for a certain fall over so dangerous a fence, let hounds run as hard as they will."

The man stared. "Men!" he repeated, "Master! I ain't got no master: it's my *lady* as I'm a talkin' of—Miss Merlin: her that came two hours ago in a po' chay. The prettiest rider in England, let who will be the other. Master, indeed! I should like to know the man who can see the way she goes. There's a many of 'em that's tried it; but bless you, she takes no more notice, but just cuts 'em down, and hangs 'em up to dry."

It was now my turn to be surprised. I confess I had never contemplated such a possibility as this; and now it flashed upon me all at once, as these things generally do. The owner of such high-bred cattle, the reckless equestrian, to whom wood and water formed but the mere items of a pleasurable excitement, was doubtless also the mistress of the fascinating Justine. I could picture to myself the sort of person likely to combine those dashing possessions. I imagined a lady of gaudy exterior, such as I remember to have met formerly out hunting in the vicinity of London, and masculine, not to say free-and-easy manners, with a bold eye, a dab of rouge, false plaits skilfully disposed, and a loud voice, enforcing a corresponding style of language, garnished with strong expressions. I could conceive that such a dame would never be content to sit down to dinner alone at the Haycock, after the excitement of a day's hunting, particularly as she seemed to render that amusement as thrilling a one as possible, but that she would naturally make acquaintance with its sole inmate, bid him join her quiet little repast, a pint of sherry, and a bottle of champagne between the two, and what would become of me then? Perhaps, ere twelve hours had elapsed, we might be drinking the palest brandy-and-water together, while I smoked my virgin weed, and she indulged in a coquettish little cigarette. Of course she smoked. It is the fast thing for a woman to do in these days, and most of us know what a pace they *can* go when they like. I saw it all, in my mind's eye—the little shyness at first, the gradual warming from acquaintance into friendship, and from friendship to intimacy; my own misgivings, struggles, subjugation, and eventual discomfiture.

I am not ashamed to confess my weakness. Any woman, who thinks it worth her while, can put her foot upon my neck. It is for this reason that I fight shy of the sex, that I am considered a bear and a bore by the majority of my

female acquaintances, and that my pretty cousins call me
The Woman-hater. There are certain allurements I cannot
resist, certain encroachments I cannot withstand. I see the
net, and walk into it open-eyed. Other men can emerge
scathless from the ordeal of Christmas games and Twelfth-
night festivities; can play at blind-man's-buff without finding
their mental vision dazzled and darkened by the game; can
hunt the slipper or the ring, round and round the charmed
circle, nor find the charm too potent for their peace of mind;
nay, can even take a base advantage of the pendent mistletoe,
with a forehead of brass, a cheek of marble, and a lip of stone.
I envy them their insensibility, their moral courage, and their
physical daring; but for my own part I think it wiser to leave
these "little games" alone. Need I say I am a bachelor?
Need I say I came to the Haycock in order to enjoy my favourite pastime, unmolested by the presence of the dominant
sex? Even Miss Lushington I had considered an unnecessary addition to the establishment, a snare to be avoided
and an enemy to be defied: but I had been somewhat reassured by the mild and motherly interest that lady took in
my welfare, and the impartiality with which she shed her
attractions on all alike. But now, if I was to be exposed to
the insidious attacks of this mounted Dalilah, beset by Miss
Merlin, not only in the free intercourse of the hunting-field,
but also when "taking mine ease in mine inn," why I had
better retire in disorder at once, and obviate the possibility
of battle and defeat alike, by a tumultuous flight.

Revolving these weighty matters in my mind, I retraced
my steps into the Haycock, and ordered a glass of sherry
and a biscuit in the bar.

Miss Lushington filled out my liquor to the brim without
a word, slamming down before me at the same time that

biscuit, peculiar to the British hostelry, of which, to judge by its flavour, the ingredients are soda and sawdust, with a dash of gravel. I munched in silence for awhile, observing cautiously the clouds that gathered on the barmaid's brow. At last I ventured an observation.

"A fresh arrival, I understand, Miss Lushington. The Haycock will be getting quite gay now, I presume."

Miss Lushington's only reply was a toss of her black head. "Do you expect any more visitors?" I proceeded, like a timid bather trying his depth. "This will be somewhat lonely for a lady all by herself, when she isn't out hunting, I should say."

Miss Lushington's bright eyes flashed. "Ladies are very different in their tastes," said she, laying a withering stress of sarcasm on this general and incontestable position. "Some women, Mr. Softly" (I have omitted to mention that my address is Cyrus Softly, Esq., Hat and Umbrella Club, London) —"some women seem to me more like men than women. In course every one to her liking. For my part, I say nothing; but this I *will* say: for a lady to come down to a out-o'-the-way corner like this—no friends, no followers; nothing but that highty-tighty maid (and if ever I catch her put her saucy face inside my bar, I'll give her a piece of my mind, see if I don't,) and hunt, hunt, hunt, day after day, and when it's a frost or what not, read, read, read, from morning till night, and never out of a riding-habit, or else a plain dark gownd with no more trimming than on the back of my 'and" (Miss Lushington, when excited, had a habit of catching her breath, and in so doing let go a certain number of aspirates, and added a few elegant superfluities of language). "Why, I say it isn't natural, and if it isn't natural, there must be something in it, don't you think so, Mr. Softly? And to

see a maid dressed out like that flaunting miss, in flounces
and fal-lals, with a velvet net to her 'air, and hear-rings like
any lady of the land! In course it ain't my place to make
remarks, Mr. Softly; but you can't prevent my thinking it
a pity and a shame, not if you was to hang me alive for it
the very next minute, there!"

Foreseeing no advantageous result from a continuance of
the discussion with Miss Lushington, and surmising also
that the strong opinion she had formed of the new arrivals
was partly owing to Justine's attractions, I left the barmaid
in her own department, placing her hand to her side for
"occasional spasms," and catching her breath loudly at intervals, as is the habit of the sex when stimulated by any
unusual excitement, and proceeded up the staircase and
along the dark passage that led to my dormitory, pondering
deeply on all that I had heard and seen.

My curiosity—more, my interest, was strongly aroused.
Miss Merlin was evidently no common character. Brave,
reserved, studious, and simple in her attire, she must be a
lusus naturæ, a flower like the aloe, blooming but once in a
century; and here she was at Soakington;—how to obtain
an introduction was the difficulty. Had I been sound again,
nothing, I thought, could be easier: a large fence out hunting; an appropriate compliment to her horse, and implied
flattery of herself; a gate opened at the right moment, and
then a bow out-of-doors, which could not but ripen to a
familiar greeting within. After that, it would be all plain-
sailing. When I got thus far, I was perfectly astonished at
myself. "Softly," said I, "is it possible—you, who have
been a shy man and a diffident all your life; who have never
been willing to burn your fingers at the shrine of Cupid,
much less scorch yourself up, body and bones and all; you,

who have had warnings innumerable among your friends, and beacons untold in your own family—can *you* be such an ass? Did not your cousin Harry, helping a comparative stranger to put on her goloshes at a picnic, become involved in a series of dilemmas which came eventually under the notice of Sir Cresswell Cresswell, in reviewing whose decision a weekly paper was good enough to remark that the co-respondent, meaning Cousin Harry, had behaved with the blackest villany throughout? Was not your brother John, accidentally offering an unknown damsel his umbrella in the street, compelled by an Amazonian mother to marry her within six weeks? has not the Amazonian taken up her abode with him for life, and has not Mrs. John Softly borne twins to her lord on two successive occasions? Are these hideous examples insufficient, and must you in your own person furnish another deplorable instance of the inevitable result when—

"'Fools rush in where angels fear to tread'?"

"Let it alone," cried Caution. "But may I not at least take a look at my danger?" whispered Curiosity. "Better bandage your eyes," answered Caution. "Perhaps she is not good-looking after all," urged Curiosity. "Don't go near her for your life!" threatened Cau. "I'll be d—d if I don't!" thundered Q.

This was the end of the argument, and I arrived at it precisely as I reached a turn of the staircase that led to my bedroom. Justine was at this instant coming down with a basket in her arms far too wide for the narrow landing: the corner was exceedingly dark and inconvenient. In common humanity I could not but stop to assist her. Not very self-possessed at the best of times, I am afraid my efforts were of the clumsiest. Between us, we got the basket in the angle of the two walls. I was inside of it, and could not possibly get out: Justine could not very well leave me imprisoned. She laughed a good deal, and blushed and pulled as hard as she could. I, too, pushed vigorously, but it struck me Justine was remarkably pretty, and that of all places in the world this was the most whimsical for a conversation with a strange young woman of lively manners and prepossessing exterior.

CHAPTER VII.

MISS MERLIN.

At length, by our joint efforts, the basket was extricated and placed upon its—what shall I say?—on its right end, in the landing. The pretty maid smoothed her hair and adjusted her collar, somewhat creased by her exertions. I made an effort to recover the usual dignity of my demeanour, conscious that I was, to a certain extent, in a false position, yet resolved to make the best of it.

"Thank you," said I, somewhat bashfully, as well as breathlessly.

"Thank *you*, sir," said Justine; laughing, I thought, rather roguishly.

"Dear! how you've rumpled your collar," I observed, with perfect innocence. Justine glanced reproachfully in my face, as she smoothed the collar down with a remarkably pretty hand, and, tilting the offending basket on the bannisters, paused for a space, as if to "get her wind" before proceeding any further. In a few minutes the process would be accomplished, and Justine would take wing and fly away. I should never have such an opportunity again—at least not for a considerable period. The basket, in all probability, contained articles of wearing apparel, either going to or coming from the wash. Without being a family man, I was aware such an occurrence did not usually take place more than once a week. I should have another seven days to wait before so favourable an opportunity would arise again. Stimulated by this reflection, I accosted Justine with considerable energy. I am not sure that I did not take her by the hand.

"Can I speak a word with you, Mademoiselle?" said I, in trembling tones. I do not know why I called her Mademoiselle, except that I was flurried and eager, and inclined to be supremely polite.

"Not now, sir," replied Justine, sinking her voice, to my great alarm, incontinently to a whisper. "Some other time, Mr. Softly" (she had got my name already): "not now, sir, *pray*. I hear somebody coming!"

"It's only a question or two I want to ask," I urged, as soothingly and reassuringly as I could; for, in truth, had there been fifty "somebodies coming," there was nothing to be alarmed at. "Something you can tell me about—about your mistress." I bounced it out, thinking it better we should understand each other at once.

"Oh!" replied Justine, this time in a perfectly audible voice. "And what may you please to want to know, Mr. Softly, about *my* lady?"

"I want to know *everything* about her," said I; slipping, at the same time, a little profile of her Majesty, raised in gold, into Justine's hand, which delicate compliment was acknowledged by the least perceptible squeeze. "When did she arrive? When is she going away again? Where

did she come from? Where does she live when she is at
home? Is she young or middle-aged? Of course she's
very beautiful, or she couldn't afford to take about with her
such a pretty maid as *you!*"

The latter clause of my sentence I considered, not without
reason, a master-stroke of diplomacy, and I strove to enhance its effect by again possessing myself of Justine's hand;
a manœuvre she neutralized by placing both her own in her
apron-pockets, leaving the basket to take care of itself.

"Why, ain't you a hunting gentleman?" asked she, in
her turn, somewhat inconsequently, as I thought. "I made
sure you was a hunting gentleman, by your broken bones;
and I thought every hunting gentleman knew my lady.
She's just come from the Castle—my lady. She'll stay
here exactly as long as suits her fancy, and not a moment
longer. Bless you, Mr. Softly, we might never stir a foot
from here this side of Easter; and we *might* be off, bag and
baggage, first thing to-morrow morning. She's a quiet lady,
mine: a quieter lady than Miss Merlin I never wish to dress
and do for; but when she says a thing, she *means* it, Mr.
Softly, and horses couldn't draw her the way she hasn't a
mind to go."

"And is she so very beautiful?" I inquired, determined
to know the worst of this Amazon at once. Justine looked
up from under her long eyelashes (she was a very pretty
girl—this Justine), and shook her head, and smiled.

"That depends upon taste, Mr. Softly," replied she,
shooting such a glance at me the while, as I have no doubt
had often done irreparable injury amongst her adorers.

"Some gentlemen doesn't admire such a pale grave lady
with dark eyes and hair. She's a slight figure, too, has Miss
Merlin; and, for as tall as she is, her waist is as small as

mine. For goodness' sake, Mr. Softly, here's the waiter coming along the passage!" and without giving me any more information as to the size of Miss Merlin's waist, or further opportunity of measuring her own, Justine darted up the staircase, and was soon lost in the sacred retreat of her mistress's apartment.

I am no busy-body, I humbly trust and believe. It is not my way ever to inquire into the affairs of other people; and when any obliging friend wishes to make me the depository of some secret which is growing too heavy for his own shoulders, I invariably beg that he will keep it to himself. There is no such false position, as to be told an awful mystery under oath of inviolable silence, which you feel sure has been administered with the same injunctions to some half-dozen others besides yourself. One of these lets it out; perhaps all six of them make it their every-day conversation; and you, the only trustworthy person of the lot, sustain all the blame of having divulged a circumstance which you have kept silent as the grave, or even forgotten altogether. I need not, therefore, say that it is not my custom to waylay waiting-maids, nor to set every engine in my power in motion to discover the antecedents of such ladies as may happen to occupy the same hostelry with myself. But there was something about this new arrival that interested and excited me in spite of my better judgment. It was like being in the same house with a ghost. A man may not like ghosts, or he may disbelieve in them, or, worse still, he may have an invincible terror of these apparitions; and although he laughs and jeers at such matters by a crowded fireside on a Christmas Eve, he may quail and shudder in his cold sheets at the dead of night, when he lies awake, thinking of all the horrors he has ever heard and read; fancying, as people *will* fancy in the dark, that he hears sighs at the door, footsteps in the passage, and something moving softly and stealthily about the room. But whether he be a courageous infidel, or a superstitious believer in the possibility of apparitions, only tell him there is a phantom belonging to the establishment, and the man becomes restless and uncomfortable forthwith. You will find him poking about the attics and offices by day and night. When you are snoring healthily in your first sleep, he will be shivering in his dressing-gown, to discover the spirit or the impostor; and it is probable that in his character of detective he will alarm more of the inhabitants of the mansion in a week than the old established and considerate ghost itself has done in a century.

Well, Miss Merlin was rapidly becoming *my* ghost. I felt a morbid desire to find out all about her. I could not rest in ignorance of the appearance, the character, and the antecedents of a lady who in her own person involved such interesting contradictions as this mysterious dame—tall, pale, and slight; with a waist as small as Justine's, and that was certainly an extremely taper one; with a will of iron (not that there was anything unusual in THAT), and four such horses as I never saw together in one stable before. Then she was a devoted student; for had not Miss Lushington taxed her with read, read, reading all day long? Probably she was *blue*; possibly she might be an authoress, and I adore intellectual women! I can never see why ignorance is supposed by some men to be such an attraction in the other sex. The Tree of Knowledge is not necessarily the Tree of Evil; and, for my part, I think the more they know the better. What can be more graceful than a woman's way of imparting her information?—the deprecating air with which she produces it, as it were, under protest, and the charming humility with which she accepts her victory when she has beaten you in argument, and swamped you with rhetoric? Oh! if Miss Merlin should turn out *literary*, it would be all over with me! In the meantime, how was I to find out something definite about her, before I committed myself in a personal interview?

As I revolved this question in my mind, I bethought me of a club acquaintance of mine—indeed I think I may almost call him a friend—whose speciality it is to know all about everybody who floats on the surface of society, not only in London, where he resides, but also in the different counties of England, and most of the fashionable watering-places abroad. Where and how he acquires his information is to me a matter of the darkest mystery, inasmuch as I never entered 'The Hat-and-Umbrella' in my life, without finding him making use of that commodious club; and I have been informed by other members, that with the exception of Christmas-Day—a festival which, in his dislike of congratulations, I am given to understand he always spends in bed—he may be seen seven times a week in his accustomed arm-chair during the afternoon, and at his accustomed table when the dinner-hour arrives. However, he is a man of universal information, a walking edition of " Who's Who?" in any year of the century. And to Quizby accordingly I resolved to write, begging him at his earliest convenience to give me all the particulars he could about Miss Merlin, stating also that we were occupying the same hotel, but wording my communication with the delicacy imperatively demanded by such topics. I hope none of my friends may ever have cause to say, but that "Softly is a confoundedly *guarded* fellow about women, you know!"

Pending my friend's reply, it may easily be believed that
I waited with no small anxiety and impatience, none the
less that the fact of my being under the same roof with Miss
Merlin gave me no more access to her society, no more information regarding her movements, than if we had been
on different continents. The very first morning after her
arrival she was off to hunt before I was out of bed, and
returned so quietly as to frustrate my insidious intentions
of waylaying her in the passage. Justine too, either taken
to task by her mistress, or on some definite calculations of
her own, avoided my presence altogether, and never gave
me an opportunity of exchanging a syllable with her. Miss
Lushington, whom I boldly confronted in her own dominions, was obviously on her high horse, and ill at ease.
There could be no question but that, notwithstanding her
simple and retiring habits, in accordance with the strict
seclusion in which she lived, Miss Merlin's arrival had completely altered the tone and destroyed the cordiality of the
whole establishment.

True to his post, my letter must have found Quizby at
the 'Hat and Umbrella,' for within eight-and-forty hours
of its dispatch, I received his answer; written of course on
Club paper, and sealed with our handsome Club seal—a
beautiful device formed of the domestic *insignia* from which
we take our name. I opened it eagerly, and after a few
commonplace lines of inquiry and gossip, I arrived, so to
speak, at the marrow of its contents.

"You could not have applied, my dear Softly," said my
correspondent, "to any man in London better qualified to
give you the information you require. Not only have I
known Miss Merlin almost from childhood, but it was my
lot in early life, when the heart is fresh and the feelings

susceptible, to be by no means insensible to her charms.
You ask me whether she is good-looking; and this, did I
not know your extreme diffidence and scrupulous delicacy
of feeling, would seem a strange question from one who is
under the same roof with its object. Beauty is a matter of
opinion. I need scarcely say that many years ago I thought
her 'beautiful exceedingly.' She was then a tall pale girl,
with the most thorough-bred head and neck you ever saw,
with the grace and elasticity of a nymph, combined with the
dignity of an empress. So haughty a young woman it has
never been my fate to come across. She had full dark eyes,
and very silky dark hair; regular features of the severe
classical type, and a sad mournful expression, that had a
great effect on me at that period. I need not be ashamed
to confess it, whilst I remained an eleven-stone man I was
romantic; but, like many others, increasing weight has
brought with it, I trust, increasing wisdom, and I have not
the slightest doubt myself that adipose matter conduces
vastly to a proper equilibrium of the mind. I thought
otherwise once, and Miss Merlin's dark eyes would have
led me to follow her to the end of the world—nay, even
over those ghastly fences, which then, as now, it seemed to
be her greatest delight to 'negotiate,' as I think you hunting men call it in your extraordinary vernacular. She had
a wonderfully graceful figure too, as a young thing, and the
narrowest, most flexible hands and feet you ever beheld. I
have waltzed with her many a time—*moi qui vous parle;*
and to think of the delicious swing with which she went
down a room to the strains of Jullien and Kœnig, the musical wonders of *our* day, almost makes me feel as if I could
waltz again. When she bridled her taper neck, and put one
little foot forward from beneath her draperies, she looked
like a filly just going to start for the Oaks.

"I have been thus particular in describing her, because they tell me she is very much aged and altered now; so that, whenever you do see her, you can judge for yourself of the difference between the Miss Merlin of to-day, and the damsel of a good many years ago, who made such an example of your old friend.

"But I never had a chance with her—never! She was a singular girl, not the least like most of her own age and sex. Her mother was dead; and she lived and kept house for her father, an old clergyman of eccentric habits and extraordinary learning. Being an only child, she was accustomed to have her own way from the first; and as her father never interfered in the household arrangements, and indeed seldom came out of his study upon any provocation, she had the whole management of the establishment, and conducted it with the decision and prudence of a woman of forty. To this I partly attribute her extraordinary self-reliance and self-control. She was attached to her father, and studied with him several hours a day. At the period when we used to dance together, I think Miss Merlin was as thorough a Greek scholar as any University don I know. She was a proficient in several modern languages, and my own impression is that mathematics and algebra were as completely at her fingers'-ends, as worsted-work and crochet-knitting are to the generality of her sex. Studying hard at the Parsonage, her only relaxation was to hunt. I have already said she did exactly what she pleased; and her father, though a clergyman, was a rich man, and though a rich man a liberal one. Consequently Miss Fanny, as she was called then, was allowed to keep a couple of horses for her own use, and very good ones she took care they should be. At eighteen there was not a sportsman with the X.Y.Z.

Y

that cared to follow Fanny Merlin in a quick thing over the Vale, where the fences were largest, and the Swimley twisted and twined about, like the silver lace on a green volunteer uniform, never less than eighteen feet from bank to bank. I always hated hunting, I honestly acknowledge it; but oh! the duckings I have had in that accursed Swimley, following the flutter of her riding-habit, that I *would* have followed, if necessary, across the Styx. The girl never looked back either, which was sufficiently provoking. No; she rode on, always in the same calm business-like manner, perfectly quiet, and perfectly straight. She cured me of following her, though, after a time; for I found it safer and easier to skirt a little, with the generality of the other sportsmen, so as to come in somewhere at the finish, and take my chance of riding with her part of the way home.

"It was hard that such devotion as mine should not have met with better success. You, my dear Softly, who are fond of that uncomfortable diversion which men call hunting, can scarcely appreciate what I had to undergo; but when I tell you that in addition to unintermitting agitation of mind, I suffered from constant abrasion of body, you will pity, though you cannot sympathize with, my distress. Apprehension, amounting to actual *funk*, is a disagreeable sensation enough; but to be partially flayed alive, and that on portions of the person called into daily use by a man of sedentary habits, amounts to a cruel and unbearable infliction. I wonder whether she ever pitied me! I am inclined to think she scarcely thought about me at all.

"At one time, however, our acquaintance seemed likely to ripen into intimacy; and it happened that at the same period a detachment from a regiment of Hussars was quartered in our neighbourhood. The Captain hunted of course, so did the Lieutenant; and two harder riders never dirtied their coats with the X. Y. Z., nor washed them, when dirty, in the Swimley brook. Also they danced, dined, drank, and flirted, as is the custom of their kind. But the Cornet was an exception to the rule. Strange anomaly! a Cornet of Hussars, who seldom, when off duty, got upon a horse; who did not waltz or give conundrums, or squeeze young ladies' hands; who retired from mess early, not to smoke nor play whist, nor get into scrapes, but to practise on the piano-forte; whose general appearance was sedate and steady, though, to do him justice, he was a good-looking fellow enough, in a manly Anglo-Saxon style, and, in short, whose whole character and habits appeared more those of a travelling tutor than a dissipated young officer of Dragoons.

"And yet Miss Merlin fell in love with Cornet Brown. Where they met, has always been to me a mystery; and when they did meet, I cannot conceive what they found to talk about, for they had not two ideas in common. He did not even read; for, with all his quiet habits, the Cornet was as ignorant upon most topics of general information, as if he had been the fastest and idlest of his kind. His sole passion was music, and Miss Merlin did not know a note. Nevertheless, she fell in love with him—over head—such a fall as she never had in her life before, even in the Vale. She gave up hunting; she parted with her horses; she altered her whole habits and disposition and appearance, as a woman will, to identify herself the more with the man she loves. A good many of us in that part of the country had entered for the race; but we saw it was all up now—Brown in a canter, and the rest nowhere.

"The Cornet, too, seemed fond of her, in his own undemonstrative way. When not practising the piano-forte in his barrack-room, he was generally to be found at the Rectory; and as he never interfered with old Merlin, who indeed hardly knew him by sight, he would have suited him as well for a son-in-law as anybody else. The thing seemed to go on swimmingly, his brother-officers laughed at him, and we all thought the Cornet and Fanny Merlin were engaged.

"But this deserving young officer had an elder brother, whose views in some peculiar points it did by no means suit that his junior should commit matrimony, and the elder Brown appeared ere long upon the scene of action. He came down to stay at the barracks, where he made himself so agreeable to the Hussars, that they seriously proposed to him that he should make interest at the Horse Guards for the transfer of his brother's commission to himself. He didn't know a note of music—the elder Brown; but he talked, and he drank, and he smoked, and he rode, and, in short, was as jolly a fellow as ever kept a mess-table in a roar. Also, he made a slight acquaintance with Miss Merlin—not, I am bound to state, with any ulterior views; for he had a wife and promising little family of his own. He was a man of energy, you see—this gentleman—and when he meant a thing, why he went and did it without delay.

"There are secrets, I am told, in all families—a fact that makes me additionally grateful that I have got none: I mean, neither family nor secrets. What arguments were used by the elder Brown in his conferences with the younger, whether he urged him by threats or plied him with entreaties, we shall never know. It is sufficient to state that he gained his point, as such men usually do, and prevailed upon the less energetic Cornet to give up Miss Merlin. Men vary much in the force of character, and I hope I know what is the wisest and the most discreet course to take in most affairs of life; but when I was his age, before I would have given up such a girl as Fanny Merlin, in consideration of any amount of threatening, reasoning, or expediency, I would have seen fifty elder brothers consigned to that place where they would have had an opportunity of comparing notes with Dives on their terrestrial prosperity.

"The Cornet, however, gave way, and wrote a most affecting letter to his ladye-love, in which he assured her of his eternal attachment and regard, vowing that 'imperious necessity would alone have induced him to forego her affection, and that although, at his brother's injunctions, he must leave that part of the country, and they would probably not meet again, yet he could never forget her, and should always look back on their acquaintance as the happiest period of his life. In conclusion, he implored her to send him some keepsake, however trifling, that he might take with him into his banishment—anything that was *her* gift would be prized and valued till death,' etc. etc.

"Miss Merlin was not a young lady to make parade of a sorrow, however engrossing. She said nothing, and the most curious observer could not have discovered from her impassive face that she had sustained so cruel a wound, for she loved the Cornet very dearly, as the sequel proved; but she complied with her weak-minded swain's request, and sent him by return of post the most appropriate present she could think of—namely, 'a pair of leading-strings and a child's go-cart'! Brown the elder positively roared with delight when he heard of this quiet and bitter sarcasm. But the Cornet took it very much to heart; I do not think he had seen his own conduct in its true light before.

"Soon after this, old Merlin died, and there was a lawsuit instituted by his next of kin to deprive his daughter of her inheritance. The general report in the country went that Fanny Merlin was ruined, and would have to go for a governess. The Cornet was not a bad fellow after all. In defiance of his brother, he came back forthwith from the North of England, and endeavoured to renew his proposals. Of course, with such a girl as Miss Merlin, this was a forlorn hope, and equally of course the young officer became more attached to her than ever, and would have broken the leading-strings and dashed the go-cart all to pieces this time; but he never once set eyes on her whilst he remained in the neighbourhood, and retired at last in a perfect fever of fury and disappointment. Whether this *contre-temps*, or the accumulating pressure of many unpaid bills, chiefly for grand piano-fortes, and other musical instruments, was the cause, I know not; but the following year Cornet Brown exchanged into a regiment serving in India, and the same paper which furnished the gazette of his appointment, also announced the judicial decision that restored Miss Merlin to affluence and prosperity.

"She gave up her hunting, though, for a time, and practised music incessantly. I have heard that in a wonderfully short period she attained a proficiency in that science, which is not usually acquired under a lifetime.

"Meanwhile the Cornet, alternating his military duties in India with a great many *tiffins* and a vast quantity of brandy *pawnee*, was invalided home in a very dangerous state of illness. The sea-voyage failed in his case to produce its usual good effect, and he arrived at Marseilles a dying man. How she heard of it, I have not the slightest idea; but Miss Merlin never was like other girls: she possessed an energy and force of will extremely rare in her sex, fortunately for ours. She started off, at a moment's notice, without taking even a maid, and crossed France in the utmost haste, to reach her old lover, and bring him home. She had forgiven him his weakness and vacillation, had forgotten all about the leading-strings and the go-cart, now that she heard he was dying.

"I am not a sentimental man, as you know, and have little sympathy to spare for those afflictions of the heart, which, in my opinion, sink into insignificance when compared with a derangement of the stomach; but it has always struck me that Miss Merlin's was a melancholy story. When she arrived at Marseilles the Cornet had been buried eight-and-forty hours. She stood by his grave on the hill above the town, with the blue southern sky overhead, and the blue Mediterranean at her feet. I think, strong and self-reliant as she was, she had as much sorrow then for her portion as she could bear.

"She remained abroad a twelvemonth, I know, for I made it my business at the time to ascertain; but what she did with herself, during that period, I have never been able to find out. Some said she had gone on into Syria, others that she was in Egypt. Archer thought he saw a person very like her eating sandwiches at Jerusalem. Aimwell is almost sure he recognized her in male attire at the First Cataract; there was a very general report prevalent that she had gone into a convent for a year on trial; but didn't like it, which I can easily imagine, and so came away again. Be this as it may, she turned up again after a time in the X. Y. Z. country, hunting more furiously than before, riding harder, speaking less, and looking graver than she had ever done; but as the Rectory was now inhabited by a fresh incumbent, and she had no settled place of residence, she did not remain very long in the neighbourhood of her youthful home.

"Since then, and it is a long time ago, she has travelled about the country, far more independently than most bachelors. In the summer she retires to some obscure town, either in the Highlands of Scotland, or on the sea-side, where she takes a quiet lodging, and devotes the time to study. In the winter she moves her horses about, to hunt with different packs of hounds, giving the Soakington country the preference, partly on account of the strong friendship which has sprung up between herself and the Earl. In fact, a room is always kept ready for her at Castle-Cropper, and she has arranged the library for the proprietor, and re-hung all the pictures in more favourable lights. So independent is she, however, in her habits, that she often prefers to remain at the Haycock, where, *if you are not afraid*, you may, perhaps, have an opportunity of becoming acquainted with her. I have now told you all 1 can about your mysterious visitor, and consign you, not without a shudder, to your fate. If she only retains half the attractions she had at eighteen, you're a gone 'coon, Softly; and mind this—it's a game like the pitch-and-toss we used to play at school. 'Heads *she* wins, tails *you* lose!' I have warned you. Adieu! *Liberavi animam meam.*

"P.S. A piano-forte is no use. She has never played a note since the Cornet died."

I appeal to any impartial man, whether such a communication as the above was not adding fuel to fire. I read and re-read it with an interest that increased on each fresh perusal. I resolved that, come what might, it should not be my fault if another sun went down without my obtaining at least *a sight* of the fair subject of Quizby's memoir. I called up, in my mind's eye, my correspondent himself. His jolly fat face, with the little eye, that twinkled pleasantly over a ready joke as over a slice from the haunch or a bubbling bumper of Bordeaux. I reflected on his imperturbable character, his consistent philosophy, cynical, perhaps, in language, but jovial, and thoroughly epicurean in practice; and the more I thought, the more I wondered, the more I longed to witness with my own eyes the peerless attractions that could have knocked my steady friend, so to speak, off his equilibrium. To-morrow morning then, I resolved, I would see Miss Merlin, or die in the attempt.

Eagerly I scanned the hunting-card for the week. To-morrow the hounds were to meet at the kennels. Castle-Cropper was but ten miles from Soakington. She could not possibly start before nine. I desired my servant to call me at eight, and retired to rest, in that frame of mind which prompts a man to shave over-night, that he may be in time, and makes him wake every half-hour lest he should over-sleep himself after all at the last.

CHAPTER VIII.

YOUNG PLUMTREE.

I SUPPOSE no man sleeps the sounder for a broken collar-bone, even when it is getting well. Determined to be up in time, even if I lay awake for the purpose, I spent what invalids call a *bad* night. I heard more than one of the small hours strike from a certain loud-ticking clock in the kitchen, that, strangely enough, was never audible in the day. At last, however, I fell into a deep sleep, from which I woke with a start, to hear my servant arranging my dressing-things and pouring cold-water into my tub. The morning was as dark as only a hunting morning can be, and a drizzling rain, glazing the chimney-pots and tiles, of which I had a commanding view from my bed-room window, by no means enhanced the temptation of leaving a warm bed. I jumped out, nevertheless, with an effort, shaved, washed, and dressed with considerable energy and rapidity, writhing into my coat in my crippled state, by a series of gymnastics similar to those with which a "navvie" struggles into his fustian jacket. The clock struck nine as I completed my preparations. I had already heard the wheels of a carriage grinding round from the stable-yard to the front-door of the inn, whilst a certain bustle in the passages, with much opening and banging of doors, denoted an arrival or a departure. There was no time to lose, if I would waylay Miss Merlin as she went downstairs. I brushed up my whiskers for the last time, and emerged from my bed-room. As I put my foot in the passage, a rush of cold air from below, apprised me that the hall-door must be standing wide-open, and I ran down in a tumult of hurry and agitation, lest I should be too late after all.

As I reached the lobby, there was a fly standing at the inn-door. An incoherent waiter, with a dirty napkin under his arm, and flourishing a Japan tea-tray wildly in his hands, was gazing vacantly at space; Miss Lushington's head peered darkly out from amidst her lemon-nets; an ostler, with one eye, held the carriage-door; and into that carriage, with her back to me, was entering the graceful figure of a lady in a riding habit; a taper little foot, in the neatest of boots and—what shall I call them?—leg-sleeves? receding from the top-step, being the only feature, if I may be allowed the expression, distinguishable amongst that dark mass of folds and draperies.

There was a fatality about it! The thing was obviously in the hands of Destiny. The door shut-to with a bang. A pretty little gloved hand drew up the window, and the fly drove off with Miss Merlin inside, on the road to Castle-Cropper.

Some men are the favourites of Fortune; others, the butts and targets of Fate. I endeavour at all times to bear my reverses with a sulky equanimity. I retired accordingly, to derive what consolation I could from an elaborate and protracted breakfast by a good fire, and then proceeded into the bar to smoke.

In these ingenious days one cannot but be struck with the many devices that exist for the discovery of character. One man finds you out by your handwriting; another by the tone of your voice; a third judges exclusively from the shape of your hat; and I have met an extremely far-seeing foreigner who professed to learn, not your fortune, as the gipsies do, but your tastes and disposition, from the lines on the palm of your hand. I think I should myself be inclined to judge of a man's style by the sort of carriage he drives. This tendency—superstition—call it what you will, prompts me to take rather a careful survey of such vehicles as I come across, and therefore it was that, observing a strange dog-cart in the inn-yard as I traversed its stones, with an unlighted cigar in my mouth, I paused to examine more minutely the unfamiliar equipage.

So slang a turn-out it has not been my fortune to meet with, before or since. Imagine a very high box, narrowing considerably towards the top, on which, judging by the cushions and hand-rail, it is fair to conclude the driver is supposed to sit, perched on a pair of extremely tall wheels, painted red, and picked out with a staring yellow. Imagine the shafts of this contrivance, perfectly straight, and of great strength and substance, nearly on a level with the withers of the unfortunate animal that has to draw it. Imagine the old machine, wickered, and lacquered, and glazed, and polished to the most dazzling pitch of brilliancy, attached to the person of a well-bred, crop-eared, vicious-looking bay mare, herself wearing as little harness as is compatible with the fact of her being fastened to anything at all, and that little of the colour and appearance of untanned leather. Add to these, a tall whip with a yellow crop, long enough to drive four-in-hand, a pair of enormous lamps, and a white bull-terrier coiled on the foot-rug, licking his lips, with a blood-thirsty expression of countenance, and winking hideously with his ominous and ill-looking eyes.

The proprietor of such "a trap," as he would probably call it, could not fail to be a study in himself. Loud accents from within smote on my ear as I approached the bar. The shrill tones of Miss Lushington's voice predominated, and I gathered from this that she had recovered her good-humour, which for the last few days had been most indubitably on the wane. Entering the *sanctum*, I stood for a few seconds behind the wooden screen—which I have already mentioned, and which admits of a new comer, himself unseen, reconnoitring the occupants of the place—to survey the visitor whose arrival seemed so acceptable to the presiding goddess. I had ample time to take a good look at him; for, whilst he discussed a glass of sherry and a bitter (a glass of sherry and a bitter—and it was not yet eleven o'clock!), both talker and listener were so engrossed with the former's jokes and conversation that I had entered completely unobserved. He was a stout young man of some five-and-twenty summers, with a whiskerless face, and a ruddy complexion, not yet destroyed, though obviously impaired, by his habits of life. His cheek, still healthy in colour, was mottled here and there, as if the vessels near the surface were kept habitually too full, and he already began to show that slight puffiness under the eyes, as if he had put his neck-cloth on too tight, which is the certain symptom of a digestion impaired by the too liberal use of stimulants. Not that *his* neckcloth was too tight—far from it. Save a scarlet knot half-way down his throat, secured by a horseshoe pin, there was nothing to be seen of the customary wisp of ribbon which has now replaced that obsolete article of apparel, so concealed was it by the fall of a turned-down shirt collar, extremely well starched, and of a singularly varied and gaudy pattern, not unlike the papering of a room. His hat, which he had not thought it necessary to lay aside, was of the " pork-pie" order, immortalized by Leech—a head-dress extremely trying to a countenance already divested by Nature of any particular expression, and which, like many other graceful eccentricities, looks as ill upon a man as it is becoming to a woman. Coat and waistcoat, I need hardly observe, were of a checked pattern, to which, for richness of hue and diversity of colours, the rainbow of heaven is a mere pale and feeble transparency. Beneath the latter, knickerbockers of course! formed apparently from some woollen fabric, designed by the inventor for a horse-cloth, and combining great strength of wear-and-tear, with an unassuming and neutral tint. Scarlet hose, imparting fulness to the calf, and general *contour* to the leg (in this instance much required, the limbs themselves being of too massive an order for elegance), sprang from the robuminous superfluities above, and a pair of exceedingly stout half-boots, much strapped and pieced, and, as it were, tattooed like the *mocassins* of a Red Indian, completed this choice and becoming costume. When I add that a double curb-chain of gold, sustaining a dozen trinkets, ornamented the wearer's stomach, and a short pipe, blackened by unintermitting smoking, graced his mouth, I have done all I can to convey a representation of the gentleman whom I now found making himself agreeable to Miss Lushington in the bar, and whom I had no hesitation in setting down in my own mind as the proprietor of the dog-cart in the yard.

He was sitting, when I entered, not *at*, but *on* the table, by the side of his sherry and bitters. Volumes of smoke, *latakia*, and something stronger, I could swear by the fragrance (and here I may remark, in parenthesis, that if the London tobacconists keep up the exorbitant price of cigars, as they have lately done, nobody will smoke anything *but* a short pipe very soon), curled upward from his mouth, and I was just too late for some irresistible witticism which had convulsed Miss Lushington with laughter. Indeed, that lady's fair hand was applied to her lips, as if to conceal or repress her hilarity, when I entered. An Oriental woman's idea of modesty is to cover her mouth; and, indeed, to keep that organ shut, as much as possible, is no bad custom for the sex to adopt. But why ladies of Miss Lushington's social standing should habitually express intense amusement by the same gesture, I cannot take upon me to explain. When the teeth are black and the hands white there may be reason for it; but Miss Lushington could not fairly be accused of either of these specialities.

"Softly! How goes it?" exclaimed the new-comer, removing his pipe from his mouth, and rolling off the table, and on to his legs, with a coachmanlike action extremely difficult to acquire. "Give us your flipper, old boy! Ah! I forgot you'd had your wing broken. Never mind; might have been worse. Won't you liquor up? Now, Miss L., look alive! those sparklers of yours were made for use as well as ornament. What's our friend's variety? An invalid ought to be taken care of, you know. Draught three times a day, and the mixture *as* before."

Greeting my voluble acquaintance, whom I now recognized as young Mr. Plumtree, of The Ashes, but of whom my previous knowledge did by no means warrant such a familiarity as he was kind enough to display, with a more stately and reserved demeanour than usual I lit my cigar, and proceeded, in self-defence, to envelop my person in its fumes.

Without being a stickler for the more ceremonious forms of politeness, or an advocate for the stilted dignity of the old school, I do not quite relish the tendency of certain individuals to be so "gallows familiar," as a poor good-for-nothing friend of mine used to call it; nor do I see that a man has a right to call me "Softly," with no handle prefixed, the third time he has ever met me in his life. "Gaudent prænomine molles auriculæ," quoth Horace; and he understood human nature, if anybody did. Besides, I knew enough of the gentleman now occupying the bar, to have no great wish to cultivate his further intimacy.

I had avoided him hitherto as much as possible. It seemed to be part of the bad luck of the day that I should be thrown into his society now. To have failed by thirty seconds in seeing Miss Merlin in the morning, and find myself the boon companion of young Plumtree at noon, was surely a combination of untoward circumstances which that individual himself would have called "hard lines."

As I smoked my cigar, rather sulkily, and watched my aversion making the agreeable to Miss Lushington—a process at which, to do him justice, he appeared singularly skilful,—I recalled in my mind all I knew of his antecedents, and could not help congratulating myself, the while, that he was no son of mine.

Young James Plumtree, then—or "Jovial Jem," as he was called by his familiars—was the only son of John Plumtree, of The Ashes, a most respectable, and, I believe, unimpeachable country-gentleman, living in the vicinity of Soakington. I have always understood that the father was a man of grave and particularly gentlemanlike demeanour, and, although an excellent sportsman, extremely averse to anything approaching slang. It was, therefore, perfectly natural that his son should turn out one of the "loudest" and most uproarious rattles of his day.

The boy had an excellent education, too—at eight, a private tutor, who could never keep him out of the stable, and into the pockets of whose sad-coloured garments his pupil was continually putting white-mice and such abnormal vermin—nay, on one occasion, this long-suffering Mentor discovered a ferret in the tail of his coat, and an eel in the crown of his hat; at twelve, transferred to Eton, where he was placed as low as he possibly could be, and, notwithstanding repeated floggings, and constant wiggings from "my tutor," persevered in the study of natural history with an ardour that could by no means be brought to harmonize with the rules of that elegant college. Corporal punishment is—or at least, in young Plumtree's day, used to be—inflicted for the following misdemeanours, of which he was habitually found guilty, viz.: Entertaining fighting-dogs, at an outlay of a shilling per week, and making use of the same in their combative capacity; associating, both in and out of bounds, with cads and such low persons, with aggressive views on personal property in the form of hares, pheasants, etc., at Stoke, Burnham, Thames Ditton, and elsewhere; keeping singing-birds in a bureau that ought to have been devoted to school-books, and white-mice in the lower drawers of the same, along with clean linen; also, and this partiality for ferrets was one of the boy's most remarkable characteristics, taking a female of that species into three-o'clock school, and producing her, so to speak, in open court; finally, never, under any circumstances, knowing one word of his lesson.

When Plumtree left college, the head master, who, like many other head masters, had rather a weakness for a pickle in his heart, took him kindly by the hand, and recommended him, with perfect single-mindedness, to devote his energies to the habits of beasts and birds, and the study of comparative anatomy, "the only mental labour, Plumtree," added the don, with extreme kindness, "for which you seem either qualified or inclined."

A lad of such tastes was pretty sure to be sent to one of the universities: and after an interval of a delicious twelvemonth at home, during which period of relaxation the young 'squire not only destroyed every rat in every barn within a day's ride of The Ashes, but also made acquaintance with every tap of beer, and struck up a friendship with every blackguard, within the same distance, this promising acolyte was entered at Brazen-Nose, and went up to keep his terms at Alma Mater, and acquire whatever knowledge was most adapted to his intellectual hunger, at that repository of learning.

Here, it is needless to observe, he rowed a great deal, smoked a great deal, drank an enormous quantity of beer, and read not the least in the world. He acquired, however, considerable proficiency in the difficult art of driving a tandem, and could conceal boots and breeches under loose pantaloons, when attending chapel on a hunting morning, more dexterously than any undergraduate of his year.

He kept the drag, too, for one season, but found his mode of life too dissipated to admit of the nerve requisite for that amusement. These dare-devil young gentlemen, you see, go out for the express purpose of breaking each other's necks. They ride, of course, directly *at* the leading hound; but that quadruped, generally an old stager, and stimulated by a red-herring steeped in aniseed, gives them plenty to do before they can catch him. It is a point of honour, I am given to understand, to turn away from nothing; and the man who can *get through* his horse quickest, is esteemed to have won the laurels of the day. It is scarcely possible to imagine an education more calculated to make a *horseman*, and spoil a *sportsman*, than the Oxford drag.

When Plumtree renounced the mastership of this dashing establishment, he devoted himself exclusively to driving, and became, if possible, more *beery* than before. For lectures he cherished an unaccountable aversion, nor was it likely that the wit and learning of the schools would prove very tempting to a man whose heart was habitually in the cellars.

Well, of course, it came to a finish at last; and Jovial Jem was rusticated; "Rusticated, by the Hookey!" to use his own remarkable words, "and recommended not to come up again. Well out of it, too, in my opinion: and as to another round, why if I do, I *do; but* if I do, I'm —!"

Old Plumtree was grievously disappointed, of course. By the way, I know very few cases in which sons do not disappoint their fathers. I suppose it would be difficult to persuade the latter that the former are not exclusively in fault. Old Squaretoes lays down a course of conduct for his child, totally irrespective of the feelings, inclination, and disposition of the latter. Then, if young Squaretoes don't fit the groove, and slide easily down the metal, he is undutiful, disobedient, ungrateful, everything that the Prodigal Son was, before he came to eating husks amongst the swine. If young S. turn out "slow," ten to one but old S., in suicidal folly, wishes he "had a spice more devil in him." If he be fast, the governor shakes in his shoes, foreseeing debts, bills, acceptances, renewals, and eventual penury. If he make a figure in the world on his own wings, taking warning by Icarus, and scorning to use the paternal pinions, his father is often jealous of his success. If, on the contrary, he remain in secure and humble obscurity, then the cry is, " Why, the lad has no spirit in him! Look at what I should have done at his age, *and with his advantages!*" Good masters make good servants. Unselfish and considerate fathers, more than people are aware of, make attached and dutiful sons.

So Jovial Jem came home, and took up his abode at The Ashes, completely upsetting the regularity of that establishment, where, in his absence, everything went on like clockwork. For his own sake, Mr. Plumtree senior gave his son a couple of rooms, shut off from the rest of the mansion by double doors of baize, through which the fumes of Latakia could not possibly penetrate, and ordered the domestics to serve their young master with breakfast and dinner at his own hours, when required, in his own apartments. By this arrangement, the heir was wonderfully little in his father's way; and unless the pair happened to meet on a summer's morning, when the old one was going to his hay-field, fresh and rosy, and the young one returning from a junketing, pale and exhausted, father and son often did not see each other for weeks. Consequently, they got on admirably. Young Plumtree swore "The Governor was a dear old bird; crotchety of course, but a regular brick nevertheless;" and old Plumtree, who always took a solemn pinch of snuff before he delivered himself of a remark, was fond of stating, very slowly and distinctly, that "Young men won't settle at once. Can't expect it, sir—can't expect it! But the lad's got something in him. If we could only get *at* it, sir! if we could only get *at* it!"

"I heard of your downer, old 'un," this agreeable young gentleman observed with great cordiality, transferring his attention from Miss Lushington to myself. "Wasn't out myself that day; couldn't raise a prad, or I'd have seen you picked up, and dissected, and all that. First day I can get away from home, says I, I'll just tool over and visit the mutilated sportsman. Thought you'd be dull, you know, with nobody but Miss Lushington, though she's pleasant company too when she's got her stockings on right-side-in."

"Come, that's a good one," observed the lady alluded to thus familiarly, with a meaning glance. "As if you didn't know of our late arrival! Oh, you're a deep one, Mr. Plumtree, you are!"

The young gentleman blushed, a real honest shame-faced blush, such as I did not believe could have been raised, after six years of Eton and two of Oxford, to save a man's life. "Get out!" said he, chivalrously ignoring the cause of his confusion. "None of your chaff, Miss L. Ain't I always ready to help a lame dog over a stile? Wouldn't I drive a hundred miles in a butcher's cart without springs, to succour a mutilated friend? Ain't I pitiful, and tender, and soft-hearted? Come, you know I am."

"Indeed I know nothing of the kind," replied the lady, bridling and tossing her head. It was Miss Lushington's plan, you see, always to give her admirer what she called a "set-down" the moment they passed an imaginary line of her own demarcation; so she proceeded, speaking very distinctly, and with her lips set tight—

"If you've driven all this way only to talk nonsense to me, Mr. Plumtree, you've wasted your time sadly. But, you'll never make me believe *that*. *I* know what I know; and others might know it too, if so be as you was to take and rile me more than I think pleasant. And you're too late, after all," added Miss L. viciously. "She was in the fly an hour before you drove into the yard: why, bless you! she's at the top of the hunt by this time, and no more chance of coming up with her than if she was the wind."

Without pausing to consider what peculiar position in the chase Miss Lushington intended to convey by her expression of the "top of the hunt," I shot a glance at Young Plumtree, who seemed, I thought, to quail considerably under the volubility he had provoked. Indeed, strange to say, he appeared completely "shut up," and at a loss for a reply. A horrible suspicion darted across me, lighting up, as such fancies do, the previous darkness with a dazzling and momentary brilliance. Could this unwelcome and unhappy young man be under the influence of a hopeless attachment for Miss Merlin,—one of those unaccountable infatuations of which we read in novels, but which, fortunately for the general comfort of society, we so seldom meet with in real life?

And yet, why not? To be sure, judging from Quizby's

letter and his frank acknowledgment of an attachment to her in his youth, the lady must have arrived by this time at middle age, and Plumtree was a mere boy (for, after all, a man of five-and-twenty is little more than a boy), actually shaving for whiskers, top-dressing with balm of Columbia, and raising an abundant crop of pimples as the result. A woman too, after she arrives at a certain point of maturity, say five-and-thirty, remains for an incredible period at that attractive stage of her charms. She has lost indeed the bright freshness of youth; but if she has been really handsome, she has gained in exchange a certain depth of colouring and intensity of expression, which are equally efficient weapons of offence.

Then, while the passing years blunt her darts scarcely perceptibly, every day adds to her experience and dexterity in their use. A *coquette* of twenty years' standing is like an old *maître d'armes* of the Empire, cool, wary, dauntless, and skilful; *rusé* in the art of destruction, and taught by a hundred combats to take every advantage, and never to throw a chance away. I have often thought, notwithstanding the dancing exploit, a man would have been safer with Herodias's daughter than with Herodias herself.

Then a young man, if he once suffers himself to be captivated by a woman considerably his senior, becomes rather childish, not to say imbecile, in the process. He goes into leading-strings forthwith, and there is no folly or extravagance of which he is incapable. Shall I ever forget what a fool young Larkspur made of himself about old Lady Foxglove, who might have been his mother, and looked as if she *had* been his wet-nurse? Nor can I cease to regret the fate of my poor friend Capon, who left college to run away with Mrs. Mallard the actress, at a period when that lady had become too aged and infirm for genteel comedy parts at any of the theatres royal, and of whom I last heard at a French watering-place, living in cheap lodgings at the head of a grown-up family not his own, nor indeed, unless scandal be more scandalous than usual, the issue of the talented Mr. Mallard deceased.

I looked at young Plumtree with a kind of loathing pity. I thought of what his deplorable state would be, when all the pleasures of his present existence should have palled upon him in the pursuit of the unattainable; when 'bacey should have lost its soothing properties, and there should be no more charm in beer; when dogs might "delight to bark and bite," and Plumtree, *quantum mutatus*, would care not which half-stifled champion was dragged gurgling and snarling "across the line;" when the three-pound terrier, eating its own weight a dozen times over in rats, would no longer excite his garrulous plaudits as he hung half muzzy over the pit; and to shoot pigeons for a fat pig, or see a man trundling a wheelbarrow backwards, and picking up stones with his mouth, would be equally tasteless and insipid; nay, when counting out the game-cock himself, prone on the square-cut turf, but of mettle invincible, from the top of his clean-cut comb to the points of his steel spurs, would be considered simply a dull but cruel pastime, and like Othello's in his fancied degradation, Plumtree's "occupation would be gone."

All unconscious of my forebodings, their confiding object pulled a square and heavily-sealed note from what I believe Mr. Poole terms the "opossum pocket" of his shooting-jacket, and handed it to me with the mock dignity of an ambassador presenting his credentials, winking demurely on Miss Lushington the while.

"Can you read?" inquired the facetious envoy. "If so, there's a bit of blotting from the old folks at home. I told the governor that as you weren't fit to do much 'scraping,' I'd best bring it over, and take back the answer by word of mouth. But you'll come, won't you? It's a crafty crib enough, The Ashes, and you'll get your health there as well as here for a day or so. I can't say much for the biting, but there's some lining with a green seal to it, that will set your collar-bone for you, make your hair curl tight up to the roots, and bring you down to-morrow morning, as fresh as a bull-calf, and as hearty as a buck."

There was no resisting such inducements as these, and indeed the letter of Mr. Plumtree senior, though extremely pompous and ceremonious, was hospitable, considerate, and kind. Though almost a stranger, he hoped that I would excuse our short acquaintance, and dine with him at The Ashes, adding, that as I ought not to expose myself to cold from the night-air, he trusted that I would take a bed.

Although such a creature of habit that I would far rather have remained in solitary state at the Haycock, I felt it would have been more than churlish to refuse so hospitable an invitation, the only drawback to which was the necessity I foresaw of driving over in "the trap" with young Plumtree. I would have given a good deal to be permitted to order a post-chaise and pair, and go over comfortably, with all the windows up; but it is of no use to struggle with destiny: I saw what was before me, and resolved to confront my fate like a man.

CHAPTER IX.

IN THE TRAP.

"You'll go with me, Softly, of course!" observed young Plumtree, otherwise 'Jovial Jem,' just as I expected. "There's a Waterborough 'bus runs right by our lodge-gate: your servant can come over with your traps. Get a greatcoat on, there's a good fellow, and we'll start immediately, if not before. A short drain of brandy neat, Miss Lushington, if *you* please. Look alive, you adorable angel, ministering spirit, I may say. Time's short, you know, roads woolly, and whipcord scarce."

"But are you sure you can take me?" I interposed, with expostulatory eagerness. "Yours is a smallish carriage, if that was it I saw just now in the yard" (how devoutly I wished it was not!). "I fear I shall inconvenience you; and, by the bye, where is your servant to sit?" I added, grasping vaguely at the last chance of a reprieve.

"Servant?" said the Jovial, drinking off his brandy at a gulp, "didn't bring one; don't want a 'shoot' when I'm driving Crafty Kate. There's only one gate to open if we go the short way, and it opens *from* us; so I catch it, you know, on the shaft, and there's no trouble in getting out. Once the apron's buttoned, never move till the end of the stage, that's my principle. Wet t'other eye? Thank you, Miss Lushington. Here's your health! Now, young man, tell the ostler to get the trap round to the front door; when I drive a gemman, I likes to take him up *like* a gemman."

"But if the harness wants altering, or anything?" I

urged feebly. "In my crippled state, you know, I can't get out. Don't you think, now?—though, of course, I should like the drive very much—don't you really think it would be better if I were to find my own way over, and you might take a man from here to open the gates and that, who could come back in my return chaise?"

"Not a bit of it!" replied the Jovial. "What's the use of that? I know the mare, and the mare knows me. *You* won't have to get out, never fear. Come, though you've got a queer wing, there's nothing amiss with your pipes. Look here, there's a yard of tin in that basket. You'll play all the way, and I'll drive. Take her in a hole shorter, Ben. Here's a game! hooray!"

By this time "the Jovial's" high conveyance—well might he call it a trap—was at the door; Crafty Kate wincing, and lifting and swishing her tail, as if nothing would give her greater pleasure than to knock the whole thing, red wheels, lamps, paint, varnish, and lacquering, all to pieces forthwith. I could not get out of it now, do what I would. Recalling in my own mind every frightful accident I ever remembered to have read, or heard of, that had occurred on wheels, and no whit reassured by an appalling fact I had always considered established, viz. that more long coachmen had been killed out of gigs, than had died any other death, I went upstairs to give my servant directions as to the clothes he should pack up, to wrap myself in a warm greatcoat, and to put another cigar in my mouth, that haply might conceal the involuntary trepidation of my nerves.

How comfortable my sittingroom looked as I left it! It was a cold raw day, and the fire burnt up so cheerily; the easy-chair spread its arms invitingly to receive me in its familiar embrace; there was the newspaper carefully unfolded and spread out on the table, with the last *Quarterly* uncut, by its side. An amusing novel, of which I had got halfway into the second volume, seemed to entreat me not to leave it unfinished, and two or three letters requiring early answers were lying with their seals opened in mute appeal. All this comfort I was about to exchange for a muddy drive, a drizzling rain, the conversation of a man I did not care about, and worse still, the probable vagaries of Crafty Kate. I confess I have no great confidence in a thorough-bred mare, that swishes her tail a good deal in harness. I thought Miss Lushington, even, looked somewhat pitifully on me, as one about to venture in a dangerous undertaking unawares. Nevertheless I mounted the trap, not without difficulty, was carefully buttoned in by the one-eyed ostler, and felt myself launched forth on stormy seas, with Jovial Jem for a pilot.

On leaving the door it became painfully apparent that Crafty Kate was in a condition of excitement, not to say insubordination, which boded untoward results. Passing between the lines of dilapidated houses that constitute the little village of Soakington, she piaffed and curvetted, and tucked her head in, and hoisted her great angular quarters, in a manner calculated to excite the admiration of all beholders—limited in the present instance to a lame duck, and two boys playing truant from school; but when we emerged on the smooth expanse of the Waterborough road, stimulated by the love of approbation, or urged by a morbid anxiety to get home, the mare took the bit in her teeth, and very nearly made a bolt of it. I confess I clung to the rail that ran round the seat, thankful even for that frail support, and notwithstanding the slight hold it afforded me, narrowly escaped being dashed out, as we turned with fearful rapidity, and entirely on one wheel, like a skater doing the outside edge, up a lane diverging at right angles from the thoroughfare along which we had been bowling at such a pace.

It was evident, however, by Crafty Kate's demeanor, that this was not the way home. She stopped dead short, stuck her forelegs out, and began nodding her head in that ominous manner, which denotes a determination to fight to the last. "Sit tight, Softly!" exclaimed the Jovial, with a fiendish laugh, as though this had been part of a programme devised for my special entertainment. "Sit tight! whilst I give my lady a taste of the silk!" and without further parley he pulled the whip from its bucket, and commenced a course of punishment on the mare's sides, which produced no further result than that of causing her to back faster and faster towards the ditch; the tall red wheels hovered on its very brink, when a bright idea flashed across the charioteer's mind. "Give us a blast of the tin, Softly," said he, continuing, nevertheless, a vigorous application of the whipcord, "and let us see if *your* blasting is not more musical than *mine!*"

I am no performer, I candidly admit, on a trumpet of any description; but a desperate crisis demands a desperate remedy, and seizing the long coach-horn I performed such a *solo* upon it as has probably never been heard before, or since. "The Jovial" left off flagellating, and laughed till he cried. The mare laid her ears down into her poll, tucked her tail close to her quarters, and went off at score. Completely blown by my exertions, we had gone nearly a mile ere I returned the horn to its case, and found breath to speak.

"But is this the shortest way to The Ashes?" said I, striving by the aid of a "Vesuvian" to relight my cigar, which had gone out in the panic. "I thought we kept straight along the high-road to the turnpike, and then took the first turning to the—"

"O, bother The Ashes!" returned my mercurial companion. "We shall get there quite soon enough. Besides, the governor never shows till feeding-time; busy about the farm you know, mud-larking as I call it. No! no! if you want to see some fun, I'll show you a game. We'll just trot down to Joe Lambswool's, at the World's End, about two miles further on, and if you *do* care for sport, I can promise you a real treat. He's going to pull down the old barn to-day; hasn't been touched, I dare say, for two hundred years. Talk of rats! why, it's swarming with them, as big as pole-cats pretty nigh, and twice as savage. He's got a *dawg* as I want to see tried, quite a little 'un, what you would call a toy-*dawg*, you know; but they tell me he'll tackle to anything alive, and knows how to kill a cat. If I like him I'll buy him; and we'll give old Brimstone a treat into the bargain," added my amiable entertainer, looking back at the bull-terrier, who was toiling behind us, bespattered with mud, his tail lowered, his tongue out, and a villanous expression of sullenness and ferocity stamped on his round massive forehead.

"I should like it excessively," I replied, with an inward shudder, belying, most uncomfortably, my unqualified expressions of delight, and the Jovial, turning on me a look of astonished approval, made a queer noise through his teeth, that started Crafty Kate incontinently into a canter.

"Well! I'm in for it now!" was my mental soliloquy, as we went whirling past the dripping trees and hedges with increasing rapidity. How could I ever be induced to blunder into such a trap as this? A wet day; a dangerous drive; a pot-house gathering, and an afternoon spent in a tumble-down barn, full of draughts I make no doubt, and by no means water-tight; watching for rats, animals of which I have the greatest horror, and circumventing the same by means of ferrets—creatures if possible more disgusting to me than their prey—all because I hadn't nerve to say ' No.' And not a chance now of seeing Miss Merlin when she comes home from hunting! Softly! this is a day's penance. You must get through it as you best can!"

A rescue, however, when I least expected it, was proposed for me by a kind fortune, to snatch me from the *ratting* part of my discomforts. The lane down which we were bowling, though of considerable length, was not that proverbial one in which there is no turning. On reaching an angle by a sign-post, the Jovial pulled up, with great animation displayed on his broad white face.

"I can hear 'em running in Tangler's Copse, as plain as can be," said he, putting up his hand in the air, and cocking his head on one side to listen. Tangler's Copse, be it observed, was a straggling woodland in the Castle Cropper country, from which it was always difficult, and generally impossible, to force a fox into the open. "Listen, Softly!" he continued, with increasing excitement; "I'm blessed if that isn't the horn! See, Kate hears it too."

I am not gifted with extraordinary fineness of ear, particularly when well wrapped up on a rainy day; so I turned down the collar of my great coat, and took off my shawl-handkerchief to listen. There was no doubt we were in the vicinity of hounds; I could hear them distinctly, running as it seemed with a good scent, and cheered by occasional blasts on the horn.

The drizzling rain struck cold on my bare cheek. Kate's

head was up, her ears erect, her nostrils dilated, and she trembled in every limb.

"Bother the rats for to-day!" exclaimed my mercurial charioteer. "What say you, Softly? Let's go hunting instead. The mare can jump like fun, and the trap can go anywhere. Open the gate, there's a good chap! In the next field but one there's a bridle-road takes us right away to Tangler's Copse."

I descended from the tall conveyance to do his bidding, dirtying my gloves, wetting my feet, and daubing my coat with mud in the process; but there is a condition of the human mind, at which it ceases to be a free agent, and I had arrived at that negative state, when we quitted the turnpike-road. Once more climbing with difficulty to my seat, I found myself bumping over the ridge-and-furrow of a large grass field, and, straining my eyes to find an egress, became aware that it was the Jovial's intention to drive through a sort of gap in the fence, where the ditch had been partially filled up. It was now time to protest, which I did loudly and energetically; but my objections were too late. "Sit tight, Softly! *Gently*, Kate!" exclaimed Plumtree in a breath; and with a bump, a jerk, and a most astounding bang against the splash-board, we were safe over, and careering along the next field.

I was glad to see a gate led out of this enclosure. I would have climbed up and down those red wheels fifty times, rather than repeat the process we had just now accomplished.

Crafty Kate, shamelessly belying the first half of her name, seemed to enter thoroughly into the spirit of the thing, swinging along at a very respectable pace, with her ears cocked, her head and tail both up, and an obvious determination to join the chase with as little delay as possible.

The vehicle sprang and jerked, and swung from side to side: the wheels bespattered us from head to foot with mud: the splashboard alone prevented us from shooting out, over the mare's back. No one who has ever tried it will wish to repeat the uncomfortable diversion of galloping in a gig.

Fortunately the rain began to cease, the clouds cleared away, and a burst of winter sunshine enabled us to see as far as the dead flatness of the country would allow.

The Jovial pulled up short, not without considerable difficulty. "They're away, by all that's lucky," exclaimed he, shifting his reins into his whip-hand, that he might give me a congratulatory slap on the back, which knocked all the breath out of my body. "Never knew a fox to leave Tangler's Copse before, and bearing right down upon us too, or I'm a Scotchman! There's the fox, by jingo! Hold your tongue, Softly!"

The injunction was quite unnecessary, for I am not one of the halloaing tribe. Moreover, my handkerchief was pulled up to my nose, and I did not myself see the cause of my companion's excitement. He was right, however; presently two or three couple of hounds straggled into the field adjoining that in which we were stationed, ran to and fro along the hedge-side, put their noses down, threw their tongues, and followed by the whole pack, streamed across the pasture on the line of their prey.

It was great fun, and a new sensation, to watch the progress of the field, as one sat an unoccupied spectator, perched in a thing like a tea-tray on a pair of tall red wheels. I can quite understand the pleasure an old gentleman has, who rides quietly out on his cob, to see them "find and go away."

A couple of simultaneous *crashes* in the fence announced

the arrival in the same field with the hounds of the Earl himself, and a hard-riding gentleman with moustaches, a visitor at the castle. Fifty yards or so to their right again, and somewhat nearer the pack, a beautiful grey horse, having been quietly trotted up the hard pathway that led to it, landed in artistic form over a hog-backed stile with a footboard, ridden by an elegant figure in a lady's habit, of whom it was impossible at that distance to recognize the face. Happening, however, to glance at my companion's countenance (who caught his breath by the way, during this performance), and observing it to become a deep crimson, my surmises that the daring Amazon was none other than Miss Merlin were to a certain extent corroborated.

Then came a bay, and a brown, and a chestnut, the latter falling at his fence, but inflicting no damage on his rider, who never let go the bridle, but was up and at it again without delay. These were followed by another bay, who refused to jump, and a dark-coated gentleman on a roan, whose heart failed him at the last stride, and who faded ignominiously away from that moment. The huntsman and first whip must have come a different line altogether, for we saw their velvet caps bobbing up and down in the distance, but could not otherwise have identified them.

The Jovial, however, was now waxing visibly impatient. "Dash it!" said he, "we may as well see the finish. I'm game, Softly, if you are. Come along, Kate!" And without waiting for the consent, which as a partner in the firm I think I was entitled to withhold, he laid the rein on the mare's back, and we were once more jolting and bumping across the fields in search of some dubious and unfrequented bridle-road.

My friend was a good pilot. I must do him the justice

to admit that quality. He seemed to know every gate and lane in the country, also to possess an intuitive knowledge of the run of a fox, with a staunch predilection for keeping down wind. I did not despair of coming up with the chase once more, and truth to tell I was not without hopes that to-day my curiosity might be satisfied with a view of Miss Merlin.

"The Jovial," on the other hand, had become pre-occupied and restless. No longer dispensing his quaint sallies and florid parables in my ear, he gave his whole attention to Crafty Kate, an arrangement to which I should have been the last person on earth to object; and although he drove that game and resolute animal with merciless rapidity, it was in a style considerably less random than before. Perhaps the influence of the brandy had died out; perhaps he felt the depression that always succeeds the excitement of seeing hounds, when it has evaporated. Perhaps he was thinking of his dinner, perhaps of the rat-catching he had missed, perhaps of Miss Merlin. We drove on for at least two miles without speaking.

In justice to my friend's humanity, I am bound to observe that we had long ago taken pity on Brimstone, and hoisted him into the cart, where he lay coiled up under my legs, sniffing them ominously from time to time, as if only deterred by considerations of the merest politeness from taking a bite out of them at the most sensitive place. I dreaded lest a jolt severer than common should be construed by this amiable animal into a personal insult to himself.

To any one who has ever tried the delusive pastime of following hounds at a distance, with any expectation of coming up with them, I may leave the task of imagining our repeated disappointments and the labour, like that of Sisyphus, undergone by Crafty Kate. The persevering sportsman will have no difficulty in understanding how we drove from field-road to cross-road, and from cross-road to highway; how the little indistinct figures and black hats, dotting and bobbing behind the hedges, were now on our right, now on our left, anon almost within hail, and then hopelessly and provokingly ahead; how we saw the hounds themselves entering Cropley Pastures, and, thinking to nick in upon them at Whitethorns, found they had taken an unexpected turn to Swillingford mill; in short, how surely, as must always be the case in a good run, the further we went, the further we were left behind, till our hopes, being suddenly raised by a butcher in a tax-cart, who had met them not half-a-mile from where we then were, and thought they must have "got him in a drain," to be as suddenly dashed into ruins again by a farmer's lad at the spot indicated, who vowed they had been gone twenty minutes, and "were running like fire," we gave it up in despair, and turned Crafty Kate's head, soberly and sadly, on her homeward way. A mouthful of gruel at a road-side public-house for the mare, and a small measure of hot ale, with a glass of gin, a spoonful of brown sugar, and a dash of spice in it, called by the different titles of "lambs' wool," "dog's nose," and "purl," but of superlative merit after a three hours' drive in the wet, restored us all, except Brimstone, to something of our earlier energy. I was glad, I confess, to have got through the drive without an accident, and looked forward to a warm house and a comfortable dressing-room, where my servant, I hoped, had already arrived with my things, more cheerfully than I should have conceived possible in the morning, when I anticipated my enforced visit to The Ashes with considerable distaste. The Jovial, too, having apparently drowned his unpleasant reflections, whatever they might be, in the hot mixture, came out once more in his normal character, accepting one of my cigars with facetious condescension, and sticking it in the extreme corner of his mouth, from which he never once removed it till he had smoked it down to the very stump.

"Mare's about told out, Softly," said he, as we drove somewhat soberly through the very gate he had spoken of in the morning, opening it by the dangerous process of running the shaft against its bars, and fending it off from the wheel with his hand. "Hard day for the Crafty: those field-roads are so blessed deep. Never mind; another half-mile will see us. I don't think you know my sisters: remarkable young women, and accomplished, 'specially Jane. I am prepared now to back Jane against any other girl in England, weight for age of course, to do five things—work cross stitch, whistle jigs, do the outside edge backwards, speak German, and make a sparrow pudding. My money is ready at The Ashes, Waterborough, this identical house of call we're coming to, that it's too dark for you to see. Catch hold, while I jump out and ring the bell."

The flood of warm light that shone out upon us from the hall was indeed a pleasant contrast to the dark cold afternoon, which had already changed again for the worse. As I divested myself of my wraps, with the assistance of a staid elderly servant, young Plumtree welcomed me quite courteously to his father's house, diverging, however, immediately afterwards, into the kind of jesting slang which was most familiar to him.

"You're wet," he observed, laying his hand on my coat, through which the rain had indeed penetrated. "Perhaps you'd like to go and dress at once. Indeed, we dine in less than an hour. Shall I show you your room? Will you have anything before dinner?—glass of sherry?—biscuit?—crust of bread and a pickle? No? then step this way, if you please. Here's your room; things laid out—hot water laid on. There's the bell: *you* ring for what you *want*, and the servants will bring you what they *have!*"

Behold me, then, like a man in a dream, dressing comfortably for dinner, in a strange house, of which I did not know the proprietor, nor, indeed, one of the inmates, except the *harum-scarum* young gentleman who had introduced me. In justice to myself, I made an elaborate toilet—white tie, black suit, thin boots—everything rigorously correct. There is no costume, in my opinion, which so marks the distinction of classes, as the plain dinner-dress of an English gentleman; and, indeed, I once heard that very invidious title defined as "a man who had got evening clothes." Passing down to the drawing-room—an apartment I had no difficulty in finding, for the door was open, and a lamp shone brilliantly from it into the hall—I had leisure to observe the articles of furniture in the passages, and to remark on the idiosyncrasy which prompts all country gentlemen alike to ornament the insides of their houses with stuffed animals in glass cases. The Ashes was rich in specimens of this description. All kinds of birds flourished their beaks at the visitors on the stairs. A gigantic pike, like a miniature shark, grinned at him over the chimney-piece, and a hideous otter snarled at him from under the umbrella-stand in the hall. A portrait, which I concluded to be that of Mr. Plumtree senior, also adorned this crowded vestibule. I studied it by the light of my chamber candlestick, not entirely, I fear, without spilling some wax on the floor during the process, in pardonable curiosity as to the exterior of the gentleman with whom I was about to dine. The picture was in all probability more valuable from its resemblance to the original, than from any intrinsic merit of its own as a work of art. It represented a florid personage, in the prime of life, attired in a bright blue coat, and yellow waistcoat, on both which articles of apparel the artist had bestowed a liberal amount of colour, sitting by a pillar of porphyry, under a crimson curtain, "with a distant view of the changing sea." His face, devoid of any outward expression, denoted that rapt state of thought peculiar, I am informed, to the highest order of intellects, and he seemed equally unmoved by the magnificence of the scenery, the gorgeousness of the curtain which overhung him, or the splendour of a heavy watch-chain and seals that rested massively against his nankeen stomach. On a table at his elbow stood a large book and a snuff-box, whilst his hand rested carelessly on the head of a black retriever dog. "If old Plumtree is like that," was my mental observation, "he must present as great a contrast to the Jovial as was ever afforded in the inconvenient relationship of father and son. I did not speak aloud, fortunately; for this conclusion brought me into the drawing-room, which, having dressed early, I expected I should have had to myself: it was not so, however. On entering that apartment—a pretty, well-furnished, long, low room, with some excellent prints and a grand pianoforte—I was somewhat discomfited to find it already occupied by two young ladies, dressed, as far as my confusion permitted me to observe, precisely alike, sitting in precisely the same attitude, and engaged over similar pieces of crochet-work. I bowed very awkwardly, and walked up to the fire, with the startling intelligence that it was "a cold evening," a proposition neither of the ladies seemed in a position to confute. This masterly manœuvre, however, gave me an opportunity

of studying both their faces, and I am bound to admit that
the one predominating idea present to my mind, during a
perusal of their features, was, "How shall I ever know one
from the other, when their brother comes down, and for-
mally introduces us?" Each of them was a rather tall, rather
large young lady, with hands and feet to correspond. Each
of them had a certain regularity of features, totally devoid
of any expression whatsoever, that might have laid claim
to good looks, had it not been nullified by the absence
of colouring and want of tone in their rather large, rather flat faces. If either of them had unfortunately taken
to drinking, she would have been a bad likeness of her
brother the Jovial. That I longed ardently for the conclusion of that gentleman's toilet is no matter of surprise,
the conversation between the Misses Plumtree and myself
being driven, so to speak, at a funereal rate, and in the
longest possible stages I gathered, however, from a certain
decision of tone in their few and disjointed remarks, that
there was no mother Plumtree, and that the vestals now before me were the presiding goddesses of the place.

At length, to my great relief, I heard a door open on the
staircase, and a manly step approaching, which I feared, even
while I listened, was too ponderous for that of my friend.
The young ladies made a rustling kind of movement, as if
to bespeak my attention. A deep voice in the hall was heard
to say, "Dinner directly!" and the portly form of mine host
walked into the drawing-room, with outstretched hand, and
that welcome on his lips with which an Englishman always
receives a guest into his castle, whether that metaphorical
building be really a ducal residence, a squire's hall, or a day-
labourer's cottage.

Old Mr. Plumtree was a great improvement on his son,
as well as his picture. Although of the plainest and most

unsophisticated of squires, he was obviously a high-bred gentleman; and his old-fashioned attire—for he had not discarded the blue coat, yellow waistcoat, and white stockings of his younger days—was perfectly in keeping with his fresh old face, round and rosy as a winter-apple; his fine bald head and stately figure, deep of chest, stout of limb, and somewhat protuberant of stomach.

"I am glad James found ye at home, Mr. Softly," said he, "and doubly glad he persuaded ye to come over and eat your mutton with us here. My daughters, Mr. Softly—Rebecca and Jane." Both ladies again got up, and we bowed and curtsied once more to one another; whilst I still remained as much in ignorance as ever as to *which* was Rebecca and *which* was Jane. "You got here before six," continued my host, evidently bent on making me feel myself at home. "Our roads are not the best travelling in the dark, but I conclude you don't make much account of roads. Broke your collar-bone at a fence? and a large one too, I'll be bound. I was a sportsman myself, Mr. Softly. I recollect in the year—"

"Dinner is on the table, sir!" announced the respectable-looking servant, interrupting his master's reminiscences at this juncture; and with a nod to me to take Miss Plumtree, which I aknowledged by diving at the nearest lady, whom I afterwards found out to be the younger sister, we filed off in great state for the dining-room, the Jovial joining the procession in the hall, and whispering in my ear, as he passed my chair, "Don't be afraid of the Madeira, it's been twice round the Cape; and if he talks about breeding hounds, mind you say 'Yes' to the governor!"

With the *carte du pays* thus spread before me, I unfolded my napkin, and went at an excellent clear soup with the utmost confidence

CHAPTER X.

THE OLD SQUIRE.

THE dinner passed off far more pleasantly than I should have imagined possible. Drawn out by their brother, and gradually losing their awe of myself as a stranger, both Rebecca and Jane found something to say, and voices wherewith to say it. Well-brought-up girls in our English society are all shy (though not half so reserved as foreign young ladies of the same age), or at all events, are taught that it is right to appear so; but we must never forget that it is as natural for a woman to talk as for a duck to swim. Let them alone a little: don't hurry them at first. If your host gives you good champagne, as in these anti-tariff days he is very likely to do, press them to have a glass. Turn the conversation upon some individual, the more notorious the better, of their own sex; but be careful to state that you cannot see what there is to admire in her yourself, and then begin resignedly at your cutlet. Take my word for it, the talking will be done for you, till gloves and handkerchiefs have to be recovered, and the ladies spread their pinions and sail away to the drawing-room.

The Jovial was also a host in himself. The presence of his sisters toned down his slang a trifle, while it enhanced his liveliness. He gave a vivid and laughable description of our day's hunting, performed in the gig, but rather hesitated and showed some little confusion when describing our first view of the hounds.

"Who was with them?" asked his father; the old man's

eye kindling, as he filled a glass of ruby port, and offered me my choice between that and a tempting-looking claret decanter. " Who was going well ? The Earl, I'll pound it ! Castle-Cropper will be with 'em, let it be ever so good for pace ; and Will Hawke, I suppose ; and who else ?

" The person that seemed to me to be going best," I here interposed, filling my glass, " was a lady on a grey horse ; a Miss Merlin, I believe, who is staying at the inn at Soakington. A most extraordinary horsewoman !"

The Jovial blushed, though he hid his confusion in a great gulp of Madeira. Rebecca and Jane interchanged looks of considerable meaning, and the former (I think) took up the running.

" How very unfeminine !" said she, turning round to me. " Don't you think so, Mr. Softly ? I'm sure gentlemen must wish ladies anywhere else, when they come out hunting. I think it oughtn't to be allowed ; and this Miss Merlin, you know, rides just like a man."

" Don't believe her !" exclaimed the Jovial, in his turn. " I've seen her out with our hounds many a time, but never on anything but a side-saddle, in my life."

Rebecca blushed in her turn. " How *can* you, James ?" said she. " Of course I didn't mean *that*. But you're so infatuated about Miss Merlin, you think she can't do wrong. And what there is to admire in her, I can't see, for my part."

" Why, she *does* ride beautifully, you know," put in Jane, apologetically ; at least, I suppose it was Jane, as she seemed more tolerant of manly exercises than her sister, and was altogether of a livelier and more attractive style. I couldn't help thinking, even then, I would give something to see her doing the outside edge backwards.

"Well, but that's a *man's* accomplishment," replied her sister. "I was speaking more of her good looks. Come, Mr. Softly; give us your honest opinion. *Do* you think her so very wonderfully beautiful?"

This was obviously a back-hander at James, who, having by this time tackled well to the Madeira, bore it with the utmost philosophy.

I was obliged to confess that, although living in the same hotel, I had never seen her, not thinking it necessary to add my opinion of Justine, nor to dwell on the circumstances under which I had made that sweet little woman's acquaintance.

"Never seen her!" repeated both ladies in tones of the utmost surprise; but while Rebecca's emphasis denoted simple astonishment, I was concerned to detect in that of Jane a covert reproach and contempt. What must a young lady of her gifts and acquirements have thought of so recreant a knight as myself? They are all alike, you see— these ladies; repudiating very judiciously, as an established principle, too great diffidence in our sex, and readier far to forgive us when erring in the opposite extreme. The Bissextile, or Leap-year, does not come often enough to allow their taking the initiative as a regular thing; so a backward swain is like a jibbing horse—the very worst description of animal you can drive, either for single or double harness, light or heavy draught.

"And what do you think of our hounds, Mr. Softly?" said old Plumtree, now putting in a word, as he sent the bottles round a second time; a signal for the young ladies to depart, and for me to open the door to let them out—a manœuvre I accomplished with the best grace I could muster, and an uncomfortable conviction that they might, and probably *would* talk me over, not without critical disapproval, immediately they were settled in the drawing-room.

As we took our seats round the fire, which sparkled pleasantly amongst the glasses and decanters on the little round table, my host repeated his question, adding, whilst his son almost imperceptibly elevated his eye-brows, " Don't you think now, *as* a sportsman, that we're all inclined to breed hounds a little too fast ?"

This was obviously old Plumtree's crotchet, and I resigned myself to my fate.

" You must get pretty quick after a fox *some* part of the day, if you've a mind to kill him," I replied ; because I had heard a huntsman once say something of the same kind. And Jem likewise put in his oar with the remark, that " slow hounds, in these days, would never get from under the horses' feet"—an observation received by his father with that silent contempt which a man would consider extremely rude to a stranger, but which, nevertheless, he does not scruple to betray towards those who have the advantage of belonging to his own family.

" Oh ! I grant you that," said the old gentleman. " A fox is a speedy animal himself, and it stands to reason that if you are to catch him, you must some time or another go faster than he does. But haste is not always speed. A man may be in a devil of a hurry, and yet slip two paces backwards for every one he advances. The same process that kills a hare will kill a fox. The keeping constantly *at* him, not the bustling him along best pace for ten or fifteen minutes. Now, your hounds of the present day are always flashing over the scent into the next field. Either you waste a deal of valuable time by having to try back ; or if your huntsman is as wild as his hounds, he gallops forward blowing his horn, makes a wide cast, and loses him altogether. Either way you destroy your own object, which I take to be the enjoyment of *riding* in a gallop with hounds that are running with their noses down, and the enjoyment of *hunting* by seeing the sagacity of a close-working pack, persevering through difficulties, and rewarded with a kill.

"I'm an old fogey, I grant you, Mr. Softly. If I do ever go out to look at the hounds, it's on a pony; and I can no more see, the way 'Jem' there goes, than I can fly; but let me tell you, I could have beat his head off, and given him two stone of weight into the bargain, when I was his age. It's not that I want hounds to stay behind with *me*, that makes me say they're bred too fast now-a-days: far from it. I like you young fellows to enjoy yourselves, and have brushing gallops, and comb your whiskers well out in the bull-finches, and sew up your horses and come home, and drink 'fox-hunting.' Ring the bell, Jem; we'll have another bottle of that claret. I think I know what riding is, if I haven't forgotten it. You see that dark-brown horse over the fire-place? That's a good likeness, Mr. Softly; and that was the best horse I ever had in my life."

Raising my eyes in obedience to my host's behests, they rested on a picture enclosed in a most gorgeous frame, representing a brown horse with rather a long back and wonderfully short legs; his tail reduced to the smallest dimensions, and his ears, so to speak, at full cock. This animal, in the highest possible condition, and with every muscle standing out from its body to a rigid degree of tension, was depicted in the centre of a flowery mead, overshadowed by large trees in their densest summer foliage, gazing fixedly at a red-brick mansion, on the further side of a sheet of water which had by no means found its own level, but was represented in the abnormal condition of covering the side of a slope. I gazed with admiration not unmixed with astonishment. Delighted with the obvious impression, my host went on :—

"I don't think I ever had one that could go on like 'Supple-Jack.' I called him Supple-Jack, Mr. Softly, on account of his breed. He was by Bamboo, that horse,—was out of a mare they called Twisting Jane ; and no pace was too good, no day too long for him. We didn't think so much of jumping in my day as they do now ; at least, we didn't *talk* about it so large ; but you might lay the rein on Supple-Jack's neck, and trot him up to any gate in this country, and he'd take you safely over it. Why, Jem there will tell you, when he was a boy, he's seen the old horse, when he was past twenty, jump the gate backwards and forwards, into the paddock by the little orchard, only to come and be fed. Jump, indeed! they couldn't go far without knowing how to jump, in *my* day."

"Well, sir, you talk of runs ; why, I rode that horse the famous Topley day, with these very hounds, when we found in Topley Banks, immediately after the long frost, and killed our fox on the lawn at Mount Pleasant, eight miles as the crow flies, in thirty-four minutes. Talk of pace, sir! you can't beat that in these flying days. I never got a pull at my horse from first to last ; and, barring a bit of a scramble at the Sludge, where the banks were rotten from the sudden thaw, he never put a foot wrong. Zounds, sir! I don't believe he ever changed his leg. The late Earl and myself got away together from the Banks, close to the hounds. He was a good man across country, but he couldn't ride like his son. There were a dozen more close behind us, but they never got near enough to speak ; and the Earl and I

went sailing on, side by side, over the Sloppington Lordship,
and all along by Soakington Pastures, not far from where
you're staying now, Mr. Softly, till we got within sight of
Tanglers Copse, where you were to-day. That and the prospect
of a nasty overgrown bull-finch, with only one place in it, made
up uncommon strong, tempted the Earl a little out of his
line, and I never saw *him* again. Supple-Jack and I had it
all to ourselves after that, and he carried me over the ha-ha,
on to the lawn at Mount Pleasant, just as the hounds rolled
their fox over, under the drawing-room window. There
was a large party staying in the house (your poor mother
was one of them, Jem), and they all thought the frost was
not sufficiently out of the ground to hunt, and so had remained at home.

"'Where do you hail from?' said old Squire Gayman,
the proprietor, who had served under Nelson.

"'From Topley Banks!' I answered, taking the fox from
the hounds, and putting him across the branch of a tree in
the shrubbery, whilst I kept a sharp look-out for the Earl
and the huntsman, and the whips and the rest of the field.

"'Why, its scarcely gone eleven?' said the Squire, looking at his watch; you haven't wasted much time this morning. When did they put the hounds in?'

"'At half-past ten to a minute,' I replied, 'and we found
and came away directly. But I haven't kept much of a dead
reckoning since, and they never checked nor hovered once
to give me a chance of looking at my watch.'

"'And how did the ground ride?' said two or three in a
breath.

"'Faith! you must ask Supple-Jack that question.' was
my answer; 'for indeed I hadn't much time to inquire.'

"Now, the flashiest hounds alive couldn't have done such

a distance at that, in a shorter time. And mark you, Mr. Softly, we had no tearing along, heads up and sterns down, and hounds tailing for a mile because they were all racing with each other. Far from it; they kept well together, and threw their tongues merrily enough every now and then, when they were 'smousing' through a fence, or shaking themselves dry after a plunge into the Sludge; but they kept always driving on. That was what did it. No hesitation, no uncertainty, no getting their heads up, and looking about for assistance. There was nobody to interfere with them if they had wanted it, for the huntsman was a mile behind, and dropping further and further astern every yard they went, and the Earl had left his horn at home, and had little breath to spare besides.

"They ran their fox unassisted, and they killed him unassisted; but then, you observe, these hounds had been trained for many a long season to put down their noses and *hunt;* and it's my opinion that they used to run so fast for the very reason that they were what superficial people call slow."

The old gentleman here filled his glass, and took a good solemn gulp at the dry port, before proceeding to the demonstration of the proposition he had laid down. "Jovial Jem" and myself followed his example, the latter giving me to understand, by the expression of his countenance, that the governor was now mounted on his hobby, and had better not be interrupted in the process of riding it to a standstill.

"It's all nonsense about hounds carrying such a head," said the squire. "It may look very fine to see them charging in line, like a squadron of dragoons, or a flock of sheep when they've been turned by a dog; but what's the conse-

quence? If they once get ten yards over the scent, it's all
up. Jealous and flashy, each tries to get ahead of his com-
rade; and the further they go the further they get from
their fox, till they're forced to stop and stare about them
like a pack of fools, and have recourse to their huntsman
after all. Then, what a pretty business they make of it!
To my thinking, it's enough to disgust any man with hunting, to see hounds cast, except of course under very peculiar
circumstances—such as ground stained with stock, sudden
storm coming on when a fox is sinking, or what not. It's
no pleasure to me, nor to you either, I should suppose, to
see them tearing along at the heels of their huntsman's
horse, neither knowing nor caring apparently where they go,
so long as they can keep out of reach of the whipper-in,
who is flogging and shouting behind them. Then they don't
half run, after all, even if they *should* be so lucky as to get
on the line of their fox again. He is *mobbed* to death, in all
probability, rather than fairly killed; and half the hounds
don't seem to care about eating him when they've got him,
instead of raging and tearing like so many wolves, as they
do when they know they've caught him for themselves.
No, sir; give me a good *line-hunting* pack that stick close
to their work, though perhaps they *do* make a little noise
over it. If the leaders should chance to over-run the scent
a bit, why the others take it up, and there is no perceptible
delay. I have seen these Castle Cropper hounds hunt
through sheep or oxen, just as steadily, though not quite so
fast, perhaps, as if they were running in a good-scenting
woodland. The present Earl, though, is breeding them too
fast. I always tell him so. He's breeding them too fast.
And I think Will Hawke is of the same opinion as myself."

"You consider Will an excellent huntsman, do you not?" I hazarded as a safe remark.

"He ought to be," replied my host, filling himself another bumper of port. "He was regularly bred for it, and entered to it, if ever man was. When he was a little chap, not three feet high, he used to help his father, who was feeder at the kennels. And I remember well the dowager Countess telling me that he knew the name of every hound in the pack long before he could answer one of the questions at her Sunday school. He used to ride the horses, too, at exercise; and being a smart little fellow, soon picked up all that was to be learned in the stable and elsewhere. One day, when he was quite a lad, and the hounds met at the kennel, as they often did, the first-whip was suddenly taken ill, and unable to get upon his horse; the other man was forty miles away, getting back some young hounds from walk. Will petitioned sorely to be put on a steady nag, and allowed to take the invalid's place; and, as he was the only person who knew the hounds by name, he was permitted to do so. We were all amused at the excitement and ambitious airs of the young neophyte, who bustled about the rides of the covert, and "sang out" to any transgressing hound in most approved form. Old Craner, who was huntsman then, was perfectly delighted with the quickness and sagacity of the young one. At last we crossed the Swimley with a cold scent, and the hounds took to running on the opposite side of the river. Craner, who was an old man, besides having an excellent situation, and not caring to risk it, voted this all wrong, and expressed a wish to stop them. Young Hawke had swum his horse halfway across before the words were out of his senior's mouth; and although he did not stop them, the young rascal!—for the scent improved immensely, and they took to running forthwith,—he elected himself into the post of huntsman for the occasion, and killed his fox in masterly style, after a good hunting run. He was made second-whip at the first opportunity, and has been in the establishment ever since. It's a good many years ago that I'm speaking of, Mr. Softly; and the present Earl thinks he's getting slow; but I'll back old Will to find his fox, and hunt his fox, and kill his fox, as handsomely as any of the young ones still."

"They all say he overdoes the letting-alone system," observed the Jovial, with a sly glance at me. "I've seen him lose more than one fox on a bad-scenting day, because he wouldn't go to a holloa, not even if it was given by Tom Crow himself, whom he ought to be able to depend upon."

"And how many have you known him *kill* by that same letting-alone system, Master Flash?" exclaimed old Plumtree with the usual impatience manifested by the senior when a son is so injudicious as to differ from his father. "That's the way with you young chaps, that think you know all about it, and the whole time you haven't even the wisdom to *know* that you *don't know!* Will Hawke's hounds will stoop to a colder scent than any hounds in England, simply *because* he lets 'em alone; and they take no more notice of a holloa than if it were a boy scaring crows. As for Tom, the first-whip, he's a conceited, ignorant chap, to my thinking; always 'clapping forward,' as he calls it, and dodging about, instead of minding his business. If I had my way with Tom, I'd sew his mouth up, take his whip from him, and put him on a horse with three legs. He'd be a precious sight more useful than he is now. At any rate, he couldn't do so much mischief. I never thought much of Tom; never liked his voice—never liked his riding—never liked his boots and breeches."

"He's a neat fellow enough, too," I interfered, rather inclined to take up the cudgels for my friend Tom, who had opened sundry gates for me, and shown other signs of civility on my behalf, the first day I was out.

"Newmarket, sir; Newmarket!" said the old squire. "Bad school, bad scholars. You can see it in the way he sits upon his horse; though he's got good hands, I'll allow, and can gallop them fairly enough. The present Earl picked him out of a trainer's stable, to ride second-horse, and he did it so *badly*, always larking over the fences in front, instead of trotting on soberly behind, that he got him out of that at any price; and, it's my belief, only made him first-whip because he'd nowhere else to put him, and didn't like to turn him adrift, being a sober respectable man enough.

"But he's not my idea of a whipper-in, though I may be wrong. Everything is so changed since *my* day, and every man who wears a red coat now seems to think he knows as much as King Solomon (with a withering glance at Jem, who was buzzing the bottle of Madeira). This Tom Crow is always going on to get a view, and putting his ugly face everywhere it ought *not* to be, under the idea that he is helping to kill the fox. That is all he has a notion of—to *kill* the fox. Now old Hawke, though he's as fond of blood as any huntsman alive, and far too much given to *digging*, in my opinion, is all for catching him fairly, or else not catching him at all.

"What's the use of a view? If a man believes his hounds (and if he don't, he'd better hang 'em and retire himself into private life as a market-gardener), he knows their game is before them, when he hears them throw their tongues, just as certainly as if he'd viewed it fifty times. And, ten to one, long before you see the fox, the fox sees you, and he's headed back again. I wish I'd a pound for every good run I've seen spoilt in that way. No, no! I never want to clap eyes on him till I've got him in my hand. I know all about him, then; and so do the hounds. Will you have any more wine, Softly? or shall we join the ladies?"

Half a glass of rich brown sherry, than which nothing sobers a man more rapidly, or settles his stomach more comfortably after an over-dose of claret; a stretch of the legs, an arrangement of the neckcloth, and I felt myself ready to confront Jane and Rebecca once more, perhaps with a somewhat keener sense of their merits than I had entertained before dinner. On entering the drawing-room, a dead silence prevailed between the two; I concluded therefore that the topic which they seemed thus suddenly to have dropped must have been one that would not bear *ventilation* (to use the Parliamentary slang of the present day) before the gentlemen. Perhaps, indeed, it may have referred to the general character of their visitor. I would have given something to know whether they thought me most knave or fool.

A well-timed observation from their father put me at last *au fait* as to the identity of each lady; and when papa said, "Rebecca, won't you give us some music?" and the one next whom I did not chance to have taken my seat replied, "Very well, papa. What will you have?" it became evident to me that, having devoted myself before, and at dinner, to the elder lady, it was now the younger sister's turn to have her share of my attentions.

Rebecca played skilfully, and accompanied herself, in a small voice, with a tolerably correct attention to time; chiefly delighting, I observed, in simple ballads of a touching and pathetic tendency, such as "Annie," "Willie, we have missed you," and a very tearful song about a person of the name of "Margaret."

Pending these melodies, Jane, whom I now discovered to be a lady of a certain force of character and an inquiring turn of mind, "put me through my facings," if I may use the expression, on a variety of subjects, concerning most of which it has since occurred to me I must have betrayed remarkable ignorance. When you have been out in the cold all day, then enjoyed a good dinner, and a good deal of it, washed down by copious libations of excellent wine, in a warm room, I believe, if you are blessed with a healthy constitution, drowsiness is the inevitable result. Then, suppose yourself placed in a very comfortable arm-chair, opposite a blazing fire, with the hum of quiet voices and the tones of a pianoforte falling soothingly on your ear, and you can exactly imagine my position.

I am aware of having confessed truthfully enough to my fair inquisitor, that I could neither play cricket, billiards, nor rackets; that I did not care a great deal for shooting; should be likely to upset if I ventured to drive four horses; and had never had a pair of skates on in my life. I feel sure, at the same time, that I sustained the contempt she could not but entertain for me with wonderful equanimity, and that I further sank my intellectual powers to a level with my physical incapacity, by an avowal of my inability to read a word of German. But Jane was not to be thus choked off: she was one of those energetic young ladies who, in their zeal to be doing, must needs have as many strings to their bow as Phœbus could count upon his lyre. She collected autographs, she discovered character from handwriting, she pestered all her friends for their old postage-stamps; though what she did with them, or what anybody does with them, even when the amount rises to a million, is to me a profound mystery. Amongst other inquisitorial objects, she possessed a wonderful book, in which the sufferer was requested to place on record his opinions on sundry matters to which in all probability he had never before given a thought;—such as his favourite authors in prose and verse, the characters he most admired in modern and ancient history, his pet preacher, and the names he should prefer to give his sons and daughters, if he had any: all topics on which it is obvious none but a man of profound forethought and reflection can be expected to have made up his mind. I have a distinct recollection of skipping all these questions till I came to the important one that required to know my favourite food, and falling asleep then and there in an abortive attempt to write the word "plum-pudding."

Jem's mellow voice, joining his sister's in one of the Negro melodies, awoke me in a state of great penitence and confusion. I was pleased to observe, however, that I was not the only culprit, for old Plumtree, with his head sunk into his voluminous white waistcoat, was accompanying his children with a grand chorus of snores. But the vacant chair next my own inflicted a tacit reproach that spoke whole pages of sarcasm; and I felt it an inexpressible relief when, voting it too late for whist, hand-candles were rung for, and the ladies betook themselves to bed, followed, after a brief interval, by the three gentlemen.

The Jovial, of course, went to smoke. Nobody now-a-days seems able to go to bed without that narcotic; but I declined his invitation to accompany him, and laid my weary head as soon as I possibly could upon my pillow.

Determined to have nothing more to do with Crafty Kate, I had taken the precaution of telling my servant to order a chaise to be ready for me at an early hour the following morning; and when I discovered that it had been freezing hard in the night, and the ground was one sheet of ice, I felt I had no reason to repent of my precaution.

We assembled at breakfast at the early hour of nine; the Jovial coming down in a shooting suit of marvellous fabrication and device, avowing his intention of going out "to look for ducks," a pastime in which I cannot but think I was wise to decline joining him. The squire was off to his farm the instant he had swallowed his breakfast, not, however, without giving me a pressing and hospitable invitation to remain with him another day. This I felt compelled to refuse. I longed to be back at my quiet lodging once more; and, like all men who have not room for a great many ideas at a time, felt that I had now got hold of one which took entire possession of me. This was neither more nor less than a morbid desire to see Miss Merlin.

I do not think either Rebecca or Jane regretted my departure. I am not a ladies' man—I know it; nor can I bring myself greatly to regret that failure in my character. But they took leave of me with cordiality and politeness, Jane even offering to lend me a book, of which we had been talking, to read in the post-chaise.

As I drew up the windows and drove away from the door, I could not sufficiently congratulate myself that I was not in that tall dog-cart, at the mercy of "Jovial Jem" and "Crafty Kate."

On my arrival at the Haycock, my first inquiry was for Miss Merlin. "She was gone to Castle Cropper," the waiter said. "Maid and things followed her yesterday. Gone to stay, sir? Yes, sir. Didn't know for how long; but the groom rather thought as she wouldn't be back under a fortnight."

CHAPTER XI.

THE SOAKINGTON FIELD-DAY.

A FORTNIGHT's frost tempted me to leave my comfortable quarters at the Haycock, and the delights of Miss Lushington's society, for the metropolis. Somehow hunting men never *do* keep away from London in the frost, and I had an excellent excuse in wanting the best advice about my arm. "The fracture had united very satisfactorily," said the great authority before whom I stripped, paying me at the same time an agreeable compliment on my vigorous state of health, and the development of my muscular system. By the time I had visited the different theatres, and read all the back numbers of my favourite magazines, at "The Hat and Umbrella," I was as sound again as ever I had been in my life. Nor did I forget, when once more frequenting my comfortable club, to cross-examine Quizby at great length on the subject which was still uppermost in my thoughts. His answers only made me the more anxious to see Miss Merlin; and I never greeted a thaw with greater delight than that which set in, just as I was beginning to get tired of London, and summoned me back to Soakington once more. At the railway station it was obvious that the hunting community, like those migratory birds which periodically leave the frozen regions of the north for warmer climes, was on the wing. Umbrellas and sticks, strapped together in bundles, discovered the white crook of the hunting-whip between their handles; there was a great demand at the book-stall for the 'Sporting Magazine' and the 'Field' newspaper; whilst half the hats hung up in the first-class carriages betrayed, by a little ring of wire just under the brim, that it was their natural destiny to be crushed in bull finches, knocked off by branches, possibly flattened and crumpled up by the projection of their enthusiastic wearers head-foremost to the earth.

Arrived at Soakington, the first person I met was Miss Merlin's dapper groom. These domestics come out in a thaw, as we see flies begin to swarm the first sunny day in spring. "The country," he said, in answer to my inquiries, "would ride perfectly well by to-morrow. Indeed, the frost was pretty nigh out of the ground now. His lady? Oh! she was quite well, he believed; leastways he might say as he knowed she was, for he'd been over for orders to-day—hadn't been back an hour. Where? Oh! at the Castle, to be sure, where she'd a-been stopping now a goodish spell. Would she be out to-morrow? Why, in course she would, if she were alive. Did I know that the hounds were to meet at the Haycock? A-purpose to draw Soakington Gorse—that's the new gorse as my lord made down by Willow Waterless. *Sure* of a run to-morrow, if you could be sure of anything on this mortal earth!"

Vindicating his character as a philosopher, by this profound reflection, my friend withdrew into the privacy of his own stable, and I betook myself to mine; there, having expressed a qualified approval of my stud's general appearance, I decided to ride "Tipple-cider," as being the best of them, and then retired to my apartments, to order dinner and prepare for the morrow.

I was a little disappointed, I confess, to discover that the bird was flown. I fully expected Miss Merlin would ere this have returned to her quarters at the Haycock. Also, I was a little tired with my journey and the late racketing in London. I am a quiet man, and I call supper after the play the height of dissipation. So I went early to bed, looking forward with keen excitement to the morrow.

The morning broke delightfully, promising one of those soft, fragrant days of which I have never seen the counterpart in any climate but our own, and which, alas! are rare even here. A calm, grey winter's day in England, with a faint southern breeze, and occasional gleams of sunshine descending on the distance, in perpendicular floods of gold, has always seemed to me the very perfection of weather.

The hounds were to meet at half-past ten. I was dressed and at breakfast a full hour before. To me, as to all bachelors, this is a very important meal. I like to enjoy it comfortably, in my dressing gown and slippers, before placing myself in the confinement of boots and breeches. I like to prop up the 'Morning Post,' or the last 'Quarterly,' or one of the magazines, against my coffee-pot, and feed my mind alternately with my body. Now a mouthful of ham, then a prophecy of Argus (pretty sure to be right) on the next great race; or a bite of toast, and a sentence on the Cotton question; or chip my egg and break the ice of a new story in 'Fraser,' at one and the same time, washing the whole thing down with a draught of such coffee as no servant but my own, I verily believe, is capable of concocting.

I have seen some men breakfast, and that in apparent resignation, with a button-hook in one hand and a fork in the other, a wife calling to them in the passage, children running in and out of the room, the gardener waiting for orders at the door, and their hack snorting and pawing on the gravel in front. I suppose "the hack," as the adage says, "is made for the burden." I am not ungrateful, when I reflect on sundry burdens that have not been made for my back.

At length, dressed, booted, and spurred, I made my way downstairs into the bar, where I found Miss Lushington, in a costume of surprising magnificence, far surpassing any of her previous dresses, in a high flow of spirits, and up to her very ear-rings in the business of her office. Notwithstanding all she had on hand, however, she did not fail to greet me with cordial politeness; and here I must do Miss Lushington the justice to observe, that whatever might be the calls on her attention, and however numerous the circle of her admirers, offering the accustomed incense of flattery not unmixed with chaff, she had always a word and a smile to spare for the humblest and most bashful individual who entered the magic ring. "Dear heart! Mr. Softly," said she, "it does me good to see you in your red coat again. But you'll surely remember what an escape you've had. You'll take warning, and not be so venturesome for the future."

I was not above feeling a sense of gratification at this allusion to my supposed recklessness, though I detected something like a smile on Mr. Naggett's rosy face, whilst it was uttered.

Yes, there was Mr. Naggett, in full bloom, armed and accoutred for the chase; sipping a fragrant concoction of gin-and-cloves moreover, as a further preparation. His horse, a large mealy chestnut, was being led up and down the yard. I saw it through the bar-window, and thought I never liked the look of an animal much less. All that art could accomplish had, however, been done, to set off its natural unsightliness. It was decorated with a new saddle and bridle, breast-plate, nose-band, and martingale complete. It was accoutred, moreover, with a gaudy saddle-cloth, rather too large, and a boot on every leg but one.

The owner, too, was got up in an alarming manner, and as he would have said himself, " regardless of expense." Mr. Naggett's coat was blue, with the brightest of buttons, bearing some raised device, in which a crown-imperial predominated. Mr. Naggett's waistcoat was scarlet, bound with yellow braid; and his cream-coloured neckcloth was secured by a red cornelian pin. A low-crowned hat, white cloth breeches, and high Napoleon boots, faultless in polish, but spoiled by a pair of thin racing spurs, very badly put on, completed Mr. Naggett's resplendent costume. The man himself seemed in the highest possible spirits; but I thought I could detect a slight tremor of the hand, despite his morning stimulant—that tremor which a horse is so apt in discovering, particularly when he is ridden at water.

" Nice morning, sir," said Mr. Naggett. He pronounced it *marning;* but this peculiarity I have observed amongst *ultra* sporting characters. " Hope I see you all right again, sir. You'll want both hands to-day—heels too, or I'm mistaken. Looks like a hunting *marning,* don't it, sir ? And there's a fox lies here in Soakington Gorse, as will give us a 'buster,' I know. Got your 'riding boots' on to-day, sir, I dare say."

I was somewhat nettled at his tone, three parts jesting, and not above a quarter respectful; and I replied, wishing to return sarcasm with sarcasm,—

" I shall follow you, Mr. Naggett, if I want to be well with them."

Such delicate thrusts were completely thrown away upon my friend's proof-armour of self-conceit.

"You might do worse, sir," said he, in perfect good faith. "I'm riding a real good one to-day. Go as fast as he likes, he can; and jump! He'd jump a town, if you'd put him at it! I know whose fault it will be if we get thrown out to-day. Your health, Miss Lushington. What, Ike! be the hounds come already?"

The latter question was addressed to my old acquaintance, the earth-stopper, who with many a low *salaam*, and a gentlemanlike air of excusing himself, which he had acquired in his palmy days with "The Flamers," and never completely shaken off, now sidled into the Bar.

"They're not half a mile behind," said the old man; and then turned to me, with a "Beg your pardon, sir," as if to apologize that he had addressed the other first. I accepted the implied compliment; and could do no less in return than ask the veteran "What would he have to drink?"

"A little gin, if you please, sir," replied old Ike, passing the back of his hand across his mouth. And I saw his wasted features glow and his eye brighten, as the liquid fire descended to those regions which people who are no anatomists call the "cockles of the heart." He was still a wonderfully tough old specimen, this earth-stopper. Last night he had been his rounds on a shaggy white pony that looked like the ghost of a horse in the dim moonlight; and to-day, having already walked half-a-dozen miles or so before breakfast, he would follow the hounds for several hours on foot, and be ready again for his work by nightfall.

I saw the old man's face brighten once more, as the door opened, and Tom Turnbull walked into the bar—not to drink anything, as I soon ascertained, but to inquire if a parcel had been left for his "Missis." By the way, I should much like to have my curiosity satisfied as to what these parcels for farmer's wives contain, that are continually left at houses of call. They are invariably small, limp, and a good deal crushed, wrapped in the softest of paper, and tied with the most tangled of string.

Mr. Turnbull looked the picture of a sportsman—low-crowned hat, pepper-and-salt coat, Bedford cord breeches, and brown-topped boots, thick leather gloves, and a blue bird's-eye neckcloth. "How goes it, Tom?" exclaimed a voice I recognized. "Fine dry morning, this. Won't you liquor up?"

"Never take anything before I go hunting, thank ye, sir," replied Tom, turning round his rosy healthy face and clear eye, presenting a marked contrast to the dissipated looks of "Jovial Jem," for it was none other who now addressed him. The Jovial had been in London, too, during the frost, and, judging by his appearance, had been engaged in a process which he termed "keeping the game alive," but which was likely to be rapid destruction to the sportsman. He looked as if he had been partially drunk for a fortnight and was hardly sober now, as indeed probably was the case. He was attired, nevertheless, in the most fashionable hunting costume—long scarlet coat with large sleeves, white waistcoat with an infinity of pockets, blue satin neckcloth and turned-down collar, well-cleaned leathers and top-boots, heavy workmanlike spurs as bright as silver, and a velvet hunting-cap. A cigar in his mouth of course, and, despite a certain nervous anxiety of manner, a merry leer in his eye, or it would not have been "The Jovial." He had driven Crafty Kate over from The Ashes, and was about to ride a steady seasoned hunter that his father had given him on Christmas-day. "Look alive!" observed this well-dressed

sportsman when he had greeted me, as he considered, with
sufficient politeness, by slapping me on the back, and calling
me "old one." "The Earl leaves the Green to a minute,
and it's ten thirty now"—words which caused an immediate
bustle in the bar and emptying thereof, nobody but Mr.
Naggett having the politeness to wish Miss Lushington
"Good-bye."

Soakington-Green, as it was called—an open space of
verdure, generally too wet for cricket, and seldom boasting
anything more lively than a worn-out pair of stocks and a
few lean geese—was all alive when we mounted our horses
and rode across its level surface. True to his character for
punctuality, the Earl was already moving off, and I did but
catch a glimpse of his long back and tall aristocratic figure
as he jogged along amongst his hounds, in earnest conclave
with Will Hawke. The pack were gathered round their
huntsman's horse, looking, as they always did, bright as
pictures. Glossy in their coats, full of muscle, ribs just visible, and plenty of covering upon their backs, they stepped
daintily along, with their sterns well up, and that sagacious
quick-witted ready-for-anything expression which is characteristic of the fox-hound. A party of gentlemanlike-looking men from the Castle, admirably mounted, followed
close upon the hounds; but my eye sought in vain amongst
the troop for the well-known form in its close-fitting riding-habit, which was beginning to take up far too much of my
attention. The tinge of disappointment I experienced was,
however, rapidly cured by a conversation I happened to
overhear between young Plumtree and a double-distilled
dandy from the Castle, riding a conspicuous white horse.

The "Jovial," whose shattered nerves could not brook
suspense so well as mine, addressing the elaborate exquisite

by the familiar abbreviative of "Pop" (his real name was Popham Algernon Adolphus Evergreen, so it *did* come shorter to call him "Pop"), asked him point-blank, "What they had done with the rest of the party?" to which "Pop," after a vague stare, and an effort to remember where he was, replied, "Party?—Oh!—Aw!—Yes. Some of the fellows were late, and went on at once to the Gorse. Emperor wont like it (meaning the Earl); but daren't blow up, because The Slasher's gone on with 'em."

"The Slasher?" exclaimed Plumtree, turning very red and forgetting in his indignation to be either slang or cool. "Who the devil do you call The Slasher?"

"Pop" gathered his wits together once more, and replied imperturbably, "Oh, The Slasher, you know—that Miss Merlin, you know. It's a name Bight gave her, you know. I'm sure I don't know why; but he's a devilish clever fellow, Bight, so they say. It wouldn't be a bad name for a horse, would it?"

"Pop" relapsing into a brown study at this juncture, it was impossible to get anything more satisfactory out of that priceless piece of porcelain-ware; and the "Jovial," blowing off his indignation in clouds of cigar-smoke, trotted on to have a look at the hounds, young Evergreen running his eye over myself and horse with a supercilious stare that, in my opinion, did no credit to his good manners. A leading duchess, however, in London, had stated her opinion that "Lady Evergreen's boy was the best-dressed and the most impudent young one of his year;" so "Pop" was very much the fashion in consequence.

A little wide of the hounds, in order to do no mischief, and a little clear of the horses, lest the four-year-old should prove too handy with his heels, I observed my former acquaintance Tips, the rough-rider, in the full glory of his profession. He had so completely singled himself out from the crowd, that he could not but attract attention. Rather neater in his dress than when I had seen him last, and with a clean white neckcloth of clerical proportions, Mr. Tips sat down in the saddle as no man but a professional horse-breaker ever *does* sit—an attitude only to be acquired by the habit of keeping constantly on his guard against the agreeable varieties of rearing, kicking, plunging, turning round, and lying down, adopted by a thoroughly refractory pupil when his "dander" is up. Tips, prepared for any or all of these vagaries at a moment's notice, kept his knees well forward, his feet home in the stirrups, his hands apart, holding the reins rather long, for he likes, he says, "to give them plenty of rope" when they begin throwing their heads about, and his short sturdy cutting whip ready in his right.

To-day, however, these precautionary measures seemed merely to arise from the force of habit, as the animal he was riding—a lengthy good-looking brown, on short legs, with long low shoulders, a long coat, a long head, and a long tail—looked as docile and good-tempered a four-year-old as ever was crossed, and played with its rusty bit, attached, as a horse-breaker's bit always is, to the most insecure-looking and weather-beaten of bridles, with a good-humoured cheerfulness calculated to inspire the utmost confidence in its rider.

"You've got a pleasanter mount than usual to-day, Mr. Tips," I remarked, coming alongside of him; whereat the four-year-old tucked its long tail in, and gave a playful kick or two, snorting the while in pure gaiety of heart. "Are you going to make a hunter of him, or have you only brought him out for exercise?"

Mr. Tips dived towards his fully-occupied hands with his head, as the nearest approach he could afford towards touching his hat.

"Never seen hounds till to-day, sir," he replied. "Sweet young horse he is, sir, as ever looked through a bridle; a kind animal, too, both in the stable and out; as mild as a milch cow, and as handy as a ladies'-maid."

Just then the object of our joint praises, startled, pardonably enough, by a tinker's caravan that had taken up a conspicuous position on the Green, shied violently away from the alarming object, and did not recover its equinamity without a succession of bounds and plunges, such as would have unseated most men ignominiously, but which produced no perceptible effect on the demeanour of the experienced Tips, his affability only becoming, if possible, more conspicuous than before.

Lost in admiration of my companion's skill—for I confess to a great weakness for real finished horsemanship such as in my own person I have never yet been able to acquire —and taken up with the movements of the young horse and the conversation of its rider, I had not remarked that we had let the hounds slip on so far ahead as to find ourselves a long way behind the whole moving cavalcade, proceeding leisurely towards the gorse. An exclamation from Mr. Tips roused me to the true state of affairs.

"Best shog on a little, sir," said he, with a sparkle of excitement in his eye. "Blessed if they haven't reached the covert already! and are putting in. There's a short cut; this way, Mr. Softly, if you'll be so good as follow me."

With these words, Tips thrust open an awkward handgate, the young one pushing it with his chest, as I felt convinced at the time, far more handily than Tipple Cider would have done, and entered a low swampy pasture patched with rushes, and stretching right away to the further end of the gorse from that where the hounds were put in. Shutting my eyes to the great probability there was of our heading the fox, and resolving to shut my ears to the expostulations that would too surely accompany such a catastrophe, I followed my leader along the pasture, rather in a state of nervous trepidation, in no measure soothed by the view I now obtained of the assembled field, amongst whom I had no difficulty in recognizing the well-known riding-habit.

Tips, sitting down in the saddle, put the four-year-old into a lurching awkward kind of gallop, and I followed him at a venture, Tipple Cider raking and snatching at his bridle in disagreeable exuberance of spirits, as if he were rather short of work.

There was a low rail at the extremity of the pasture, fortifying what had once been a gap into the covert itself, a shelter I was most anxious to reach before the eagle-eye of the Earl could spy me out in so untoward a position. I had already made up my mind for a considerable *détour* which would bring me to a friendly hand-gate (I hate the foolish practice of jumping when hounds are not running), when I saw Tips charge this said rail with the utmost coolness; the four-year-old resenting such an unnecessary demonstration, by turning short round, and kicking out violently at the offending timber.

"Give us a lead, Mr. Softly, if it isn't taking too great a liberty," said Tips, as quietly as if this cool request were the most natural thing in the world; adding, as a clinching argument, "*You're* on a hunter, *I know*."

The rail, though not high, was strong and ugly. There

was a nasty deep blind ditch on the taking-off side, and nothing but gorse-bushes to land in. I did not seem to care much about entering the covert at this point; but whilst I was deliberating the matter in my own mind, and Tipple Cider was doing all he could to get at the rail, tail first or anyhow, a horn resounded from the opposite side of the covert; the music of hounds running, which had greeted us ever since we got within ear-shot, suddenly ceased: though I could see nothing of them, I could distinctly hear the rush of horses galloping up the adjacent pasture. It was evident they had gone away; and equally incontestable that we had lost our start. Tips blazed up into excitement at once; he made no more ado, but caught the four-year-old short by the head, rammed both spurs in, and, notwithstanding an abortive kick or two, forced him over the rail, striking it hard with fore and hind legs. Tipple Cider, fired with emulation, took the bit in his teeth, and had me over it, clear and clean, before I was aware. The next instant, leaping and plunging through the gorse-bushes, I was following Tips at the best pace I could muster, to get after the hounds.

My blood rose with the motion, my horse dropped to his bit, my pilot chose an easy, though devious path; if everything had gone right, I think at that moment I could have ridden fairly and boldly enough.

As we rounded the slight acclivity on which the gorse was planted, a beautiful panorama was spread out before us. Already two fields ahead, the hounds were running hard, evidently with a capital scent, followed at different intervals by the scattering field, all fresh as fire, and every man taking the place to which he felt his skill and daring entitled him. Nearest ourselves I recognized Mr. Nagget, striding away on the mealy chestnut with a great display of enthusiasm and hard riding, his feet stuck out, his elbows up to his ears, and his blue coat-tails flying in the wind. He was diverging, nevertheless, slightly from the line of chase, and making vigorously for the gate, which old Ike, whose active feet had already taken him there, was hurriedly unfastening. Two or three dark coats and the second whip seemed also inclined to avail themselves of this convenient egress; the body of the field, however, were charging the fence boldly (a fair hedge-and-ditch), making for the places that had been leaped by their leaders in the first flight. I saw Plumtree jump it on his steady hunter; but I observed by the way in which he pulled the old horse out of his stride, upsetting the equanimity even of that experienced animal, that his nerves were by no means up to the mark. The Earl and Will Hawke, a hundred yards or so ahead of these, were close to the hounds. "Pop," too, on the white horse, had got a capital start, and was blazing away as if he had a second horse in every field, and a spare neck in his pocket. Rather in front of him, and alongside the hounds, rode the dauntless Miss Merlin, sailing away on "Lady-killer." I recognized his long swish tail even at that distance; taking everything as it came in his stride, and diverging neither to right nor left.

Even at the pace I was going, my heart beat faster at the sight. If such were wanting, this was indeed an additional inducement to catch them at any price. I caught hold of Tipple Cider's head, and for a few resolute minutes I do believe the deluded animal thought he had got a regular "out-and-outer" on his back.

The hounds bent somewhat to the right. Tips, who had an eye like a hawk, perceived it in a moment; and turning round on the saddle, good-naturedly motioned me to follow him. By diverging a little, we got upon a succession of sound headlands, with fair easy fences; the hounds kept turning towards us, and we began to overhaul them rapidly. Excited as I was, I could not but admire the masterly manner in which the rough-rider handled the young one at his leaps. We were getting on gloriously. The first flight, including Miss Merlin, although a couple of fields distant, were scarcely nearer the hounds than ourselves. I rejoiced to think that I should drop amongst them, as it were, from the clouds, and assume my place in the front rank.

A momentary hesitation, another down-wind turn of the hounds, and there was but one fence between ourselves and the pack. My leader charged it resolutely; I prepared to follow him. It was an ugly place—a down-hill gallop at it, a high straggling fence, sedgy banks, and something that was more of a watercourse than a ditch running on the far side. Tips was as eager as a glutton, but the young one's heart failed him the last stride; and, although his rider had him in such a grasp that he could not refuse, the powder was out of him, and he jumped short, dropping his hind legs, and rolling into the next field. Tips was hardly clear of his horse before he was on him again; and I do not believe he lost half-a-dozen strides by the fall. Why did I not follow? My heart failed me. I thought it would be rash to go where another horse had fallen, though I had seen exactly how it happened; and Tipple Cider was shaking his head, as much as to say, "Why won't you let me have a drive?" So *I went to look for another place.*

That sentence explains everything. Need I say how, the further I rode along the fence, the deeper and wider it became? Need I confess that I was eventually compelled to creep ignominiously through a gap in a green lane, the disappointed Tipple Cider grinding my leg against a tree and crushing my hat amongst its branches, in his disgust; or that I proceeded along this convenient alley as far as it lasted with renewed hopes, dashed by a bitter sense of vexation and shame? A stern chase is a long chase, by land as well as by sea; and there is no process, in my opinion, so utterly disheartening as that of trying to catch hounds in a run.

Sometimes I heard their notes, borne by the westerly breeze in tantalizing harmony on my longing ears. Sometimes I caught sight of a few scattered riders in the distance, a lot of cattle herded together in a corner, or a flock of sheep formed up in military line, and not yet recovered from their panic. I rode on like a man in a dream; minutes seemed to lengthen themselves into hours, and I was surprised to find my horse so fresh after such prolonged exertions. At last, rounding the corner of the well-known Tangler's Copse, and speculating vaguely how I should ever cross the Sludge, supposing the chase to be still forward in the same direction, I caught a view of the whole assemblage, not a quarter of a mile off, on the opposite side of the brook. It was obvious they had killed their fox, after a capital run. Horses were being led about, men on foot were standing in groups, some were in the act of remounting—it was probable that the run had been over some little time. Distinct against the sky stood out Miss Merlin's graceful figure, leaning forward to caress the redoubtable Lady-killer, who had carried her so well. In close attendance, I made out the white hunter of the exquisite "Pop." I should think that poor beast must have had enough of it.

I was deliberating in my own mind whether I should

not be fool enough to ride at the Sludge in cold blood, when my motions were decided for me by a general break-up of the distant party; Miss Merlin and her attendant cavaliers taking the direct road for the castle. It was evident she did not at present mean to return to the Haycock. Moodily and dejectedly, I too took my homeward way. I was disgusted with myself—disgusted with hunting—disgusted with life. I should have liked to know what the hounds had done, too; but I felt I could not have brooked the good-humoured curiosity of Mr. Tips, nor the self-sufficient pity of Mr. Naggett, who would be sure to swear he had gone better than he really did.

Espying these two sportsmen at a turn in the road gradually overtaking me, I set spurs to Tipple Cider, and rattled back to the Haycock as fast as I could trot. Arrived there, I found the dapper groom in marching order, getting out his horses for a journey. He had received orders that morning to move them on to Melton; and I have never set eyes on Miss Merlin from that day to this.

THE END.

www.ingramcontent.com/pod-product-compliance
Lightning Source LLC
Chambersburg PA
CBHW030428300426
44112CB00009B/900